*Cycling is something that you do, not something that is done to you…
It's immediate and direct. You pedal, you make decisions. You're vitalised.
You're alive!… You fight against alienation and impersonality, you build
consciousness and identity… The salvation of the world is the development
of personality and identity for everybody in it. Much work, many
lifetimes. But a good start for you is to get a bicycle!*

Richard Ballantine

The Bike at the End of the Puddle. Hikarigaoka Park, Tokyo. Photo: Ben Torode.

About the Author

Jim McGurn has 40 years of experience as a writer on cycling, including books such as *On your Bicycle, a Social History of Cycling*. He has also co-published *Bicycle Design* and magazines on cycling, in German and US editions. His *Get Cycling Guide* for beginners has appeared in over 20 regional editions.

In the background he has kept up a professional interest in languages and has written three school textbooks. He enjoys giving talks on the families of languages – and on cycling, of course. He sees himself as a populariser, and certainly not as an academic.

In 2008 Jim and wife Sally founded Get Cycling, a Community Interest Company. They have a son with Down's Syndrome, and their social enterprise specialises in helping people with disabilities to cycle. They also founded Everybody's Cycling, a charitable Community Benefit Society specialising in bike try-out roadshows for the general public.

After many years in social enterprise Jim returns to his old career in the form of *Cycle Magic*.

Cover artwork: Janet Attard

Cycle Magic

Jim McGurn

Company of Cyclists

Published by Company of Cyclists, York, UK.
www.companyofcyclists.co.uk

ISBN 978-1-0682336-0-9

Author: *Jim McGurn*

Design: *Frozen Marrow*

Printed in Latvia

*For my wonderful family and especially
for my wife Sally whose sacrifices and
enthusiasm for this book helped, more
than anything, to make it happen.*

Photo: *Steve McKay*

Borin van Loon.

Forward

One unforgettable day, in the mid-seventies, I was kicking my heels as a young student out of term time. Taken by a whim I bought a shabby old track bike sitting outside a second-hand shop. It was light, fast and single speed. It was magic. I was totally hooked and in the following week only the need for essential bodily functions could keep me off that bike. Then I read *Richard's Bicycle Book*. Richard Ballantine was the cycling guru of the time and his writings deepened and broadened my love of cycling and changed the lives of many others. I just hope that *Cycle Magic* will help excite and inspire in similar ways.

This is a guide, practical and otherwise, to the wide worlds of cycling. I hope that it will encourage enthusiastic cyclists to discover more, and will inspire beginners and novices to experience the beauty, joy and wellbeing which the bicycle creates. Cycling is a solution to so much which is wrong with the world and at the same time gives us a unique and practical way to get about and care for the environment. If Jesus were ever to return he'd choose to ride a bicycle as the equivalent of the modest donkey.

I have included contributions from writers, photographers and illustrators whom I admire and have worked with – whose expertise plugs the many gaps in my own knowledge and abilities. I have tried to weave it all into a coherent whole but I expect most readers will dip into the book as they please. I have worked on a very wide canvas, balancing easy reading with heavier stuff. No-one will enjoy or appreciate everything in this book – it wanders perhaps too widely for that. But I hope it will give pleasure, deeper understanding and greater confidence while helping to lift the status of cycling generally.

In Cycle Magic I have chosen particular makes of cycle purely as examples. No aspect of the editorial, whether pictures or words, has involved any exchange of benefit. I have selected impartially.

Cycle Magic suggests how pedal-power can find its way into many areas of human activity where it has never been particularly welcome, often for illogical reasons. But cycling quietly challenges so many prejudices and failures of imagination. I sense its happy days are coming back.

Jim McGurn

Contents

The Magic of Minimal

The bicycle gives so much and takes so little. It's a neat collection of triangulated sticks holding slender, air-shod wheels – a humble arrangement bringing colossal benefits. It's one of the finest examples of engineering design, built around the human body: so minimal yet so practical. So life-enhancing, healthy, harmless and light on the planet. To ride a bicycle is to keep mind and body in a happy place while we simply have fun getting around. Your bicycle is a marvel in action, but useless without you.

Our bicycles are a true form of independent private transport. We travel freely, quickly, anytime, door to door. We access routes closed to motor traffic and have easy parking. Cycling brings us closer to the life of our neighbourhoods. We can stop any time to chat or explore rather than just transit through without thinking.

Some of us have turned inwards, towards private pleasures at home, or we travel in motorised comfort sealed off from the world outside with all its confusion, weirdness and identity challenges – yet on a bicycle we can discover happiness and community.

If bikes are so good why are they not fundamental to human activity in 'developed' societies? Perhaps they're too cheap, too simple, too universal, too harmless, too quiet, too status-ambivalent for their own good. Perhaps it's because bikes require us to make our bodies do something useful when we've spent over a century taking the physicality out of everyday living. The powerful logic of cycling presents a challenge to many aspects of western culture.

Author and public intellectual Stephen Pinker includes the bicycle as one of his Seven Wonders of the World. We ask it to take forces equivalent to ten times its own weight. Cycle designer Alex Moulton pointed out that *'Our fuel is non-fossil, pleasant to consume, and easily renewable'*. Maria Lowe tells us that a cyclist can ride 3.5 miles (5.6km) on the calories found in an ear of corn. And every hour you spend cycling comes back to you three times over in extended life expectancy. According to Professor Stuart S Wilson, *'If we compare cycling to walking we find that our energy consumption for a given distance is reduced to about a fifth (0.15 calorie per gram per kilometre). In fact, on a bicycle you improve your efficiency rating to number one among moving creatures and machines' (Scientific American 1973).*

You might say that the bicycle is the perfect machine.

Mick Orloski

CHAPTER 1
The Cycling Story
How we changed the bicycle and how it changed us

The Running Machine

Unexpectedly, in 1817, out of central Germany, came an invention which would catch the fancy of the fashionable world and begin the evolution of the modern bicycle. The wooden *Laufmaschine* (*running-machine*) was a balance bike, offering simplicity, good ergonomics, and the ability to follow a single line on rough ground.

The inventor was Baron Karl von Drais, District Forestry Officer in the Duchy of Baden. He experimented with four-wheeled machines until, in a massive leap of the imagination, he worked out that steering adjustments could unlock those secrets of balance which make cycling possible. It was a big intellectual advance since virtually every form of transport had four wheels and there was no natural predecessor for the bicycle.

Riders of running-machines jolted over the solid ruts and sank deep into the soft ones. Also, the constant pounding could injure feet. Nevertheless thousands found the running-machine worthwhile. On good roads its speed was unmatched: it was four times faster than local post coaches.

In 1818 Drais sent one of his forest huntsmen to demonstrate the machine in Paris. This man failed to shake off a crowd of mocking children and got off several times to push. Then a bystander leapt on the machine and tumbled off. A crucial nut was lost and all was abandoned.

Races and exhibitions restored some prestige and Paris began to warm to the *Draisienne*, as they called it. The craze reached England in 1819, kindled by a machine copied and refined by Denis Johnson of London, who had entrepreneurial skills which von Drais lacked. Nicknamed 'dandy-horse' and 'hobby-horse', Johnson's machine was produced in quantity. He had on his doorstep the novelty-seeking sporty bucks of Regency London. Notable figures took to scooting around the streets and parks.

There was a short-lived craze on the eastern seaboard of the United States in mid 1819, as the British craze was losing wind. Hobbies (known simply as *velocipedes* in the USA) were being made in Boston and elsewhere, but interest was most intense in New York, where the timid rode at nightfall along the Bowery. By late 1819 the American craze was in its final spasms.

Disappointment had soured von Drais's innocent, open nature, and he had turned to alcohol. Following a brawl in a tavern he lost his employment and was suspected of insanity. He continued to produce inventions, but success eluded him. He spent his latter years as a travelling showman and died impoverished in 1851, aged 66.

The running machine never really went away.

The Great Velocipede Mania

A race in Bordeaux, 1868.

With the arrival of the pedal, feet left the ground and the *velocipede*, or *boneshaker* craze began. Direct drive to the front wheel meant the rider had to both steer and power the same wheel. Velocipedes had a framework of wrought iron and their wooden wheels were held in compression by iron tyres. It was cartwheel technology: tension-spoked wheels had not yet arrived.

'Velocipeding' first surged in Paris, in the 1860s. Parisian Affairs correspondents wrote of *"machines like the ghosts of departed spiders, on which horrible boys and detestable men career about the streets and boulevards."* A writer for *Le Galois* announced that *"Velocipedists are imbeciles on wheels."* Others expressed delight: *"Oh, Velocipede! Camel of the Occident!"* wrote one journalist.

Velocipede racing took on the paraphernalia of horse racing with trackside bets and riders dressed as jockeys. At night in Paris velocipedes with swinging lanterns attached darted among the carriages like fire-flies. Velocipeding lent itself so easily to creature similes.

By 1867 the USA was enjoying its own 'velocipedomania'. Riding schools were gorged with pupils and *The Scientific American* declared that *"for the majority of civilised humanity, walking is on its last legs"*. Henry Ward Beecher, the celebrated pastor, hoped to see *"a thousand velocipedists wheeling [i.e. riding] their machines to Plymouth Church."*

The lamentable road surfaces took their toll. By the end of April few respectable citizens were still riding velocipedes in the USA.

Back in Europe the Franco-Prussian War of 1870-71 wiped out the French velocipede industry, and British manufacturers seized their chance. The factories of the West Midlands produced in quantity, with technical advances.

'Extraordinary Velocipede Feat' was how *The Times* proclaimed a day ride from London to Brighton in 1869 by John Mayall and companions. They set off accompanied by a *Times* reporter in a coach. Mayall arrived first, after 53 miles (85km) in about 15 hours. The Chinnery brothers walked the same route about 3½ hours faster the following month.

The demands of athletes and tourists induced manufacturers to develop lighter machines with larger front wheels and smaller rear ones. The wooden-wheeled boneshaker was evolving into the imposing steel-wheeled high bicycle, which some now call the *penny farthing*.

A Michaux bicycle from 1868.

Higher, ever Higher

The reign of the mighty wheel

In the 1870s and early 1880s high streets and marketplaces up and down the country would echo to the rumblings of high bicycles on cobblestones as uniformed club riders prepared for the 'off'. At the bugle call for 'assembly' the captain took the head of the column. At the call for 'mount' each man would place a foot on the mounting step on the frame by his rear wheel, hop along behind his rolling machine and then project himself up and forward into the saddle.

They rolled through sleepy streets, past bemused townspeople and bewildered horses, to surge out into a serene countryside with only occasional horse traffic. At the bugle call for 'double file' the riders could relax and chat, powering their great wheels along in a rhythm unbroken by freewheelng or gear changing. The club bugler heralded the club's approach and villagers out for a walk stepped well back against the hedge, eyeing warily such a parody of a foxhunt.

The clubmen bumped along turnpike roads neglected since the arrival of the railways. The bicycle clubs brought new prosperity to country inns which had not seen such custom since the days of the stagecoach. The clubmen would stop for a drink to wash road dust out of their mouths and perhaps tuck into a 'capital repast' or a 'cold collation'. This might be followed by the singing of popular songs and the club anthem.

So high was the profile of rider and machine that sidewinds brought steering problems and headwinds could force a rider to walk his machine home. As darkness fell each would dismount to light the oil lamp hanging from the hub inside the spokes of the front wheel. Slowly and carefully, peering for potholes, the clubmen would return to the commonplaces of town or city life.

Every so often there was a 'monster meet' of bicyclists. One was held at Hampton Court Palace

The Apolda Bicycle Club, Thuringia, Germany.

near London, where 2177 riders formed a colourful but ceremonious procession six miles long. These were not only displays of finery, riding skill and discipline, but also shows of solidarity, and public evidence that bicyclists were both respectable and numerous.

The high bicycle was reaching the peak of refinement in the early 1880s: the front wheel had become as big as the rider's leg length would allow, giving more distance per revolution and more comfort over rough roads. Wheels, made of steel, were strengthened by new tension spoking techniques. Hollow-tubed competition machines weighted around 20lbs (9kg). Direct

A cycling club in Plymouth, UK.

drive, a minimal backbone and solid rubber tyres rendered bicycles elegantly uncomplicated.

The high bicycle was never safe. The rider sat directly above the straight front forks, always in danger of being pitched forward. Going downhill some slung both legs over the handlebar, hoping to be projected clear should the front wheel hit a pothole or obstacle. As there was no freewheel mechanism the rider slowed himself down by back-pressure on the pedals, an opportunity easily lost when wheeling downhill with feet up and pedals whirring out of control.

These majestic machines appealed to athletic and adventurous males proud to be mastering the fastest vehicle on the roads. Riding in a club gave some protection against the ridicule, insults and stones which came the way of wheelmen.

Rural Britain, in the slough of an agricultural depression, did not always take kindly to excited and noisy young men from the towns, whose uniforms could be hurtfully compared to the gaudy garb of a German band, and whose bugle calls could bring derision.

Bicyclists were very much at the mercy of the public and of the rivalry of professional carters in particular, who had been long used to empty roads. In 1876 the driver of the Watford to St Albans coach lashed an overtaking bicyclist with his whip, and his conductor brought down a following bicyclist by flinging an iron ball

attached to a rope into his spokes. The carters were successfully prosecuted.

Within a few years the inherently unsafe high bicycle was to be brought down by a radically new form of low, chain-driven cycle: to be called, for obvious reasons, the 'safety' bicycle.

The Kendall Green Bicycle Club, Washington DC in 1884. The Star was an alternative format of high bicycle, developed and made popular in the USA. American clubs first copied British club customs but many switched to regular military titles, and even committee posts were militarised.

To which add a Wheel

In the 1870s and 80s tricycles offered a more reputable and supposedly safer alternative to the extremes of high-wheel riding.

Tricycles were expensive and so a marker of class. Technical developments were rapid and only the wealthy could upgrade to the latest models and had the space to store large cycles.

Some high bicycle clubs bought a tandem tricycle or a side-by-side 'sociable' for the use of individual members, many of whom used this 'club bus' for their courting activities.

By 1885 women tricyclists were generally accepted. However, sensitive ladies of rank could still be assailed by roadside comments from the lower orders. In the United States, where tricycling was uncommon, women founded their own tricycling clubs for common protection.

Tricyclists had no need to dismount when stopped. Also, they could go at extremely low speeds without balance problems, and so gearing could be very low. However, a typical touring tricycle, loaded with luggage, could be beaten by quite gentle hills. *The CTC Gazette* of May 1884 carried advice from a reader:

66 *When touring in a hilly country, it is better to fasten a rope, about four yards long, to the ends of the footrest, and draw the machine up unrideable hills instead of pushing it, as the rope goes round the waist and the arms get a rest... I have pulled my 'Humber' up the Brunig Pass, in Switzerland, for one and a half hours without fatigue.* 99

Hilly descents could be lethal as any of the three wheels might hit a stone or pothole. As tricyclists sat *in* their vehicles more than *on* them, they were more likely to be entangled in their cartwheeling machinery in accidents.

The arrival of the safety bicycle caused tricycles to also become lower, and the lower centre of gravity made them more manageable and more stable.

The Coventry Rotary was a radical departure in tricycle design. It was two-track as opposed to the normal three.

The Safety Bike arrives

High bicycles and safety bicycles sharing a track in the Netherlands, 1892, at a time of transition. Photo: archiefeemland.nl

After years of high wheels the big idea arrived: geared transmission to the rear wheel, allowing wheels of inclusive sizes. High-wheel riders could look down (in both senses) on the squat new safeties, yet the newcomers performed astonishingly better, particularly in sport. It began with the 1885 Rover, designed by Englishman John Kemp Starley, which set the fashion to the world. In the following ten years low safety bicycles swept high bicycles away and were essentially what most of us ride today.

Then, in 1888, John Boyd Dunlop gave us pneumatic tyres, increasing comfort and speed. Shortly after, Dunlop and Edouard Michelin in France introduced wire-on tyres. In 1892 the Michelin Company organised a road race from Paris to Clermont-Ferrand to demonstrate how their tyres were so much easier to repair than Dunlop's. Nails were scattered on the road in places, with a Michelin repair team waiting conveniently nearby. A Michelin cycle won the race.

Bourgeois France hailed the safety bicycle as a symbol of the nation's enterprise and vigour, of modernity and democracy. The French *Cyclists' Yearbook* proclaimed: '*Each century completes its course with a great upheaval. 1793 was marked by blood and the guillotine, 1893 by rubber and ball-bearings.*'

In Germany the freedom, mobility and privacy which cycling gave were more than the authorities could tolerate. Cyclists needed 'bicycle passes' and contended with road bans, restricted hours of riding, enforced single file and ten-metre gaps between riders. Policemen hid behind trees or in ditches to pounce on transgressing cyclists. Ironically, Germany was one of the first nations to provide bicycles for its policemen and local militias – agents of social control.

As the new safety bicycle entered everyday activities it brought issues of compatibility with one's profession. For example, should off-duty military officers cycle in uniform? Henri Desgrange, later to found the Tour de France, lost his job with a law firm when his client complained that his activities as a champion sprint rider were incompatible with the dignity of the law.

The Boom Years

In the mid 1890s the moneyed classes of Western Europe, and then the USA, were captivated by the chain-driven safety bicycle with its pneumatic tyres. It could be ridden by both sexes, and was comfortable, liberating, exciting and novel.

Bicycles were hugely expensive. Many were ridden on country estates, others were transported to public city parks by personal carriage, to be ridden sedately up and down. No-one had ridden on two wheels as a child so riding schools sprang up in the capitals of Europe. Cycling became a significant part of upper class social events, such as musical gymkhanas, where women tended to wear white, as for tennis: it betokened innocence and the ability to afford large laundry bills.

In 1896 Britain and France had about a million cyclists each, Germany had half a million, and estimates for the USA range from two to four million. In the following three decades numbers of cyclists were to rise five-fold, in Britain and France at least.

Most of the park practitioners were women, exhibiting leg-of-mutton sleeves, hour-glass waists and voluminous skirts. Nor were their bicycles spared such triumphs of taste. They were multi-coloured, some matching the colour of the

Leisure events were adapted to include cycling.

lady's dress, and some men's cycles were liveried in their regimental colours.

Many of the Hyde Park cyclists were in London for the 'summer season', a round of dress balls, garden parties, receptions and carriage outings. These events were often adapted to include cycling. Wealthy families parked their cycles ornamentally in their wide hallways, and employed uniformed boys to take charge of visitors' bicycles and clean them.

By autumn 1896 many had tired of ceremonious park cycling. Also, it was becoming too easily gatecrashed, as any upstart could turn up with a bicycle. Besides, cycling required effort and sometimes it rained. The mania for exclusive novelties was to remain dormant till the motor car arrived. The socialites had added prestige to the cause of cycling and established women's right to cycle.

The cycle craze in France had started earlier than its British counterpart and French cyclists faced fewer social constraints. Polite Parisian society cycled in the Bois de Boulogne. Unlike their British counterparts they were prepared to cycle energetically and enjoy themselves. It was important to be seen, to perform and to sparkle. Society life revolved around cafe talk, banquets, cabaret, duels, circuses and new technological marvels, such as the cinematograph, the electric bulb and, of course, the chain-driven safety bicycle.

Cycling in France showed a greater social mix than in the UK: students, artists, bourgeois, government ministers, and even the President of France, Casimir-Perier appeared, tandeming round the Bois each morning with his wife and children. Members of the old French aristocracy cycled with gusto, joined on Sundays by less privileged wheelers enjoying their one day off in the week. A carnival atmosphere reigned and Sunday cycle dress was so bizarre that it became a tourist attraction. As early as 1892 the Prince de Sagin delighted onlookers by riding his 'little steel fairy' in a loud striped suit and a specially designed boater.

At dusk the Sunday revellers headed for home, their cycles festooned with purloined flowers and Chinese lanterns.

In the riding schools of Amsterdam, which were probably the best in Europe, novices could be coached by splendidly uniformed instructors. Helpers steadied cyclists by grabbing special leather waistbands, and walls had protective padding. All riding was jollified by a pianist.

In Germany the sophisticated middle classes of the big cities did not allow their governments' restrictions to exclude them from the international craze. In Berlin cyclists successfully supported their own candidates in municipal elections. German interest in cycles designed for special purposes intensified and in 1898 a magazine reported that 500 tricycle taxicabs were plying the streets of Berlin.

The boom was brief but its legacy long.

An English lady of means photographed for a fashion magazine around 1897. Note her waistline.

Prince Ludwig Ferdinand and Prince Alfons of Bavaria, around 1897.

With its fundamental design established, the bicycle had begun its journey towards universal mobility, personal freedom and social progress.

Liberation Came Riding

The bicycle helped free women from domesticity and isolation, despite tides of opposition from both sexes. Cycling was instrumental in women's escape from late nineteenth century outdoor clothing which featured ankle-length skirts over multitudes of petticoats. Also on the way out were tightly corseted waists and heavy, substantial hats.

American cyclists were among the first to wear bloomers, in around 1893. These 'bifurcated nether garments' caused a sensation. Women founded their own cycling clubs, for which bloomers were often standard dress, and there were 'bloomer dances'. British women cyclists, and many others in Europe with the exception of the French, stuck to their long, heavy skirts – often literally so, as it could be a sweaty business.

The tyranny of the long skirt caused manufacturers to design drop-frame bicycles, which were inevitably heavier and technically awkward chain-guards and dress protectors were needed.

A young French lady at ease with life, hand confidently resting on hip, holding a practical hat and wearing culottes. She is painted here in oil by her father, Léon-François Comerre, in 1893. 'Bicyclette au Vésinet', Courtesy: Musée des Beaux Arts, Paris.

For the great majority of women the bicycle was not an implement of radicalism but a means of social integration.

It took considerable courage to wear rational dress in Britain. In 1895 *The Clarion* magazine wrote: *'Few would believe how insulting and coarse the British public could be unless they had ridden through a populated district with a lady dressed in rationals. And the poorer the district the more incensed do the people appear.'*

As bicycles became more affordable for working people, they increased what is known as the 'marriage distance', with a corresponding broadening of the gene pool. Working-class marriages to people within the same parish went down from 77% before 1887 to 41% between 1907 and 1916. Marriages to partners living six to twelve miles away increased from 3% to 9%. It is likely that this new courtship mobility was pedal-powered: few had the energy to walk six or more miles to another parish after a long, hard working day.

Royalty
Rides

Czar Nicholas II of Russia was a dedicated knight of the whirring wheel. As a young man he had organised an informal kind of cycling club for the princes of Europe. They rode together at Fredensborg in Denmark, where the royal families of Europe got together each year. The Romanovs were keen cyclists, and Prince Alexei, later to be assassinated with the rest of his family, was cycled round the Palace Gardens by his uniformed minder.

The monarchies took to cycling in a big way in the late 1890s. Some went for spins around their private parks, some gifted bicycles to friends. As a general rule, the more despotic the monarch the crasser their taste in bicycles. Archduke Ferdinand of Austria's machine was a splendid beast: nickel-plated throughout, monogrammed, and with handlebar grips of ivory inlaid with gold.

The more liberal royal families, especially the Danish one, turned out to watch professional cycle racing. In the Netherlands Queen Wilhelmina went on regular bike rides with her daughter, Juliana. The royal families of Scandinavia and the Netherlands cycled for pleasure, but also to be closer to the people. During World War Two, King Frederick IX of Denmark and his wife, Ingrid, cycled round Copenhagen to show solidarity with the people during the German occupation.

When Juliana became Queen of the Netherlands in 1948 she kept up the Dutch tradition of royal cycling, and was enjoying cyclists' picnics in the 1970s. She is shown below on a cycle tour of the island of Terschelling.

The British royal family did not cycle for long. Queen Victoria's daughter, Maud, was a 'maid of the wheel', whose activities were fondly reported by the Lady's Realm:

❝ Princess Maud was, as we have often heard, wooed and won during those long rides in the glorious deer forests around Bernstorff, when she and the handsome Prince Carl, (of Denmark) so often found themselves handle to handle, far in advance of the rest of the royal party. ❞

Edward Prince of Wales, who had enjoyed cycling while living it up on the French Riviera, became a committed motorist. In 1906 he was bragging about doing 60mph on the Brighton Road, at a time when the speed limit was only 20mph.

Alexei and his carer.

Queen Juliana of the Netherlands.

Princess Elizabeth, to be Queen of the United Kingdom.

Cycling travels the World

A Japanese manufacturer of clothing fabrics produced this advertising material around 1903. However, women were not encouraged to cycle and often rode disguised as males.

BY 1896 the passion for safety cycling had reached far beyond north west Europe and the United States. Excitement and curiosity had been carried abroad by cycle-loving diplomats and colonials, by the hectic enterprise of manufacturers, and by the influence of London and Paris fashion on the international middle class.

The extent of the vogue is suggested by Scottish journalist John Foster Fraser's travelogue, *Round the World on a Wheel*. Fraser describes how, in 1896, he and his two companions were escorted by cyclists from Budapest, and later by the wheelmen of Nyireghaza (North East Hungary), who rode with giant sunflowers on their bicycle headsets. In India they cycled with colonial dignitaries and in Japan they were welcomed by the Unreliable

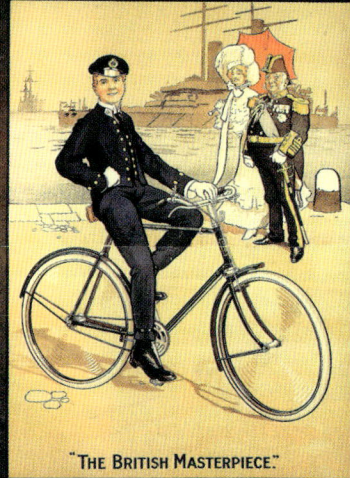

RALEIGH

"THE BRITISH MASTERPIECE."

THE ALL-STEEL BICYCLE

Cycling travelled with empire, and was seen as an ambassador for western technology.

Wheelmen of Yokohama, a club composed of "Scotsmen and humorists". Had he taken a more northerly route Fraser would have encountered the five thousand cyclists of St Petersburg or the members of the Moscow Society of Velocipede Lovers. To the south he would have been welcomed by the colonial wheelers of Johannesburg, by the Sultan of Zanzibar, who was to become one of Raleigh's best customers, or by the Ameer of Kabul, who had, in that euphoric year of 1896, ordered bicycles for the ladies of his harem.

New markets were also being created in Latin America and Japan by American cycle manufacturers. Reports of cycling activity at the very outposts of western civilisation were relayed back to the self-congratulatory cycling public of the industrialised nations.

China, around 1898.

The Moscow Society of Velocipede-Lovers gifted Tolstoy (then aged 67) a bicycle and helped him to learn along the paths of his estate.

The Nizam of Hyderabad Bicycle Boys' Corps taking part in an annual military parade in the city, probably in 1897. Many Asian potentates bought tricycle rickshaws to be pedalled by their servants seated behind.

Animal Encounters

As they ventured forth cyclists encountered creatures which had never before seen a bicycle. Horses bolted and cows were liable to stampede. Farmers claimed their frightened cows produced less milk, and few cyclists paid for the farmyard fowl they ran over.

Aggressive dogs were a concern and readers of cycling periodicals swapped advice on how to beat the menace. One kept a pocketful of stones to throw at dogs, another recommended liberal doses of cayenne pepper; yet another carried a lead-weighted stick strapped down one fork. Some carried gunpowder-filled firecrackers or ammonia squirters. There were even a cyclist's revolver which could be pulled out of the handle-bar grip.

The periodicals press ran racy stories of cyclists pursued by lions, bears or wolves. *The Captain*, a British magazine for boys, ran a story of plucky explorers fighting off a pack of wolves.

Cycling Boom USA

Riverside Drive, New York, was the place to be seen on your bicycle. There's a very unusual triplet tandem in the background, and what looks like a companion cycle.

A 'police patrol tricycle' operated by the Dayton Ohio Police Department. The felon was handcuffed to his seat.

Cycling became a formidable part of the social scene amongst wealthy Americans, from around 1894 to 1896. For example, New York City's 'Four Hundred', the self-defining social elite, held social evenings and gymkhanas which were occasions for elaborate set pieces. In the Balaclava Melé, for instance, four male cyclists wearing fencing masks used canes to strike at plumes fixed to opponents' headgear. For the ladies there was serpentining down lines of bowling pins and there were cycling versions of dances such as the Virginia Reel. Over on the western seaboard Seattle's many cycling groups regularly rode the 25 miles of urban bicycle trails which were built with part funding from cyclists. There were over 20 bike shops on Seattle's Second Avenue alone, and it's estimated that there were 10,000 cyclists in a city of about 100,000 citizens.

Cyclists held meetings, races, and parades to promote the improvement of roads and cyclepaths and to protect cyclists' rights. A popular cyclepath was the ten mile long Lake Washington route. There was an increase in long distance leisure cycle-touring, supported by a complex of ancillary services. There were maps and guides, signposts, 'dangerous hill' signs, repair shops, and cyclists' hotels. Along the routes were stalls from which farmers, who were badly affected by an agricultural depression, sold their produce. There were trains to take cyclists a little further on their tour, or back to their cities.

Cyclists from the cities sought a controlled contact with nature, combined with a maximum of urban culture. The 'service corridors' along which they cycled represented a new form of urban growth. Cyclists who strayed beyond these 'corridors' risked the dangers of a hostile environment, and many carried firearms.

Cycling also became a feature of city life. In New York bicycling policemen became adept at stopping runaway carts and coaches, by riding alongside to grasp the panicking horse's bridle. The New York Police also hired the speed-cycling star, Mile-a-Minute Murphy, to catch transgressing cyclists.

Bicycle manufacturing in the United States was dominated by the Pope Manufacturing Company: pioneers of mass production techniques. Pope sold his wares with panache. One ploy was to offer a fifty dollar reward to anyone who returned a stolen Columbia, still in good condition, to its owner – but only on conviction of the thief. *"It is grand larceny to steal a bicycle; it is arrest and conviction to steal a Columbia"*, he declared.

The Bicycle and the Bush

John William Thistleton on the bicycle he rode to the Mt Ragged gold rush, 1895. Note the puncture repairs. State Library of Western Australia.

It required no food or water, was two or three times as fast as a horse or camel, and never ate poisonous plants. It was easy to maintain and could travel vast distances over very inhospitable terrain. It could also carry 150lbs (70kg) of luggage. It is no wonder the bicycle was quickly and widely adopted by Australians in the remote outback. It simply made many journeys possible.

All kinds of rural Australians used bicycles: shearers, clergymen, boundary riders, cycle express messengers, pipeline checkers, rabbit fence patrols, swagmen, and dentists.

The bicycle was particularly useful to prospectors in the Western Australian goldfields, where the scarcity of water and fodder made difficult the upkeep of horses and even camels. Across the sheep-raising states of Eastern Australia the bicycle was transport for gangs of itinerant sheep shearers. There was an attachment which connected to a bicycle to pedal power hand-held shears.

The Australian bicycle market was dominated by American and Canadian imports. The typical bush bicycle had no brakes and riders typically slowed themselves down by pressing their feet against the front tyre. Thorn punctures were a regular problem and often had to be repaired without water. One trick was to blow tobacco smoke into the inner tube and spotting where smoke escaped. If repair was impossible the tyre could be stuffed with grass, rope or strips of hazel, or the bicycle could be 'ridden on the rims'.

In his book, *The Bicycle and the Bush*, Jim Fitzpatrick points out that the role of the bicycle has been largely ignored as it could not compete with the romantic appeal of man and horse in the Australian landscape: the basis of most Australian outback legends.

Cyclist and camel rider set off on a long journey together. Camels created smooth surfaced pads (pathways) for which cyclists were grateful. State Library of Western Australia.

Professional racers in France, 1914. The artist has dressed the spectators in the upper class fashion of ten years before. It is also unlikely that such people would attend an event so overtly commercial, with cycle racing intermingled with donkey racing and dog cart racing (note the inset pictures). Lyons Municipal Archives.

Wheels for Winning

The keeping of international records, which began around 1880, made it possible for, say, an Australian cyclist to compete against a competitor in Norway who had died before the Australian was born. Competitors and spectators were captivated by the pursuit of improved performances, statistical calculations and tabulated results often turning on fractions of a second. The kind of systematised, record-hungry sport which the industrialised nations imported largely from England depended on specialisation and hierarchical power structures run by trainers, race organisers, handicappers, time-keepers and administrators. However, cycle sport also developed in less intensive ways, with more informal and community-based events in the smaller towns and even villages of the industrialised world.

Throughout Europe the defenders of amateur cycling were being outflanked by commercialised professionalism. In the USA the League of American Wheelmen (LAW) had taken early control of cycle sport but was unable to fend off the many-headed advances of professionalism. In an attempt to maintain standards they tolerated limited professionalism but promoters and riders complained that the LAW suppressed their earnings by banning Sunday events, and by limiting purses and the number of events. In 1893 the National Cycling Association, or 'Cash Prize

English racing men in 1890. Anerley Bicycle Club.

A substantial crowd for a women's race at Herne Hill Velodrome, London, 1930s.

League' was organised. The LAW finally gave up control of racing in 1900 to concentrate on the promotion of good roads.

In the UK the National Cyclists' Union had become alarmed at the perceived dangers of racing on the open road. The police, the press and the public were complaining of large numbers of riders, paced and pacing, hurtling recklessly along public roads. A ban was brought in which held until the end of the Second World War. British cycle sport was effectively isolated from continental developments in road racing. British riders turned to the introverted and almost masonic sport of time trialling, involving separate, individual performances against the clock. In contrast with the chaos and ballyhoo of a massed road race, time triallists avoided drawing attention to themselves in the interests of their sport's survival. They used secret codes and arcane directions to identify meeting points, usually on quiet country roads. At the break of dawn they would set off one by one, dressed in inconspicuous black.

Elsewhere in the industrialised world major road races became epic national events, with folk heroes battling against unrelenting competition, challenging geography, severe weather and unpredictable incidents. All were excitedly reported by press outlets which often had close commercial interests.

The professionals of the 1890s were public figures: stars created and cherished by the cycling press. In France cycle racing supported a daily sports paper,

le Vélo, which had a circulation of 80,000 in 1894. The public could relate to *géants de la route* drawn from their own class and sometimes from their own town. Furthermore, their heroes were often endearingly small men. British crowds warmed to Jimmy Michael, the first British rider to win a professional world championship, who was little over five foot tall (1.5 metres). His main achievements were on closed circuit track, not on road.

The bicycle forced the issue, common in many sports, of amateur versus professional status. It provided new and exciting spectator events. It had, in turn, been refined by technology in the service of sport, becoming a marvel of grace and efficiency, soon to be available to almost everyone.

Time-trialling in the UK, 1930s.

Cycling in the Age of Traffic

The end of the cycling vogue among the wealthy was a heavy blow for manufacturers worldwide. Around 1898 prices began to plummet. Cheap American imports flooded Europe. By the turn of the century the UK industry had saved itself, seen off the 'American Invasion', and was making good, reliable cycles, at prices within the eager reach of the better-off working classes. There was no immediate transition to mass cycle use in any country. That needed time and even lower prices.

The average cost of a bicycle in 1909 was £4, which was three weeks' average earnings in the UK. Working-class buyers needed hire purchase schemes, and sometimes formed clubs to buy their cycles through mutual guarantees. Gradually bicycles were coming into the hands of those who had the greatest need for cheap and independent mobility. Several factors operated closely together. Workers' higher wages enabled them to buy the machine and the local newspaper; their literacy enabled them to use the newspaper to read advertisements for bicycles and local events, their shorter working week gave them time for such journeys, for reading, and perhaps for writing letters. Most working-class buyers were young bachelors on regular incomes.

In 1923 a Dutch historian said this about his country's network of cycle paths:

66 *Just how useful cycle paths have been in the intellectual development of country people is beyond calculation, but together with the bicycle and the acetylene lantern, which made it possible to take lessons and to attend courses and meetings, they fulfilled a leading role in the intellectual development of the farming population.* **99**

In France there were about four million bicycles in circulation by 1914. There was a strong tendency for the skilled urban working classes to set up competition oriented cycle clubs. Among the earliest such clubs were the Societé des Cyclistes Coiffeurs-Parfumeurs and the Union Cyclistes des Postes et des Télegraphes.

There is evidence that the general level of cycling activity in Britain rose after the demise of the Society boom. At Easter 1898, for example, 50,000 cyclists were dispatched by train from Waterloo Station in just a single week, a large increase over the previous year's figures. Many of the middle and upper middle classes continued to cycle-tour.

The very personal pleasures and benefits experienced by the new cyclists cannot be measured solely via

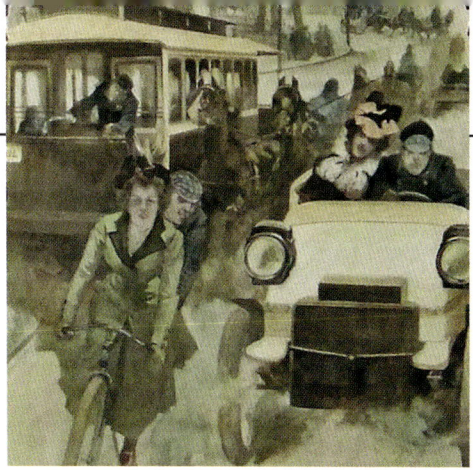

From the cover of Leslie's Weekly in New York.

club membership or bicycle production figures. For example, you can't quantify the delights experienced by Irene Pickering on cycle rides in the Ripon area around 1904:

❝ *Dad was very fond of cycling; he used to go cycling in his dinner hour. When we were little tots during his rides he would sometimes, during closing time, put me on a cushion on the crossbar and I held onto the handlebars and Reg sat behind and held onto Dad and he cycled all around, in the villages and the moors. I loved the moors and am still thrilled when I hear the song of the curlew.* ❞

The automobile speed limit had risen in the UK to 20 mph by 1903, making it more attractive to those of the moneyed classes. The number of cars increased five-fold in ten years, and the motor car became the proving ground for class privilege. In 1906 Lord Northcliffe wrote: 'Lady cyclists were formerly a great danger, as they were apt, when a motor car was heard approaching them from behind, to fall off their machines, apparently in terror; but this distressing spectacle is now comparatively rare.'

For many cyclists motor vehicles came as an interesting and logical extension of cycle technology and leisure patterns. Others were less happy. In the words of one of H G Wells's characters,

The first decade of the 20th century, in England at least, had little motor traffic and is possibly the closest cyclists ever came to paradise on earth.

❝ *The world had thrown up a new type of gentleman altogether, a gentleman of most ungentlemanly energy, a gentleman in dusty oilskins and motor goggles and a wonderful cap, a stink-making gentleman, a swift, high-class badger, who fled perpetually along high roads from the dust and stink he perpetually made.* ❞ (*The War in the Air,* 1908).

The passage refers to motorcycles, and it may have been that their existence helped smudge the class distinctions which increasingly attached to cycles on the one hand and motoring on the other.

Faced by falling membership, most of the major continental cycle-touring organisations began to recruit and represent motorists. Some, such as the ANWB in the Netherlands, did so unhindered and some, like the Cyclists' Touring Club in the UK, met strong opposition from members. The question went to court and the judge disallowed the proposal: a decision which showed remarkable insight.

A 'velomobile' from Sweden, in 1912. A low-budget solution to cycling in cold weather. The owner added a further invention: thermal pedals, containing a cylinder of powdered charcoal.

From War to War

Wheels for almost everyone

The motor car was beginning to entice those who could afford it, but by the late 1920s cycling was becoming easier, safer and more comfortable, thanks to the new freewheel mechanism and to hub gears. Other advancements included rim brakes and all-weather hub brakes replacing inefficient 'spoon brakes' applied to the tyre.

The enormous Raleigh factory in Nottingham was claimed, in 1926, to be the most self-contained in the world. It produced its own gas and electricity and drew water from its own wells. It was a huge metropolis of machinery turning out 3,000 cycles a week.

The bicycle because a packhorse of desperation, helping refugees escape war. Here citizens of Antwerp load up everything precious as the Germans advance in 1914. Belgian National Archive.

The upsurge in walking, climbing, cycling and camping was potent between 1929 and 1933, years of economic slump. The Great Outdoors was cheap, reviving and relatively close. Bicycles also became general utility vehicles, with torrents of cyclists entering and leaving factory gates at end of shifts.

As the century progressed cyclists were losing out to the motoring few. In 1936 the number of cyclists killed and injured was two and a half times what it had been eight years before. The government seemed to care little.

In the Netherlands and Denmark cycling was an established and respected culture. In Germany the liberating ethos of cycling was subverted by the National Socialists' strident philosophy of physicality. Their 'Day of the German Cyclist'

Wartime fuel restrictions on private transport led to alternatives such as this machine in occupied Denmark sometime between 1940 and 1945.

A police dog squad in Bucharest, Romania, demonstrate their mobility in 1936.

Wiki Commons.

The Dutch enjoyed an annual Tandem Day. Here they celebrate the occasion at Schiphol Airport in 1936. This image has a certain poignancy given that the German invasion was just four years in the future.

in 1933 included a vast cycle rally of uniformed party members in Berlin. Eleven years later, on retreating from the Netherlands, German soldiers were to steal and take with them around half of all the Dutch people's eight million bicycles.

In the USA cycling had largely lost out to the automobile but was revived a little by petrol shortages during the Second World War. So sudden was the demand for bicycles that in April 1942 all retail selling of cycles was 'frozen' for three months, after which limited numbers were released to defence workers.

In France the bicycle helped many city-dwellers to keep starvation at bay. They could cycle out into the countryside and, avoiding police control points, bring back farm produce and game.

Wartime austerity gave cycling a short reprieve in the industrial world. The post-war peace was to lay the bicycle low.

Eriol tandems in France were probably a sub-brand of Raleigh.

Wheels for the Workers

ARBEITER-RADFAHRER-BUND "SOLIDARITÄT."

Known as the 'Red Hussars of the Class Struggle', the Workers' Cycling Federation, Solidarity (*Arbeiterradfahrbund: Solidarität*), were known for their propaganda and electioneering activities, along with their impressive cycle parades. Founded in 1896, they sent out 'Enlightenment Patrols of Social Democracy'. One method for evading identification in those years of repression was to throw handfuls of leaflets at crowds while cycling quickly past. By 1913 the Federation had an impressive 150,000 members, a chain of co-operatively organised cycle shops, a co-operative cycle factory in Offenbach and a circulation of 167,000 for its newspaper, *The Worker-Cyclist*, all despite energetic state attempts at control, including blacklists, infiltration by spies and straightforward proscription.

The Federation was ideologically averse to offering valuable cups and prizes at its sports meetings, and so lost some competitors to middle-class cycling events, where the prizes could be substantial. This put the middle-class clubs into a quandary. They were ideologically committed to encourage the working classes to develop their physique on behalf of the Fatherland, but were upset at seeing their prizes carried off by sturdy newcomers, many of whom 'trained' daily on heavyweight delivery cycles.

One of Hitler's first acts upon assuming power in 1933 was to criminalise cycling unions, which were associated with anti-Nazi political parties. Brownshirts were sent to villages to confiscate bikes.

The British counterpart was the Clarion Cycling Club, which was founded nationally in 1895 and reached a maximum membership of around 8000 before being incapacitated by the First World War.

Members of the Workers' Cycling Federation Solidarity exhort comrades to "Get out of the Bourgeois Sports Clubs".

The club was born of the Clarion Fellowship, a sporting and charitable socialist movement. It emphasised outdoor leisure pursuits: fellowship and fresh air, away from the cities. In 1941 the historian R K Ensor was to write that the Clarion movement's newspaper:

66 mirror(s) admirably their hobbies and ideals... cycling, literature, music, arts-and-crafts, 'rational' dress, feminism, vegetarianism and back-to-the-land – all gaily jostling one another in a generous and Utopian atmosphere of socialist enthusiasm. 99

The movement's father figure was Robert Blatchford, whose gifted socialistic writings drew in thousands of converts despite some distasteful jingoism and military-mindedness.

Clarion fellowship was reinforced by the club badge, the wearing of red caps (by some cycling clubs) and by a rag bag of little rituals such as the shout of "Boots!" on spying a fellow Clarionette cycling, who would be expected to respond by shouting "Spurs!"

In the USA the Labour Party initiated a Socialist Wheelmen's Club in 1898. It had a uniform of light brown jacket, blue sweater and tie, and a cap of socialist red. Shortly after the club's foundation the members rode en masse from Boston to New York distributing their literature on the way.

Cycling in France was boosted by the introduction of the 40-hour week and paid holidays, as part of the leisure policy of Leon Blum's socialist Front Populaire government, elected in 1936. In the few years left before the war Parisian cyclists almost monopolised the roads as they left the city for their weekend tours of the countryside.

Struggle and Change

The peoples of Europe and America gave a high priority to recreation. They filled sports stadiums and cinemas, holiday camps and seaside resorts. Many thousands of European cycle-tourists continued to take quiet, private pleasure in meandering through rural lanes and villages. The cycle industry in the UK tried hard to revive the association of cycling with the delights of the countryside:

" *Don't you sometimes long to get away from it all? Away from the streets of serried houses... only a few miles away is a different land... Sheltering amongst the trees you see the spire of the village church – beyond it that quaint old thatched cottage where the good wife serves fresh*

The Cyclists' Manual from 1954 associated cycling with rural wholesomeness.

eggs and ham fried 'to a turn' on a table of rural spotlessness, for everything is so clean in the country... Rosy health and a clear brain is what Raleigh gives you! **"**

British manufacturers struggled to make cycling aspirational.

Appealing for steel, around 1960. Ironically the bicycle looks heavy and outdated compared to the item of streamlined aluminium roaring past.

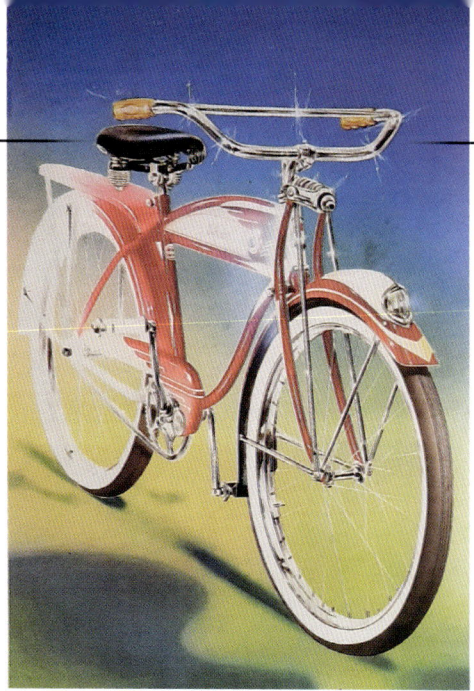

But the public was avid for new sensations and consumer goods, and the most evident was the motor car. So imperative was the motoring cause in Britain, and many other countries, that it made cyclists seem like unenterprising and insignificant social stragglers. They began to be treated as such.

Governments worldwide showed little interest in controlling road transport and it might, in any case, have seemed politically questionable to deny working people a luxury which the affluent minority had long enjoyed. The total number of kilometres travelled by British cyclists dropped steadily from about 23bn in 1952 to just under 4bn in 1974. The Cyclists' Touring Club lost members, before a revival in the period after 2000, and a change of name to Cycling UK.

In the 1970s the bicycle became a symbol of progressive politics along with environmental and spiritual wholesomeness. It embodied the lofty countercultural ideals of peace, love, unity and dissent. According to a pedal-power manifesto in the seventies the bicycle was *"perhaps an interface between East and West… the machine which makes us all brothers and sisters."*

Cycle makers in the US concentrated on the youth market. This is Schwinn's B Series cycle, popular from the late 1940s onwards. They were heavy machines with motorbike styling: imitation tank, whitewall tyres and spring fork.

With climate change threatening the planet, the language has grown more messianic. The bicycle is now *"our greatest invention"*, *"the most benevolent machine,"* *"rideable art that can just about save the world."*

Wiki Commons.

Workers from the Rog bicycle factory at the May Day parade in Ljubljana, Slovenia, 1961. They are celebrating the making of their 200,000th bicycle.

Wiki Commons.

Photo: Sascha Kohlmann.

Some northern European countries have been more responsive to new ideas. In 1975 the Dutch government recognised that it needed a 'steering' rather than an 'adaptive' policy towards traffic, and started a substantial programme for the building and improvement of cycle paths both in towns and across country. Dutch planners made sure that motor traffic is either physically prohibited or else forced by careful road design to slow down to cycling speed, and in which all services and facilities are sited within walking or cycling distance.

The last 30 years have also seen the creation of national and international networks of (largely) traffic-free paths for walkers and cyclists. Each network is typically the work of a national not-for-profit, such as Sustrans in the UK, liaising with local governments. The networks in European countries, are co-ordinated under a transnational organisation, Eurovelo, and Rails to Trails are building long distance paths in the USA.

The American bicycle boom developed along recreational rather than utilitarian or specifically radical lines. It intensified in the late 1970s, boosted by the development of a strong popular interest in health and fitness. Cycling in the United States has secured an assured and popular status, but mostly with the affluent classes. Its popularity had no great effect on social attitudes to motoring since the two are rarely seen as competing with each other.

In Germany the bicycle became a major component and symbol of 'alternative' politics and counter-cultural lifestyles. The more radical have tended to reject conformity and consumerism in cycling matters. Recreational cycling became a hugely popular activity in Germany, helped by a vigorous programme of cycle path construction. The German cycle industry is one of the strongest in the world, selling to a home market which demands high quality.

The provision of cycles has certainly changed. Strong commercial investment in cycle design has brought reliability, style and new directions. For example there are now around 30 different formats of cycle for carrying children.

The rise of the mountain bike brought new energy and riders to the cycling scene, and advances in MTB technology soon benefitted all forms of cycling. The turn of the century saw a boom, in northern European countries, in the kind of road-riding clubs common in France, Italy and Spain: with fast cycling on lightweight bikes and wearing lycra.

Some argue that this has caused a cultural shift away from fun and discovering the world, towards a macho world of speed and Strava.

Pool noodles make space in Germany.
Photo: NorbertM/@radelflieger

Activists make space in the UK.

Perhaps the most significant transport activity in Africa and Asia is the local carrying of vital goods, such as farm produce, water and firewood: between farms, villages and local market places. For centuries this has been done using head, hands and shoulders, or by bullock-cart. The bicycle has made such short distance transport more practical and efficient, improving the lives of hundreds of millions.

In South America load-carrying cycling also became significant. In Bogotá, Columbia, a major bakery had constant problems maintaining the 90 vans which supplied its 20,000 sales outlets. In about 1983 it replaced them with 1200 carrier tricycles. Distribution costs fell from 27% to 8% of total costs and a thousand new jobs were created.

In some developing countries high levels of transport cycling in cities is perceived as a problem by the authorities. At one point the Indonesian government banished 40,000 tricycle rickshaw taxis from Jakarta's roads.

However useful the trishaw may be, it has brought daily misery to many of those it employs: with long hours, heavy loads and high temperatures. Low incomes leave the drivers (and their families) malnourished, and drivers are typically worn out and short lived. The progress of cycling has never been even across the globe.

In 'developed' countries the 'new cyclists' of the 1970s and 80s were, in general, more demonstrative and impatient for change than older, established cyclists. In their turn pre-existing cyclists pointed out they had been 'keeping the faith' during the dark years, and that the aggressive or flamboyant behaviour of the newcomers harmed the status and image of cycling.

A cycle placed by the Cambridge Cycle Campaign. Anger and sorrow at cyclists' deaths on dangerous roads have become expressed in the form of white bicycles parked at accident scenes. This has become a form of remembrance and protest in many parts of the world.

The 'bike lift' by around 100,000 people at Budapest's Critical Mass in 2013. Critical mass rides in big cities are sometimes officially sanctioned, but are more often 'spontaneous'. Some argue that the antagonism caused by such events are outweighed by the net benefit. Participants see them as asserting and celebrating the bicycle's place in a modern city: not a protest but a demonstration of the social space cyclists deserve and claim.

At national level in many countries a handful of under-funded campaigners have faced the comfortably financed and well connected representatives of the road construction companies, car manufacturers, road hauliers, fuel industries and motorists' associations. Campaigners and advocates have countered with low budget techniques to spread awareness and calls to action. Their methods seek maximum impact and media attention.

Perhaps the world's most effective campaign has been Le Monde à Bicyclette, based in Montreal. One of its leading activists, Bob Silverman, argued that 'when the system accepts cyclists, cyclists will accept the system.' Many advocacy groups prefer practical measure to get people cycling: through roadcraft training and repair and maintenance tuition. Others techniques are more demonstrative, including urban 'races' between a car driver, a public transport user and a cyclist, all timed for how long they took to arrive at the same destination. Cyclists usually win.

All traditional techniques of persuasion were sidelined in the big cities by a form of cycling which simply met people's needs. Bike share schemes became an alternative to ownership, positioning the bicycle as a ready and culturally neutral tool for travel. Urban local authorities have made bike share schemes a major part of their active travel programmes, with operating contracts given to international private companies. Over two decades these refined their techniques and technology and the phenomenon seems to have succeeded. However, these programmes rarely provide for the rapidly increasing number of specialised, larger cycles such as cargo bikes and cycles for people with disabilities.

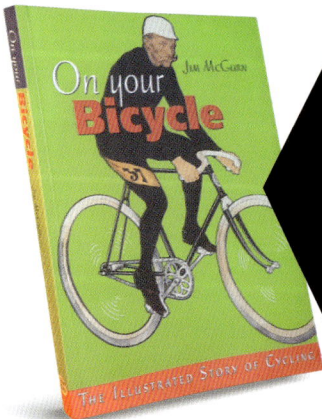

If you have enjoyed this short history of cycling, and want to read more, you may be interested in another book by Jim McGurn: *On your Bicycle, the Illustrated Story of Cycling*. It was first published by John Murray and this is the updated second edition published by Company of Cyclists. ISBN 978-1-0682336-1-6. It has 208 pages with 120 mono and colour images. You can order online for £16.95 including UK postage. Cycle Magic can also be ordered this way. To find out more, including non-UK postage costs, visit *companyofcyclists.co.uk*.

Looking Back with Love

Some of the splendour of British cycling heritage is recreated by Sarah and Hannah Loose on the platform of a heritage railway station. Photo: John Styles.

Members of veteran cycle clubs are a breed apart. Not all are collectors, but most find pleasure in restoring, or simply owning and riding fine, venerable technology. Regional groups organise regular rides and national get-togethers, so bystanders can sometimes see a whole parade of cycle history passing before their eyes. Dress varies: some go all the way, scrupulously, and some just wear clothing which is not overtly modern. Not all have a firm grasp of sartorial history: top hats, for example, were not worn by wheelmen in the era of high ('penny farthing') bicycles. Some members ride high bicycles competitively, sensibly wearing helmets and with little attempt at traditional clothing.

Members share advice, spare parts and happy memories. There are clubs and branches worldwide, but mostly in northern Europe and the US. The UK has the Veteran-Cycle Club. Annual events, each in a different part of the world, are organised by the International Veteran Cycle Association, based in the USA.

Two enthusiasts from Northumberland make it a family affair.

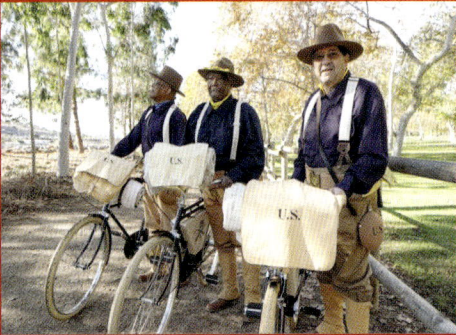

▲ *The first US bicycle corps, formed in 1896 and made up of Black riders, is honoured by US Army veterans who replicated the bicycles and uniforms to ride in commemoration.*

▲ *Veteran cycle enthusiasts prize Mochet Velocars produced in the early 1930s in France. Very few originals made it to the USA so some enthusiasts there, such as this couple, have made their own, to preserve the concept and have fun. Photo: International Veteran Cycle Association.*

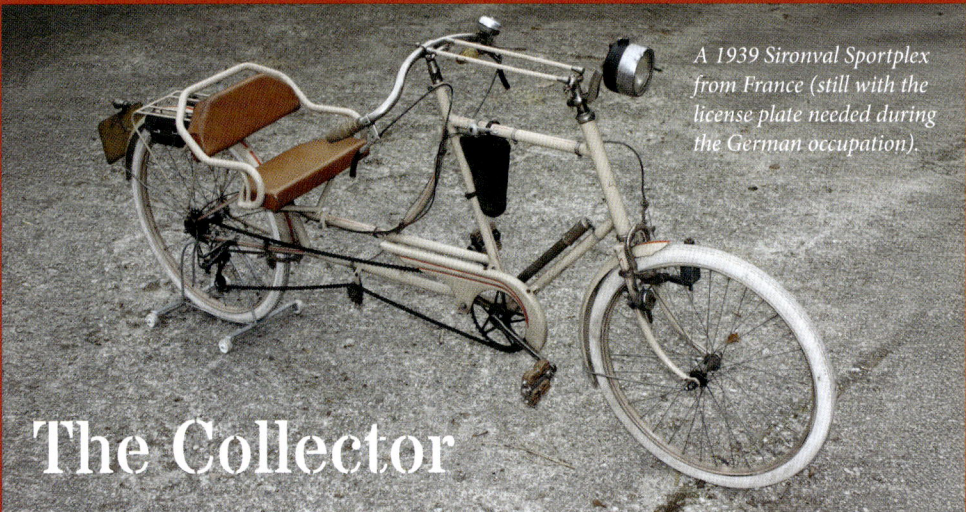

A 1939 Sironval Sportplex from France (still with the license plate needed during the German occupation).

The Collector

Some simply find pleasure in owning and caring for remarkable cycles. One such collector in Germany cherishes mostly early 20th century cycles. Known simply as AJ, he has put nearly 4000 images of his cycles on Flickr. It's essentially a museum in pictures. Search Flickr for AJ collectvelo.

▶ *A 1910 Dürkopp Diana from Germany with fixed wheel, a single high gear and wooden rims. This will probably have been a track racing machine.*

CHAPTER 2
A World full of Cyclists
People, Places and Cultures

Photo:
Edgar R. Batte,
from the series
Play (Uganda).

Going Dutch

Wikimedia.

Living by water and a cycle route. Dutch by design. Photo: Nanda Sluijsmans.

66 *The Dutch have one of the most physically active populations in the world, largely because it is built into their urban fabric. They also have the happiest children in the world, largely because they can move freely and independently from around eight.* **99**

So say the Dutch Cycling Embassy, committed to spreading the word worldwide. Dutch children do seem especially healthy, confident, self-reliant and socially adjusted, and most of them grow into adults that way. Somebody riding a bicycle in the Netherlands is not defined as a cyclist, in the same way that someone walking is not defined as a shoe user. When almost everybody uses a bike then cycling is far from being a sub-culture.

The solid, conservative design of the Dutch bicycle and its enormous social visibility have come to symbolise the national identity. Many say it represents the old Protestant virtues of simplicity,

hard work, respectability, the common good: and an egalitarian outlook, with all bikes and their riders equal in the eyes of the Lord.

The cycling experience is not the same all over the Netherlands. The heavily populated south of the country consists mainly of the Randstad. This is a huge conurbation of 7.5 million people formed by Amsterdam, Leiden, The Hague, Rotterdam and Utrecht. The Dutch have built a complex transport system throughout the Randstad, with cycle paths as an intrinsic part. However, in a city like Amsterdam, despite all its cycle paths, bicycle journeys can be stressful, especially for foreigners. Everything happens so quickly, and the natives tend to ride with limited mercy for non-native cyclists. Some visitors find this really exciting. The challenges of inner city cycling are not representative of cycling in the Netherlands in general: outside the city you find cycling to be a relaxing, peaceful and well-organised experience.

North and east of the Randstad is a treasured area which the Dutch call the *Groene Hart* (Green Heart). It does have significant towns, such as Gouda, but is kept from major new urbanisation. It's a heavily wooded expanse of nature reserves and low-impact outdoor leisure facilities. The Dutch go to great lengths to preserve the Green Heart: they even chose to tunnel a new high-speed rail line under part of it. This breathing space is where the people of the Randstad like to go cycling for leisure and is a superb cycling holiday destination for anyone wanting a good mix of nature and small historic towns.

In the north of the Netherlands the provinces of Drenthe, Friesland and Groningen are far less densely populated. Groningen is in the very north. Its capital, also called Groningen, has the highest cycling levels of any city in Europe: at 55% of total mobility. However, it's Drenthe which is generally regarded as the foremost cycling province of the Netherlands, with thousands of kilometres of cycle paths through forest, over heathland and along canals.

Drenthe is also famous for the *Drentse Fietsvierdaagse*. Every July over 12,000 ordinary Dutch cyclists of all ages enjoy four days of riding round the Province, with community support from towns and villages en route. There are now 60 or so smaller *Fietsvierdaagse* events in other parts of the Netherlands

The Netherlands has become the role model for any industrialised country hoping to place everyday cycling at the heart of its culture, and the 30,000 kilometres of cycle path certainly help. The country may have an intensive road network and a fine public transport system, but large parts of this densely populated country would congeal into one enormous urban traffic jam if millions were to opt out of cycling. The share of cycling in total mobility is 26% for the Dutch, compared to 18% in Denmark. If the level of cycling in the Netherlands were replicated by all other countries, annual global carbon emissions would reduce by 686m tonnes.

A helping hand after a cycling accident in Amsterdam. This photo coincidentally captures the variety of cycles now common in the city: a traditional 'granny-bike', a modern, stylish van Moof, an OV share-bike and (carrying the child) a solid Batavus 'personal bike' with easy step-over.

A street scene in Utrecht – all kinds of bikes for all kinds of people.

'Dinking' is common practice in the Netherlands and Denmark. Photos: Mikael Colville-Andersen.

There is some interesting background to the Netherlands' cycling success. In 1959 the Dutch discovered they were sitting on the largest gas field in Europe, in the province of Groningen. Its exploitation allowed the country to radically improve its national infrastructure, including

Riding on the front rack is sociable but not as common as riding on the back. A third technique, often used by children, is standing on the rear rack with hands on your friend's shoulders.

flood defences, polder creation and the welfare state. It was also spent on infrastructure for cycling, helped by a widely supported popular campaign highlighting road safety measures to protect children, and equity issues. When Dutch neighbourhoods were destroyed to create space for motorised traffic, casualties rose. In 1971, the year traffic accidents peaked, they claimed the lives of 400 children. Then the true cost of gas extraction was discovered: earthquakes and subsidence across the region, and a compensation bill still being paid. The gas field has now been closed, leaving around 450bn cubic metres of gas underground. The right wing government wants to re-open the gas fields with, oddly, electoral support from the people who live in areas affected by the earthquakes. In the meantime cycling had become a national necessity.

The Dutch investment in cycling infrastructure came about because the people demanded it. Perhaps this pressure was not as intense as in other industrialised countries because the Netherlands had next to no car industry of its own. And perhaps it also helped that smaller, more heterogeneous nations can better focus the self-confidence and power of the people. In the Netherlands this triggered national protests, radical revision and a serious rethink, beginning in the 1970s, of the country's transport and land use policies. It entailed a dramatic shift in favour of walking, cycling and public transport. It had become clear that mobility systems and land use systems are strongly interdependent. The task was to coordinate the planning of both so that all new investments now translate into more cycling, walking and public transport. The Danes, Swedes and Germans also moved in these directions.

The Dutch laid new paths, busy cities were traffic-calmed, and ambitious innovation was applied, an example being the immense bike park in front of the Central Station in Amsterdam housing 11,000 bicycles, some of them in an underwater garage.

The statisticians played their role. The Dutch estimated that for the £0.5bn invested annually in bike infrastructure there are total economic health benefits of £19bn.

Dutch urban and transport planners organised into a Cycling Embassy in 2012, offering consultancy and expertise across the globe. The Danes offer similar. A Dutch design manual for bicycle

traffic has inspired many of the bicycle planners in the western world, although there's a general recognition that many countries find it hard to apply radical planning measures to pull back from mass auto use, especially in the cities. But the problem would be even worse without the shining lights of the Netherlands and Denmark.

▲ *A traditional Dutch cargo tricycle. This one is a hire cycle: often booked by people transporting heavy personal goods. Students use them to move to new accommodation. Photo: Mikael Colville-Andersen.*

Many Dutch teenagers enjoy pleasant, sociable journeys to and from school. Active travel at its best.

What makes a good Dutch 'city bike'?

It's a bike to take you as you are. Expect an upright riding position, easy riding geometry, a comfortable sprung saddle, perhaps an open frame for either sex to get on and off easily, and a sturdy rear rack for large shopping panniers (and occasionally for giving lifts to friends). Most will have a full chainguard, skirt guards on the back wheel, a parking stand and a built-in security lock passing through the rear wheel.

Also expect hub brakes at the centre of each wheel, seven or eight gears in the rear wheel hub and a possibly a front hub dynamo to give you lights – Dutch wheel hubs are busy places. So much is fitted within the hubs to give maximum, carefree reliability in all conditions. Don't expect a really low gear for hills – the Dutch don't do hills. Higher value cycles may also have a quick-release lever so you can adjust the handlebar position in seconds. Components and accessories will be of quality, to withstand the kind of weather the Dutch care to cycle in.

Photo: faceme, Wiki Commons.

You can also expect your average Dutch bike shop to be populated by mainly electric cycles. That's the way the market is moving, but it means a lot of nice non-electric city bikes are being pushed onto the secondhand market.

If you are really keen to go native you can ride an *omafiets* (granny's bike). This is a certain type of lower cost, basic and heavy city cycle, usually single-geared. These are OK as utility machines for getting round town, but they are typified by having only one brake, and that's a back-pedal brake – riding with only one brake is illegal in many countries but not in the Netherlands.

This Gazelle Classic is the traditional omafiets with a back-pedal brake and three hub gears.
This export version has a front wheel hub brake.

This e-assist bike from Sparta has a mid-drive motor, a frame-integrated battery, front suspension and disk brakes.

It's not all hub gears and grandma bikes

The Dutch may be famous for their utility cycling but there is also a strong culture of club-based sports cycling.

Above are the 'captains' of the *Immer Weiter* ('Ever Further') Cycling Club out for a team-building ride. They claim to be the first ever Dutch cycling club – founded in Deventer in 1871. Oddly, their name is German.

Many successful professional cyclists on the international stage are Dutch and professional cycle sport is followed avidly. Peter Post and Joop Zoetemelk are famous names in Dutch cycling. Mattieu van der Poel is a modern cycling hero for the Dutch. Here he competes at the Milan-Sanremo in 2023. At 296km (185 miles) it's currently the longest professional one-day cycle race.

Denmark does bikes

Cool dad with four kids in Copenhagen. Photo: kristoffertrolle.com.

There's a strong 'cycle chic' sentiment in Denmark and particularly in Copenhagen. It promotes cycling as being compatible with looking and feeling good. Photo: Mikael Colville-Andersen.

Copenhagen ranks as the world's best capital city for cycling, and the figures are astonishing. For every citizen €40 is spent each year on cycling infrastructure, with an approval rate of 97% amongst Copenhageners. Three quarters of cyclists happily keep riding all through the long, dark, Danish winters. Ten years ago 35% of all trips to work or school in Copenhagen were by bike (and lots more on foot). That cycling figure is now 49% and growing, thanks largely to investment and innovation.

What is it about Copenhageners that makes them take to the bicycle every morning come rain, sleet, or snow? Are Copenhageners more eco-conscious than the rest of us? Are they all health freaks? Is it all to do with Danish DNA? None of these. It's all to do with infrastructure: a network of simple, protected and connected facilities for cyclists of all ages and abilities. This comes in the form of traffic-calmed streets, demarcated bike lanes and separated cycle tracks. No user manual required.

Nørrebrogaden (right) in Copenhagen is the street with the highest level of cycle traffic in Europe. The prominent public trip counter reinforces commitment to cycling. In the year after such counters were installed in the city 10m cyclists had passed a counter, the equivalent of twice the population of Denmark.

On some streets there are even 'conversation lanes': ideal for slower or less confident riders. It works because each conversation lane is next to a separate lane for faster riders. There are green routes running through parks, by waterfronts, railway lines, and sometimes highways, but well buffered from motor traffic. These paths help stitch together the network of on-street bike lanes. The design of these off-street greenways still maintains a separation between pedestrians and bicycle riders through different surface colours. Some, like the harbour ring, are better suited for recreational riders, while others, like the region's ever expanding cycle highways, provide long stretches of comfortable and uninterrupted routes for commuters.

People of all ages cycle in Copenhagen not only because it's safe, but because it feels safe. There is only one serious accident each year for every 5.7 million kilometres cycled, and these are people who don't wear cycles helmets. The number of seriously injured cyclists has decreased by one third in the last decade, and polls show that more than three quarters of residents feel safe when cycling.

The famous bike traffic counter.

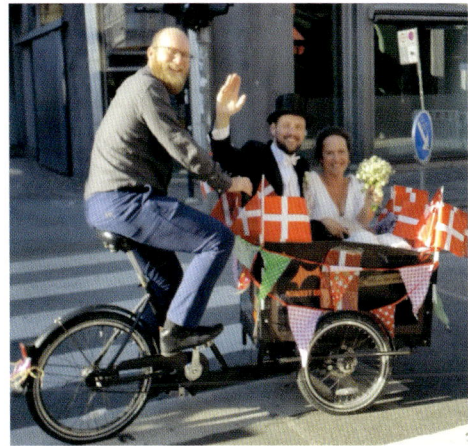

Getting married. A limousine car might not have accessed the place they needed to be.

Looking stylish on bikes, day and night. All photos this page: Mikael Colville-Andersen.

Mikael Colville-Andersen.

With safer infrastructure come more bicycle riders. And with more riders comes the safety in numbers, linked to their mass and their visibility.

The city council has a goal of three lanes in each direction on 80% of its network. To really tie the city together cycling infrastructure needed to be even more connected. Copenhagen is bisected by a harbour and smaller canals, so large gaps had to be bridged. The Quay Bridge (Bryggebroen), completed in 2006, was the first of many new connections built over the harbour. Traffic planners had predicted 3,300 daily bicycle crossings for this bridge, but within months of opening more than 9,000 were counted, of which one third were former car drivers. In other words

the existence of this strategically placed bridge has actually created cycling trips. And the latest numbers show that more than 20,000 now cycle across the bridge daily.

Next to the Quay Bridge is the Cycle Snake (Cykelslangen) Bridge, so named because of its 220 metres of delightful curves sweeping cyclists across the harbour. It has been called Copenhagen's cycling skyway.

Nordisk Cryobank's Sperm Bike for transporting sperm donations to fertility clinics around Copenhagen. Photo: Mikael Colville-Andersen.

The Cyclists' Snake Bridge. Photo: Dissing Weitlingen.

Copenhagen rush hour. The snow plough has cleared just one lane of the bike path, which explains why they are all strung out. ▼

The bridges make the cycling experience more special. They brighten up the commute of tens of thousands. But in the late afternoon it's different. Commuters cycle back from work in a more relaxed style. Some cycle two abreast, chatting and laughing. They are joined by parents on the school run, chugging along on their cargo bikes with their kids up front. All of this watched by people lining the bridge, enjoying the late afternoon sun, having a drink, and just watching the evening pass by. It's a rush hour like no other.

The Island of Fyn (English: Funen). Away from the cities Denmark is a cyclists' paradise. The 'mainland' is the peninsula of Jutland, but to the east there are 1,419 islands, 78 of them inhabited. The rural cycle path networks link the villages and towns, but they also take you over bridges between islands, and to ferry points. Photo: visitfyn.com.

Belgium – land of cycling surprises

Belgium is an under-appreciated cycling country. It has delightful bike-friendly historic cities such as Bruges and Antwerp, but Ghent has been the city to watch. It's divided into segments, like slices of a cake. Motorists are not able to move laterally from one to the next, or get close to the city centre, making life much easier for cyclists and walkers. People with disabilities can buy very cheap vouchers for cycle rickshaw taxis.

Belgium is crossed by over 1000km of international EuroVelo routes, with 15 new cycling superhighways under construction. Everyday cycle paths are more common in the Flemish-speaking north of the country– regions such as Flanders, Limbourg, Antwerp and Brabant, where paths connect most villages and towns. In the French-speaking regions of southern Belgium the cycle paths are not as good and in some cases non-existent in towns.

Wiki Commons.

Ghent old town. Photo: Slywire.

In some regions of Belgium, particularly the northern Flemish-speaking provinces, they use a system of cycle network routes known as the *'Fietsroutenetwerk'*. Each intersection or *'knooppunt'* (connection point) on the cycle network shows a unique number. Signs are then placed along the route giving you directions to the next numbered intersection. At each intersection there is a map showing you all the further numbered intersections on your route. You just look at the map, decide your route, note down the numbers and then follow the well marked signs. It's cycling by numbers, and has been adopted throughout the Netherlands.

'Citycycling' offer cycle tours of Ghent's famous street art and graffiti art zones.

On the beach at Blankenberge, near Ostende, the crazy bikes of the Velodroom (Velo-Dream) have been giving pleasure since 1933. At the end of each season the whole wooden edifice is taken down and stored for the winter.

The province of Limburg has created unusual attractions on its cycle route network. In the Pijnven Nature Reserve in Bosland you can cycle through the tree canopy for 700m, ten metres above the ground.

In Bokrijk you can cycle beneath the water level of a lake. Photos: Visit Limburg.

France – projects go national

Personal and share-scheme cycles on the Champs-Élysées. Few had believed it possible. Photo: Ninara, Wiki Commons.

France is the spiritual home of the bicycle. Cyclists are generally respected – in the country's great expanses of rural delight, but not so much in its cities. This is starting to change. The French government's *Plan Vélo* is boosting cycling levels everywhere, but particularly in the cities, and Paris is leading the way with determination. It's removing 60,000 car parking spaces, laying down new cycle paths and bringing in pro-cycling legislation. There is now an east-west route along Boulevarde Haussmann and right past the *grands magazins*, pushing cars out of the picture. Paris has become a joy to ride around.

The Vélib hire scheme and others are popular, and parents and children commute in the morning on two to three person e-cargo bikes. By 2024, with the city's bike-sharing and cycle path programme

still far from completion, 11.2% of journeys in the Capital were by cycling and only 4.3% by car.

Already well established is the '*Paris Respire*' (Paris Breathes) project, with sectors of the city closed off to cars every Sunday. The quays of the Seine are always car-free, as are scenic trails in the Bois de Boulogne and Bois de Vincennes. The city is vigorously pursuing the 15-minute city concept, so that all significant facilities and services are within a fifteen minute active travel journey.

Plan Vélo is not just about facilities. It supports behaviour change through persuasion and incentives. For example the government has a €5bn investment fund to finance innovative businesses in the cycling sector.

Outside the cities cyclists from around the world are drawn to the country's famously cycle-friendly rural roads, which partly make up the network of well sign-posted long-distance cycle routes. This includes the ten different EuroVélo routes crossing the country. The French know what cycling treasures they have, and market cycle tourism energetically. It's no surprise that France has become the second biggest market for cycle tourism in Europe. There's an impressive website which puts some delicious touring ideas and useful information on your plate. In several languages

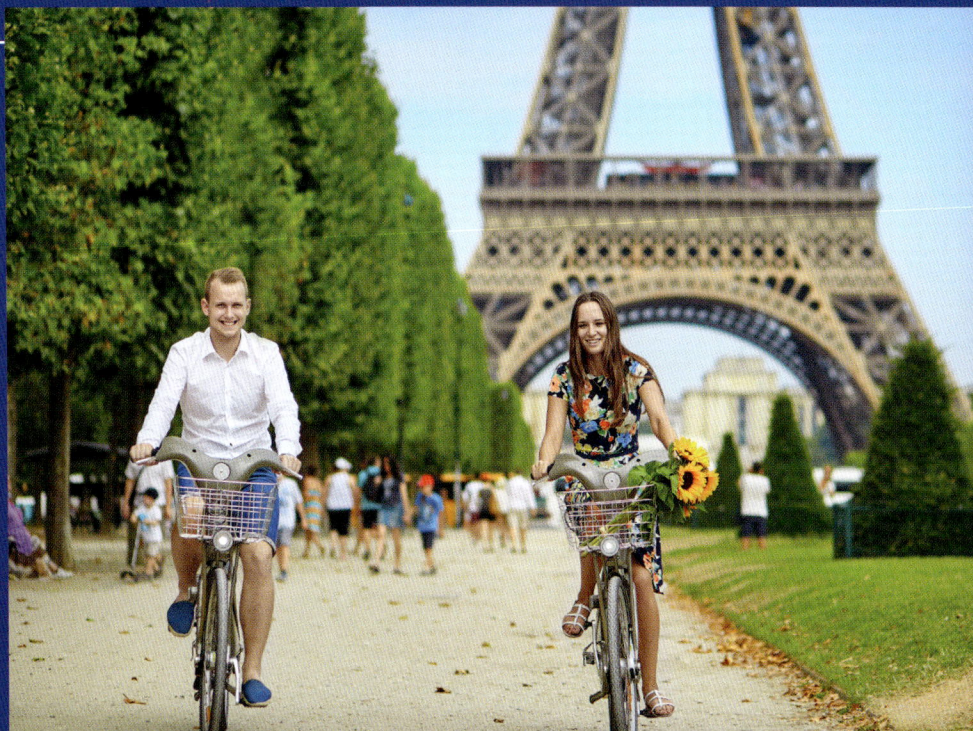

francevelotourisme.com presents a detailed route-finder facility with downloadable route maps, including a topographical profile of each route chosen. The site also gives access to *Accueil Vélo*, a national accreditation scheme guaranteeing a high quality of welcome and services for cyclists, covering accommodation, restaurants, cycle repair services and more.

Canal des Deux Mers - from sea to sea

For many years the *Canal des Deux Mers* has been a popular cycling route linking the Atlantic Coast to the Mediterranean. However, it has until now been a piecemeal affair loosely connecting four different routes. Now there is a continuous and 'official' *Canal des Deux Mers*, starting in Royan in Poitou-Charentes and ending on the Mediterranean Coast at Sète. The route takes cyclists through many regions of France, each with its own character. It follows the Gironde Estuary to Bordeaux, then the wonderful Roger Lapebie bike path linking through to Sauveterre, then onto the Canal de Garonne. From here it's the 'normal' tried and tested route through to Toulouse and the start of the famous Canal du Midi cycle path. *Photos: Lauragais Tourism.*

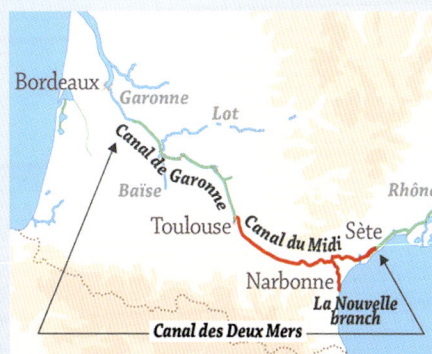

The cycle path under the Bir-Hakeim Bridge over the Seine. The network is being joined up.

The Veloscenic (Véloscénie) is a well-signposted cycle route taking you 450km (280 miles) from Paris to Mont Saint-Michel. Long stretches are 'greenways', linked by quiet roads. Go to veloscenic.com. Photo: Joel Damase.

Winter cycling in the Place d'Italie.
Cycling round Paris has become a joy.
Photo: Roman Bonnefoy.

Wikimedia.

Germany powers change

Photo: *Rückenwind Bike Tours.*

With more than 260 major bicycle routes, a strong cycling infrastructure and an enormous cycle holiday sector, Germany is regarded as the foremost cycling country in Europe. Cycle-friendly hotels, guesthouses, restaurants and repair facilities have sprung up along the major tourist cycle paths, making them service corridors for cyclists. Many are attracted to the wide paths alongside Germany's large rivers, which give fairly flat but eventful cycling. The route along the Weser river, for example, runs from the North Sea to Hannoversch Münden: a total of 450km. Another popular route follows the Danube, with the German part running through imposing landscapes from Donaueschingen to Passau. From there you can ride on to Vienna (the most popular section), to Budapest or even as far as the Black Sea.

Existing routes are being supplemented by a superhighway network dedicated exclusively to bicycles. One of the new routes will follow abandoned railways for 100km, to connect ten big cities in the Ruhr area. This is expected to remove 50,000 cars daily from the area's roads. There are similar projects at different stages of completion in other big population centres.

According to German statisticians 30% of households in German cities of over 500,000 inhabitants use the bicycle as the sole mean of transport. More than 80% of Germans use bicycles, especially for rides of less than 15km. The Berliners have gone one step further–the city has 620km of well used cycle paths, placing it amongst cities with the highest rate of bike commuting in the world. Berlin has 710 bicycles per 1,000 inhabitants.

Each region of Germany has its distinctive character, and since reunification new regions have been open to discovery. Regional differences are matched by the many local versions of German, which range from the Frisian 'Platt' of the North Sea shore to the rugged dialect of deepest Bavaria. But everyone understands standard High German. Culturally, too, Germany is a varied land. Until around 150 years ago 'Germany' was no more than a very loose grouping of relatively independent bishoprics, principalities and kingdoms. This has led to the development of all sorts of local cultural peculiarities–best discovered on a bicycle!

Cycling city Münster

The figures can speak for themselves. Münster is blessed with around 500,000 bikes – averaging 1.67 per inhabitant, The station's cycling facilities are the largest in Germany, with secure parking for 3,500 cycles, a cycle repair service, a bike wash and a rental service charging just €9 per day, and €25 for an ebike. Further rental facilities and bike dealers are dotted around the city. In fact over 100 cycling related businesses are registered with the city council. The story goes on. Munster has 450km of urban cycle paths and cycle roads, linking to 255km of cycle paths located off the main roads on access routes. This all explains why Münster has been voted Germany's most bicycle-friendly city several times. It would be a very different city without the *Leeze* – the local dialect word for bicycle.

Münster has something else special to offer. It is located at the heart of Münsterland, a region which seems made for cycling, giving visitors 4,500km of themed cycle routes and circuits taking in plenty of historic moated castles and nature reserves. The region uses the system of numbered junctions on cycle routes long common in the Netherlands, which is only four hours away by bike.

Münster positions itself as a green tourism destination and the people of the city enjoy the benefits which flow from that.

This was once a multi-storey car park attracting too many cars into the city. It's now Münster's mobility hub, supporting cycling and other forms of active travel.

Parking areas in Münster for sixteen cargo bikes.

The Promenade is a famous cycle and pedestrian path where the old city walls used to be. It encompasses almost the whole city. Photos: City of Münster.

The Spezialradmesse (Special Bike Show)

Once a year a small town in the very south of Germany hosts a bike show dedicated to alternatives in cycling. The International Special Bike Show in Lauchringen brings together 130 exhibitors and 10,000 cycling enthusiasts from many countries. It's an inspiring mix of bike makers, inventors and dealers: part exhibition, part social occasion, part information exchange, and part a celebration of diversity and progress. There's room for people to present new design concepts alongside exhibitors who have been coming to the 'Spezi' for decades and are producing successful commercial products which have finally moved more mainstream, such as recumbents, and cargo cycles.

Around the exhibition centre is a moving menagerie of pedal-powered creations, as imaginative cycle builders, and artists in kinetic metal, add to the fun. This is the 'Biest' created by Hase Cycles.

Exhibiting at the Spezi: an Urban Arrow e-bike pulling a Carla trailer with overrun braking.

German manufacturers are good at covering the needs of older cyclists, with low-step over bicycles and comfortable tricycles. (Photo: Hase Cycles)

The German bike industry

Underpinning Germany's relationship with the bicycle are the small and medium size businesses producing the high quality cycles which German customers expect. Graduates of engineering and commerce, energised by their love of cycling, have built up significant businesses developing new cycling products and concepts. A whole generation of creative designers and cycle makers are producing innovative cycles, and they are well supported by equally committed cycle dealers and by a buying public willing to spend good money on cycles of quality.

▲ *The Strada, a one-up-one-down tandem trike by Urban Fahrradbau.*

▲ *The Hase Pino cargo bike is a multi-purpose family cycle, featuring that enduring staple of German bicycle design: its ability to carry a crate of beer.*

◀ *Electric bikes are big business in Germany and German companies, such as Bosch and Heinzmann are making and developing high-end motors, electronics and batteries, competing well with Far East manufacturers. This e-bike from German company Riese and Müller incorporates a Bosch mid-drive motor.*

The UK struggles to catch up

The UK may have been the birthplace of the bicycle as we know it but it still has a long way to go in supporting cycling. Public investment in cycling has been battered by financial austerity and poor transport investment choices. How much cycling infrastructure could have been build with the money wasted on the HS2 rail line? However, the Labour government, elected in 2024, has reversed some of the cuts to active travel budgets. Its spend on cycling appears to be settling at around £10 per person per year. You don't get a lot for that.

Only around 13% of UK adults cycle at least once a month and the proportion of people cycling at least once a week has fallen to its lowest recorded level. Out of 28 European countries, the UK comes 22nd for 'cycling modal share' (2%), and 25th for the proportion of people using a privately owned bike or scooter (including electric) on a typical day (also 2%). Regional mayors have been given devolved powers for transport, and in particular active travel. This may make a difference in the big cities. London, whose mayor has long held meaningful powers, has already shown what can be done for cycling, and 13% of all journeys in the Capital are now by bicycle.

Claiming space

Sometimes what seems like a small change, costing virtually nothing, can bring enormous dividends. This was the case in the UK when, in 2023, the UK's Highway Code was altered so that drivers overtaking cyclists must leave at least 1.5m (5ft) of space from the cyclist at up to 30mph (48kph), and with a wider gap at higher speeds. Other countries are doing similar, but it's a big thing in the UK, which has few traffic-free cycle paths in its towns and cities. The concept seems generally to have worked. The Highway Code also now gives examples of how cyclists should ride defensively in the centre of the lane to block dangerous overtaking.

The Yorkshire Dales are a demanding but popular cycling region.

The National Cycle Network

The UK may be falling short in pro-cycling measures but the country does offer cyclists its quiet and attractive country lanes and bridleways.

The National Cycle Network has created 12,763 miles (20,540km) of signed cycle routes throughout the UK, including 5,500 miles (8,500km) of traffic-free paths. The rest of the network is on mostly minor roads with light motor traffic. The Network is managed by Sustrans, a national charity employing around 800 staff throughout the UK.

Sustrans have been developing and maintaining this ever expanding national asset for over 40 years, in co-operation with local and statutory authorities and landowners. They are aware that parts of the Network are not as well connected with each other as they should be, and their Connect2 programme tries to correct this. It remains a serious problem that large stretches of the Network are on 60mph (96kph) roads. Also many people have to use 60mph roads to access the Network in the first place. Some of the 60mph roads on the Network itself are lightly trafficked, but not all. Sustrans' routes across the UK are shown on an interactive map found on the Ordnance Survey website.

It seems odd to some that a nationally significant part of the UK's transport infrastructure is created and maintained by a charity which is partly dependent on lottery funding alongside some small financial support from government and other sources. Sustrans certainly do a good job, but their powers as a charity are limited. All 60mph roads on the Network should be reclassified to be cycle-friendly, with much lower speed limits.

Jason Patient

At rest in Rutland, England's smallest county. Its motto is 'Multum in Parvo'– a lot in a little. Country lanes can take you through the best of the UK's countryside. Our own favourite cycling regions are Suffolk, the Welsh Borders, the Scottish Lowlands and rural Yorkshire.

Sun and sea, bikes and bodies. The annual Brighton Naked Bike Ride symbolises cyclists' sense of vulnerability about traffic and the environment. Photo: Kevin Meredith.

Route 63 of the National Cycle Network passing Moira Furnace, and (right) a lakeside bike path in the National Forest. Photos: Jim McGurn.

It was once a scarred and treeless landscape after centuries of coalmining. Now the 9.8 million trees of the National Forest cover 25% of the designated 200 square miles (51,800 hectares) and the planting goes on. It spans parts of Derbyshire, Leicestershire and Staffordshire, and aims to link the two ancient forests of Charnwood and Needwood. A quarter of a century of planting means that large areas of the forest are now mature or maturing and wildlife is well established. A network of paths takes cyclists on circular routes through the lush woodland and parkland, and by well established lakes. The Ashby Canal runs through the Forest, with Route 63 of the National Cycle Network running alongside, passing Moira Furnace Museum and Country Park. There's also Conkers, a large, eco-friendly visitor attraction close to a modern eco-friendly youth hostel. The National Forest makes a very worthwhile holiday destination for cycling families.

A stylish participant in London's annual Tweed Race: a strange and very English celebration of traditional quality clothing and manners. Photo: Pat Meagher IG:Paddym01.

Through Space and Time

On the UK's National Cycle Network

The Sun is the width of your outstretched arms and the Earth the size of your thumb. You're doing 'warp-factor' on a 10km (6 mile) stretch of a Sustrans cycle path taking you south from York. The route is a scale model of the solar system, with the planets to be spotted and learned about along the route, with all sizes and distances to scale. Riding the planets gets you thinking. Here we are, clever apes full of busy on a fragile planet. We have invented the flint axe, the steam train, pot noodles and ChatGPT. And just before the end of the first industrial revolution we invented the bicycle.

The York Solar System is a journey through time, as well as through space. You feel history on all sides. You've come close to an old Roman road and the site of medieval gallows. You're on a section of the National Cycle Network which was once the domain of thunderous steam trains. It was previously part of the East Coast Main Line, made redundant in the early 1980s by rerouting to avoid subsidence from the new Selby Coalfield. The current path

The ice giant of Neptune is a tiny blue ball.
Photo: Rob Ainsley.

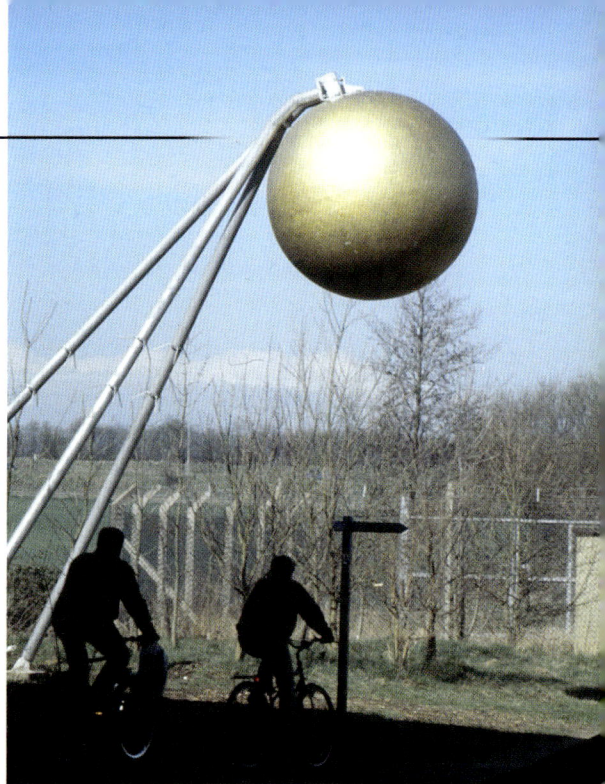

takes you past the village of Bishopthorpe, named after the stately palace of the Archbishop of York, banished to this rural retreat by Henry VIII. The path takes you across the river bridge whose engine was kept permanently in steam to open the swing bridge for tall-masters heading for York. Down below you can see the revetements of the wartime anti-aircraft guns, keeping the bridge safe for trains, including the Flying Scotsman. Over to the left is the still pretty village of Fulford (from the Old English 'foul-ford') close to the eponymous battlefield where King Harold's army defeated the invading Scandinavians in 1066, before rushing south to lose it all at Hastings. A bit further on you bump gently over bulges in the path as the roots of trees remind of the enduring power of nature. A touch further is a path-side pool which is home to great crested newts.

Riding on that famous path you become part of its story. Wars have passed, the trains are gone, the coalfield is closed and the path is now the leafy domain of bicycle, shoe leather and a lot of wildlife. On a bike we can experience close-up the physicality of nature, history and culture. Even on the most familiar routes, cycling lets you travel further than the distance you cover.

The York Solar System is on Route 65 of the NCN. It was created in 1999 by three University of York scientists: Dave Coulthard, Peter Thompson and Willy Hoedeman.

Brazil's bikes-only city

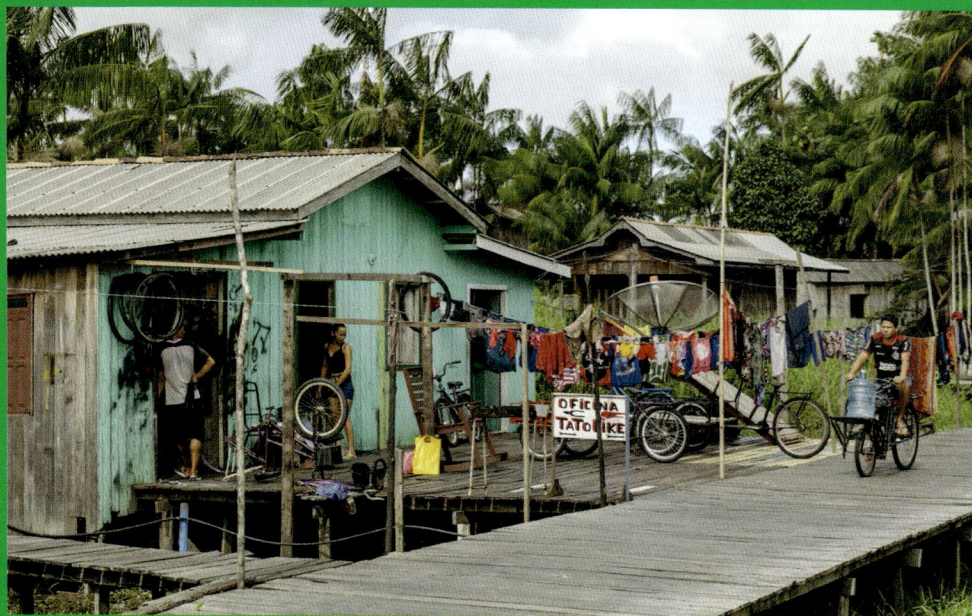

In Afuá, an isolated town on the Amazon River, the only ambulance is a pedal powered quadricycle. This *bicilance* gets you to the town's small public hospital, or to an ambulance boat which takes you on a long journey to the regional hospital. All taxis in Afuá are pedal-powered, and goods are carried by cargo cycle or boat. Motor-cycles, cars, vans and trucks are forbidden.

The reason is simple: Afuá, population 38,000, sits on the often inundated floodplains at the mouth of the Amazon. So the town largely consists of houses built on wooden platforms on stilts, and this just can't support motor vehicles. In between are waterways, and the locals jokingly call their town the Venice of the Amazon. Afuá may have a small carbon footprint but its poverty and income inequality are amongst the worst in Brazil. Less than 3 in 10 residents have access to running water, sewage mains or rubbish collection.

Even if Afuá were open to motor vehicles they could not make it into the town, as there are no access roads. The town had been offered an access road in 2010 by Pará state but turned it down in favour of a riverboat. This was a bold decision by this small community in Brazil's forgotten far north. Those Amazon towns which have received road connections have grown with their 'backs to the river', as locals put it. Research in Brazil and Colombia shows a downside to road access: nearly all Amazon deforestation occurs within a few kilometres of roadways.

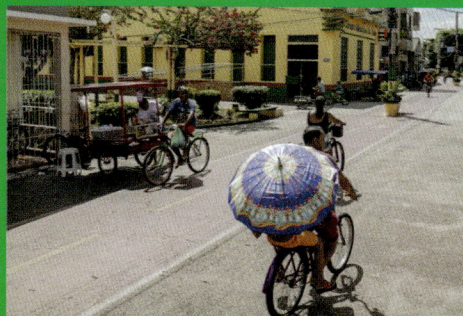

This story is based on a report by Mac Margolis, with support from the Rainforest Journalism Fund in partnership with the Pulitzer Center. Photos: Stefan Kolumban.

Cycling revivals in the USA

Recreational cycling is big in the USA but there are few examples of strong, everyday cycling culture. One such is Portland, in Oregon, where people have developed their own, unique cycling identity. Some of this is helped by infrastructure: the 640,000 inhabitants enjoy 650km of cyclepath. There's a lively community cycling centre run by a very imaginative cycling promotion group, BikePortland, coming up with community initiatives which set them apart.

Sunday Parkways. These are family-friendly closed-road cycling events using the city's largest public space – its streets – to walk, bike, roll, and discover active travel. Each ride passes through a number of 'activated' city parks filled with local food vendors, bike repair stations, community stalls, kids' activities and more. Portland's Sunday Parkways are rotated around the city so that all neighbourhoods take turns to benefit.

Pedalpalooza. Each year BikePortland organises a month-long festival of cycling with a wide spectrum of activities: from gentle led rides to serious races. In between are more exotic goings-on, such as cycle-jousting, 'bike plays' and mass rides with themes such as the clown ride and the cat ride for which people and bikes are dressed feline.

Bike Drives. BikePortland's Community Bike Drives identify children from low income families who have no bike. The volunteers provide each child, at no charge, with a refurbished cycle, a new helmet, and basic safety education. The bikes are delivered door-to-door every spring, summer and autumn, serving over 75 different families each time, and to over 300 qualifying children each December.

Portland is called the Rose City, but cycling promotion is not all flowers. As in any population centre there are competing views as to transport. The municipality is supportive of cycling, but BikePortland needs to keep up multiple campaigns challenging harmful new roadbuilding schemes.

Having fun moving house in Portland. Photo: Tim Davis.

However, the city is generally aware that its reputation for cycling boosts the economy, with a slant towards green tourism, and cycling generally attracts people to live in the city.

The Finch family in Portland gets around by bike… Emily and six kids! Photo: Jonathan Maus, Bikeportland.

Photo: Gerald Fittipaldi, Creative Commons

Davis loves bikes

The League of American Bicyclists has awarded 208 universities and colleges, in 47 states, the status of Bicycle Friendly University. The University of California Davis is always amongst the awards. The city of Davis is often called the Bicycle Capital of the USA. Its civic symbol is a penny-farthing. Why so much cycling? In the 1960s student numbers were about to skyrocket. Realising that the city was not going to cope with the extra traffic the cycle-loving chancellor pushed for a 'bicycle-riding, tree-lined campus' with cyclist-specific roundabouts. Prospective students were told not to bring a car but to buy a bike.

The city of Davis itself joined in with this 'bicyclisation' and now 98% of its main streets have some form of bicycle provision. Despite all this the campus and city suffered a halving of its cycling modal share during the 1980s, but this has since largely recovered.

Problem policing?

The social justice demonstrations following the murder of George Floyd in 2020 saw a deployment across dozens of US cities of police on bikes using controversial crowd-control tactics,

Officers on bikes are more mobile than the protesters. Arriving at the scene they hold their cycles sideways like a barricade or shield. Moving in unison, a relatively small number of officers can push back a large crowd. Seattle was among the first departments to use these techniques and they have been taught to police departments across the world. The Seattle Police Department itself has received many complaints about the use of undue force by their own bike squad.

Photo: Seattle Police.

Under construction is the Great American Rail-Trail stretching almost 6,000km from Washington DC in the East to Washington State on the Pacific Coast. This multi-use trail crosses 12 states. It was launched in 2019 and will eventually connect over 145 existing paths. Much is already open and progress can be followed online.

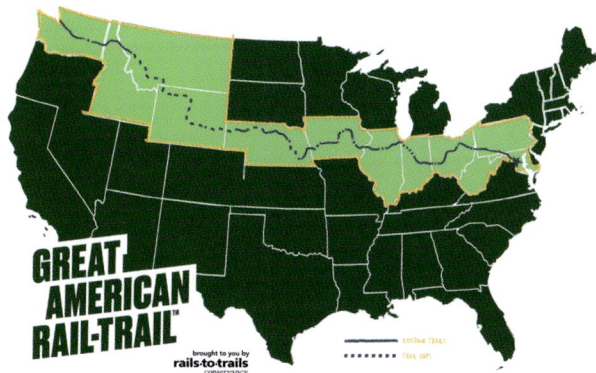

GREAT AMERICAN RAIL-TRAIL™

brought to you by rails-to-trails conservancy

Burning Man
Strange times in an American desert

The Neverwas Hall Art Car.
Photo: BLM Nevada. Wiki Commons.

Fantasy has no bounds. A solar car trundling round at 3.5mph, with rear bike rack. Photo: Kevin Meredith.

For a week each year Nevada's Black Rock Desert is the unlikely venue for a unique festival of creativity. Burning Man attracts around 80,000 people to a kind of temporary city based on radical self-expression and self-reliance. Comfort is not planned in, as shown by the muddy mess of 2023.

Bikes and trikes are a big part of Burning Man – some are grunge-decorated beach bikes used to get around the concerts, artworks, and workshops. Others are creative home constructions mostly in mad-max or movie-gothic style. Static structures are put to the flame at the end of the event. They say it's about letting go of ephemeral possessions. Participants are expected to take home their own trash. However, after the 2023 event, there were 5000 abandoned bikes.

The elemental inhospitality of the desert has led to questions about the wisdom of throwing such a party on a warming planet, given the motor traffic it generates, and the carbon release – not least from the ritual finale of burning the huge effigy of 'the Man'. Also there has been a trend towards more wealthy 'bucket list' participants, turning up with air conditioning and other luxuries. Like all dynamic human creations Burning Man is changing, as is the climate.

Photo: Ryan/Debbie/Owen BaTese: Wiki Commons.

Getting High on Bicycles

At Clustered Spires

This is the USA's only race of its kind: an intense hour of thrills and spectacle around the historic downtown district of Frederick in Maryland. The annual Clustered Spires Bicycle Race has been creating thrills and theatre since 2012, attracting competitors of all types and genders. It's a spectator-friendly criterium race (meaning it consists of multiple laps) around the 0.4 mile (644m) course. There are two qualifying heats before the big event.

Riders come from many countries, including Sweden, Belgium and the UK. Most are local Marylanders. They saw the race, became intrigued, tried high riding and were hooked.

Why Clustered Spires? It doesn't refer to the participants (although it could do) but rather to the skyline of Frederick with its many churches.

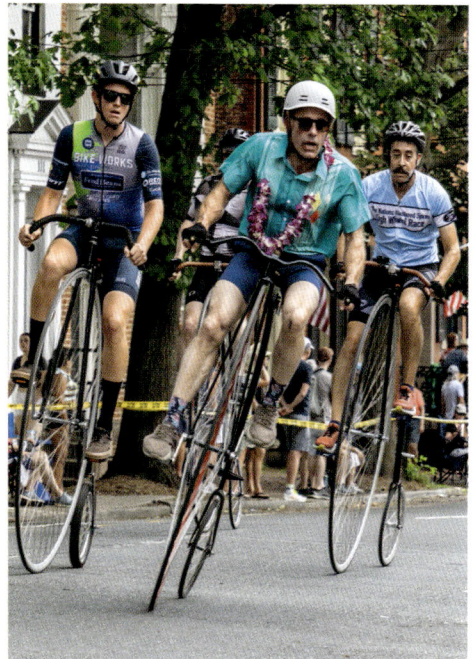

Photos: Acroterion. Creative Commons.

Bikes keep Cuba moving

Pedro Szekely

Here's what not to do in Cuba. Don't tell people how much you love your bike, and how delightful it is to cycle on those almost empty roads, through lush countryside, in the glorious sunshine. Eyes will be rolled heavenward. They'll quietly wonder why you've come all this way to ride, sweat and tire yourself out under the hot Cuban sun! Don't tell them the bicycle has changed Cuba for the better and helped the battered economy. Don't tell them that cycling gives them more individualised, affordable mobility than cars or the bus system, and that it has shaped the country's character and ecological credentials.

It's not just the hot climate which has caused many Cubans to dislike the bike. Recent history has also played a part. The fall of the Soviet Bloc brought a sudden crisis to the island. From the early 1960s the Soviet Union had been Cuba's main supplier of vital materials, including food and oil.

It accounted for 80% of the island's international trade, and it was heavily subsidised. When it all abruptly stopped Cuba fell on its knees and most services ground to a deadening halt. Cubans were suddenly forced to walk everywhere, usually tired and hungry, and in every weather. They needed alternatives for many things, including transport, and millions took to bikes – out of necessity.

Over a million Chinese bicycles arrived and were given out to students and workers. These bikes were both prized and resented. Many were sold on for much-needed food. Bike theft became rife and the constant fear of it caused stress. The bicycle is still associated by most with sacrifice and misery.

In the late 1990s Venezuela began sending oil in exchange for Cuban specialists (mainly doctors, dentists and engineers). Transport systems improved

Daniele Zanni. Wiki Commons.

and cycles began to disappear, along with the infrastructure which had supported them.

Right now Cuba is in a further economic and transport crisis and the old Chinese bikes are returning. As before, many Cubans have a low calorie intake, yet have long, hot rides to work, at which point the job itself might require manual labour. The famous Chinese Flying Pigeon appears to be the first choice: valued by young men for its robustness and strong back rack used partly for carrying family members around. Just the same, the switch to cycling has been a challenge, especially for the less fit and the elderly.

Powerful influences have swept through Cuba: Spanish colonialism, then American and Soviet expansionism, then Cuban socialism. The country remains a unique and fascinating blend of Caribbean culture. If you visit there enjoy your cycling but be careful what you say on that subject!

Trishaws are common in the cities and popular with tourists. They are made in local workshops where scrap bicycles are welding into new forms. This photo is from 2009 when Cuba was trying out alternative forms of public transport. Photo: Philippe Antoine. Wiki Commons.

Finland cycles – all winter, too

City of Oulu

City of Oulu.

Pekka Tahkola, winter city activist.

It's the fourth most northerly city in the world, just 100km (60 miles) south of the Arctic Circle, on the edge of Lapland. Oulu sits by the often frozen sea and lies under snow for five months of the year. Mid-winter temperatures can drop to -30C (-22F), with just four hours of daylight. Yet Oulu, a city of 225,000 inhabitants, proudly calls itself 'the winter cycling capital of the world'.

42% of Oulu's residents cycle through the long, dark, snowy winter and 12% of all winter journeys are made by bicycle. These are percentages that other countries can only dream of, even those with mild weather. Oulu's citizens see winter cycling as part of their culture, their communal spirit, their state of mind. It also keeps them active all year, and so happier and healthier, both mentally and physically. Winter cycling also increases exposure to sunlight and vitamin D when the days are short.

A local lad made this happen. Or at least he was pivotal. Pekka Tahkola, born in Oulu, studied traffic engineering and urban planning before working as a consultant promoting cycling and wanting "to see real change". He is close to the community, listening and advising on cycling matters.

Tahkola's data shows that there is absolutely no difference in winter cycling levels, whether the outside temperature is zero or minus twenty. It helps that Oulu's a small city with a still growing network of 900km (559 miles) of combined

Finland has set a national goal to increase number of trips made by bicycle to 30% by the year 2030.

pedestrian and cycle path. It also helps that the superb infrastructure is well maintained. The city's heavy-duty snow ploughs clear the cycling and pedestrian paths before they clear any road. They plough down to a thin hard-packed snow layer to avoid problems with freeze and thaw. For perfect quality they plough with minimum delay, and a bike lane could be ploughed 12 times during the previous night's snowfall. Citizens ride sensible bikes for the conditions, and some fit specialised snow tyres. Oulu has dealt with other winter cycling safety challenges. The paths are well-lit during the dark winter months, and there are 320 underpasses so that children, in particular, don't have to cross roads.

Digital signs on major cyclepaths inform cyclists of the achievement levels of the snow-ploughing teams.

"When people ride, the snow gets compacted and slowly accumulates. But we need to keep the snow layer really, really thin," says Tahkola. So thin that you can still see the bicycle symbols on the ground, for safety reasons. All paths have been built for shared use and built wide to allow good mechanical maintenance.

In the winter 60% of trips to schools in Oulu are by bike. In one of Oulu's biggest schools, Metsokangas, more than 90% of the children get to school by bike or on foot, according to the school's headteacher, even during the coldest winter months: thanks partly to traffic calming measures keeping cars at bay. Monitoring cycling to school one day, Tahkola found that, with a temperature of -17C, an astonishing 1000 out of 1200 children had arrived at school by bike. Others had walked, skied or come by kick-sled or car. Children as young as seven cycle through snow to school unaccompanied. They grow up with it, so don't complain. It's part of Oulu's way of life.

In 2013 the Winter Cycling Federation was founded in Oulu to promote winter cycling internationally and has since held conferences around the world. It has helped in the transformation into active cities of places like Almatyevsk in Russia, and Astana in Kazakhstan. Tahkola organises Winter City Masterclasses in Oulu and communicates online with participants from other winter cities like Anchorage, Minneapolis and Montreal.

Africa – a continent of cyclists

A cycle of wellbeing

Jacinter Atieno Owuo, a Kenyan health worker, learned to make good use of a bicycle she was given:

66 *My neighbour who had been having pregnancy complications was about to deliver at home. I quickly rushed to my neighbour's house and helped the lady on my bicycle then carried her to the main road a distance of about 6km, where we keep a bicycle ambulance with the local shopkeeper and proceeded with the journey to a referral hospital where Eunice delivered normally to a chubby baby boy, who is doing great. I am so proud of my bicycle as it helped save her life and that of her baby.* 99

Her bicycle came from CooP-Africa as part of their Bike4Care programme. They provide modified bicycles for community health workers and bicycle ambulances for health centres. These cycles greatly increase the number of clients seen in a day and help preserve care workers' energy so they can work more effectively. On top of all this, care workers find that a Bike4Care cycle helps serve as a marker of professionalism.

Education comes with a bike

Walking long distances to school is another example of human energy misapplied. World Bicycle Relief, running a programme in Zambia, found that students who received a bicycle demonstrated a 28% increase in attendance rates and a 59% improvement in academic performance.

Students and teachers walking more than 10km to school are not going to be in top form for their lessons. CooP-Africa's Bike4School programmes provide bicycles on credit for students and teachers, and run school activities to promote the use of bicycles and improve access to education. Basirika Anitah, a student in Uganda, has this to say:

66 *A bicycle is another teacher. A school without a teacher is like a home without a bicycle, because a student can't understand without a teacher in class and even a student from very far can't reach school early enough without a bicycle.* 99

Business on bikes

Coop-Africa's bicycles improve health care and education, but their Bike4Work programme also supports people in earning a living. Pheobe Atieno Awino, a businesswoman in Kenya says:

66 *I sell tomatoes, onions and maize at the local market, which is 4km from my house. Once a week I go 10km to the market in town where I can earn more. The bicycle has helped me so much!* 99

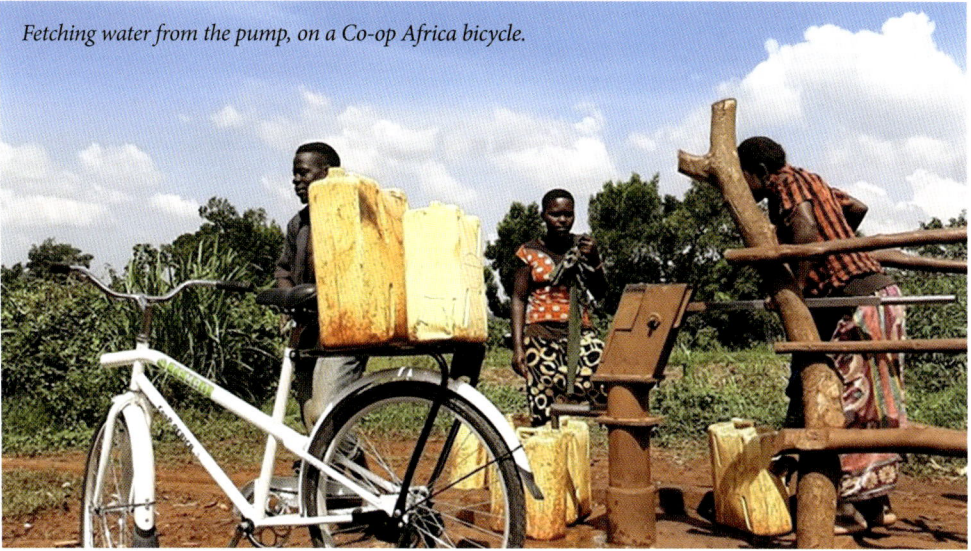
Fetching water from the pump, on a Co-op Africa bicycle.

Bikes still reign in Eritrea

Not all parts of Africa have entered a phase of inappropriate technology and transport inequality. Eritrea may be politically questionable but its capital, Asmara, is probably one of the best capital cities to cycle in. It has very little motor traffic, a pleasant climate and a distinctive cycling culture. It was never intended to be so cycle-friendly: an economy held back by conflict with Ethiopia meant the city was blocked from the conventional path of industrialisation and congestion. Eritrea has a long history of self-reliance that began during its 30-year war for independence from Ethiopia, after which its international isolation has magnified the costs of importing bicycles and spare parts. Eritreans all seem to embrace the *bicicletta*, meaning bicycle in the local language, Tigrinya, which borrowed the word from the Italians in colonial times. The Italians also bequeathed their love of competitive cycling, and the Eritrean national team is successful internationally.

The task ahead

Positive stories inspire, but every day across Africa approximately 261 pedestrians and 18 cyclists are killed. So it's not surprising that wealthier Africans seek to 'buy their way' out of walking and cycling, by becoming motorists. More than a billion people walk or cycle in Africa every day to reach work, home, school and essential services, but largely on streets and roads which are unattractive, unsafe and uncomfortable, creating a negative spiral for everyone.

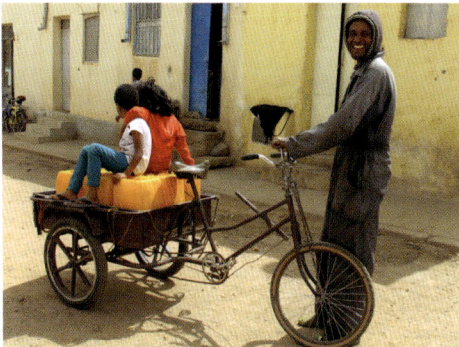
A street scene in Asmara.
Photo: Elizabeth Blair.

The Eritrean men's racing team.
Photo: Solomon Debre.

The Buffalo Bike

The Buffalo Bike is specially made for African conditions and heavy load carrying. It has been developed by World Bicycle Relief and supplied through 60 retail and support centres in six countries, giving new life opportunities to owners and to local maintenance and repair experts. Some cycles are supplied within specific support schemes, and others have a purchase price, usually with payment over a period.

The new Buffalo Utility S2, incorporates an innovative two-chain two gear system operated by a half-turn back-pedal activating a switchable free-wheel. This removes the complexity of sensitive external components. Having two gears is a major advance for African riders.

The AK2 Freewheel system, patented by World Bicycle Relief, was a winner in the Eurobike Awards 2024. The development group of SRAM, Trek, Giant Group, and Karasawa contributed product design expertise and they conducted over two years of rigorous research and testing in the diverse landscapes of sub-Saharan Africa and South America.

The AK2 Freewheel system.

Head-carrying in Cairo

Photo: Pad-manaba01. Wiki Commons.

Bread deliveries in Egypt – an unusual urban example of head-carrying but throughout rural Africa it's a common way to transport goods such as crops or water. Head-carrying can cause long-term injuries, which is a reason for the growing use of bicycles to carry the load, leaving the head free for other tasks - a concept declined by this gentleman.

Elephant Bikes in Malawi

The UK's Royal Mail has delivered something special in Malawi over the last decade. Around 20,000 Malawians are riding Elephant Bikes, which are in fact ex-Royal Mail bikes refurbished through offender rehabilitation programmes by the Krizevak Project in Staffordshire. They are distributed through not-for-profits in Malawi, one of Africa's poorest countries. These bikes could tell a tale of rejection, cultural displacement and a happy role in their new home.

Soweto spins

In the townships of South Africa they call it spinning. It's art, performance and low-budget inventiveness all in one. It's rooted in the energetic youth culture of the townships. They fabricate cycles with long 'tails' which can be spun round obstacles, put into challenging reverses, and ridden in other crazy ways. The spin is created by wrapping lengths of cut-up plastic round the rear tyre. For well pimped cycles and impressive riding there are prizes such as coveted bike parts.

Photo: Heather Mason, 2summers.net.

A harvest on the move in Madagascar

The island of Madagascar, in the Indian Ocean, is one of the ten poorest countries on the planet and bicycles are heavily used for transporting goods. Here farmers in the Malagasey region of Madagascar transport their harvest on bicycles, which are only just visible beneath the loads.

Photo: Colourbox.

The Best Investment

The peoples of Africa will want to walk and cycle for many decades to come. They need low-tech transport systems, and our planet needs them, too. By financing better cycling and walking infrastructure the rich countries of the world will make Africa happier, healthier, more equal and more mobile. This is surely the most effective and easiest investment in getting to net zero. The First African Bicycle Information Organisation (FABIO), based in Uganda, put it this way:

66 *Politicians may tell us that bicycles are a sign that we are not advancing. We ourselves have seen that cycling is a socio-economic tool. It works now – we don't have to wait for someone to rescue us with better public transport.* 99

The long route to school in Zambia. Photo: World Bicycle Relief.

China – cycling's ever-changing fortunes

For students bike sharing comes more natural than bike ownership.

The Chinese like big projects. Through the port city of Xiamen runs an elevated 7.6km cycle path: the longest in the world, with bike roundabouts, cycle parking, and service pavilions.

Beijing, too, is thinking bike, with new bike paths being created, lined with newly planted scholar trees to give shade. The famous torrents of cyclists are unlikely to return. In the late 1990s the government introduced a bicycle reduction policy, while investing in car production for economic growth. Owning a bicycle was no longer a prerequisite for marriage the way a car or apartment is today. But progress is being made.

One propellant has been the bike-share phenomenon. There are now more share bikes in any one of the nine largest Chinese cities than there are in the entire United States. At one point there were 30 cities worldwide with bike share schemes operating more than 5,000 bikes, and 24 of these cities were in China. Success has come after the infamy of poor state control which led to oversupply and a chaotic exercise in boom-to-bust. In Beijing there were 25 separate schemes with an estimated 950,000

cycles. By 2017 hundreds of thousands had been withdrawn from the streets to be parked in bicycle graveyards which took on bizarre patterns revealed by drone photography. The main problem was the

Xiamen's 7.6km elevated bike route, the world's longest. Photo: Dissing & Weitling.

Vendors of household cleaning goods still pedal city streets. Photo: Paul Jeurissen.

lack of any regulatory framework for these bikes to be introduced gradually and integrated into existing public transport systems. The situation was made worse in that dumped bikes became a serious recycling problem thanks to their digital locks, micro-sized solar panels, and solid tyres.

Fairly quickly regional governments brought order to the situation. More mature and stable bike sharing companies emerged and the phenomenon is now booming. It's not a huge mystery why China would want to invest so heavily in bike share: it has the world's largest population, is rapidly urbanising, and is trying to cut down on traffic and pollution. What's impressive is how quickly the country has implemented enormous programs in so many different cities, and after such a shambolic start.

Then came the famous dumpling story. In 2024 four students put out a social media post suggesting a cheap 50km night-time bike ride from Zhengzhou to Kaifeng to enjoy the famous local dumplings. It went viral, and around 200,000 students turned up, mostly on share bikes. This was more than the local authorities could manage, and the government

found it unsettling to see so many young people becoming autonomous together. There were even mentions of similarities to Tiananman Square. One young man, asked by a foreign reporter why he was riding, turned to the camera and replied in English: '*Because it's my responsibility!*' Although somewhat enigmatic this became a meme shared by young people across China, and similar rides are starting up elsewhere in other regions. The true significance of the phenomenon is not yet clear.

Gone forever? Beijing cyclists, 1978.
Photo: Wiki Commons.

The Japanese go their own way

Kosuke Miyata

The Japanese certainly cycle plenty: around 16% of journeys are by bike, which is very close to the percentage in iconic Denmark. Most bike trips are under 5km (3 miles) and mainly for shopping, followed by social activities, and then by commuting. Bikes are utility vehicles and often regarded as disposable: 65% of them sell for no more than 30,000 yen (under $300/£200). 60% are step-through city cycles or *mamachari* (literally 'mothers' bikes').

Oddly, the popularity of cycling has little to do with cycling facilities. Bike lanes are virtually non-existent in Japan. What is offered instead are 'sharrows' or paths shared with pedestrians. Cycling on footpaths was made legal in 1970 and has become the norm.

Yet cycling in Japan is fairly safe. Cyclist fatalities are around 2.3 per 100 million kilometres. Calculated in the same manner, the figure for the Netherlands is around 0.8, and in the USA it's around 5.3. So risk for cyclists in Japan is right in the middle, just like its mode share, even though the country has such poor infrastructure for cycling.

Fukushima yogurt deliveries.

The Japanese have some interesting designs for everyday cycles. Photos: Mikael Colville-Andersen.

In high density, land-scarce locations such as train stations and commuter hubs it's common to park your bike in automated facilities deep underground. ECO Cycles bike storage is now found in many Japanese cities. You introduce your bike to a complex miracle of mechanical engineering which tucks it away deep underground until you need it back. An ECO Cycle with a 200 bike capacity takes up around four square metres of surface space. The same 200 bikes parked above ground would consume around 25 square metres.

How, then, does cycling work in Tokyo? How did there come to be a cycling culture in this megacity, and how did it survive, in relative safety, without dedicated infrastructure? Blogger Byron Kidd (aka *Tokyo By Bike*) attributes it to the people themselves and a culture of patience called *gaman*. But there are many reasons. Public safety comes about through a culture of compliance. Laws are largely abided by, and overall crime is low. Tokyo also has a good local railway network with compact, convenient neighbourhoods around it, coupled with streets and alleys that are relatively calm. This all makes driving both less necessary and slower-paced than in more car-centric cities. Bike parking facilities surround train stations and businesses, so shopping by bike makes sense, and cycling can be easily integrated into a multimodal commute. Biking is affordable, while it is relatively expensive to own a car, especially in urban areas. Nearly all arterial streets are built with only cars in mind, but footpath cycling is allowed on most of them. And the sheer number of cyclists in Tokyo means that pretty much everyone is used to the presence of people on bikes.

Japan's cycling culture, developed as a spontaneous byproduct of many things that were not planned or designed for. It preceded full-scale motorisation and survived it. It is mysterious, and it has worked. The urge could be to leave well alone, but all is not ideal. Despite a 16% mode share and the known societal benefits of cycling, cyclists are often treated more as a problem than a solution by the news media, the police, and the government, both nationally and locally. And hundreds of people on bikes still lose their lives each year.

Japan needs high-quality, protected bike infrastructure, and more car-free and traffic-calmed streets. For decades, Japan has relied on its compliance culture to keep cyclists safe. That is no longer enough.

This account was based on work by Kosuke Miyata, a Tokyo-based cyclist and a member of the Cycling Embassy of Japan. His full report appeared in Transportation Alternatives' Vision Zero Cities Journal in 2019. The original, available on-line, cites sources not included here.

Images: GEKIN.com

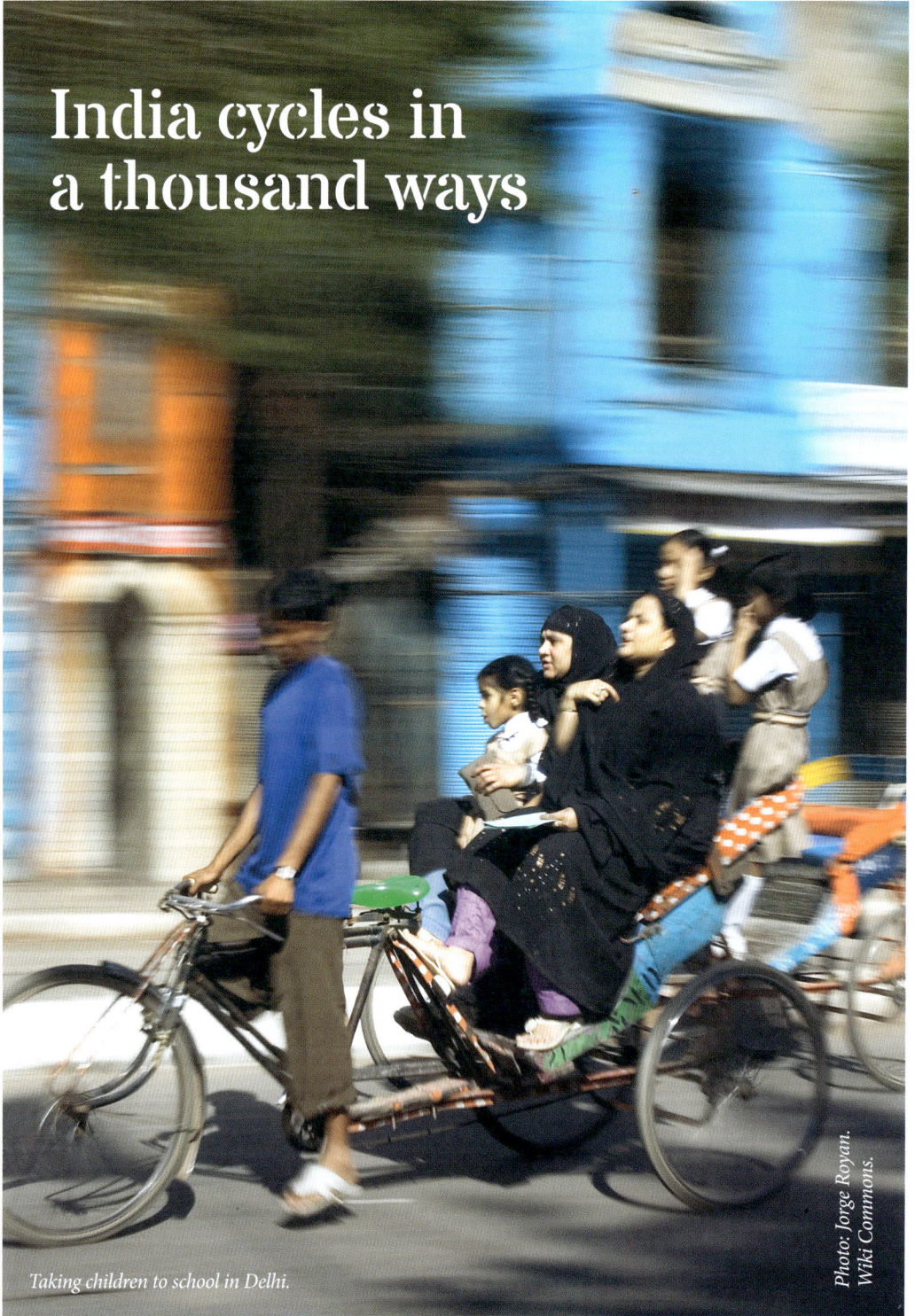

India cycles in a thousand ways

Taking children to school in Delhi.

Photo: Jorge Royan.
Wiki Commons.

Traffic on the edge of chaos, bullying drivers, hit-and-runs, pollution: there are few Indian cyclists riding for the love of it. They have other reasons for being on the road, and status is not one of them. Changes may be on the way.

Most lower income families in Indian cities work in service sector jobs – drivers, maids, security guards, sanitation workers, vegetable vendors, etc. Public transport is not a great experience, and costs money, so many on low incomes make the rational choice to cycle or walk to work. In fact the primary commuting mode in the top 53 cities in India is cycling, the highest being 57% and the lowest being 17%. This still compares well with the levels of active travel found in the famous cycling cities of Europe.

Cycling is also a livelihood. Cycle rickshaws are becoming 'Uberised' in the big cities. Then there are vending trikes of all kinds, and others which transport goods, including waste. Cycling also gives employment to those who maintain and repair these hardworking machines.

The average trip length (excluding walking) in Indian cities is between 2.5km and 6.9km and these are distances ideal for cycling and walking. The bicycle has sustained in India despite the formal planning systems, not because of them. Cyclists have remained an invisible group for Indian city planners, until now. The Government of India has finally worked out that something needed to be done. They financed experimental pro-cycling investment in 20 'lighthouse' cities, using as criteria the quality of life, economic development and social inclusion. Most cities' bids included strong cycling components. Critically important was that this programme was aimed at smaller cities, because they were the cities which could offer space for experimentation and inclusion.

At least 18% to 20% of the total work-based trips in smaller cities are by bicycle, giving cycling support and advocacy a good start. Smaller cities can trial new thinking, creating examples of good practice for the big cities.

One such city is Ranchi. While global cities are aiming to increase cycle share to between 10% and 15%, smaller Indian cities like Ranchi have already achieved it. Compared to cities like Mumbai, Bengaluru and Delhi, where non-motorised transport accounts for 35% to 37% of total trips, the non-motorised share

Photo: Sue Darlow.

The bicycle is the emblem of Samajwadi, a socialist political party founded in 1992. Photo: Sue Darlow.

A still from the film Pedalling to Freedom, a documentary set in Tamil Nadu, showing the mobility and independence which bicycles can bring to Indian women.

in Ranchi is close to half of total trips. It helps that smaller cities mean shorter journeys.

Key initiatives include vehicle-free days, road safety awareness and motivation campaigns. Ranchi's new public bike-share scheme has removed the economic burden of owning a bicycle (interestingly it costs eight times more to own a bicycle in India than in China which has four times more bicycles than India). Cycles are now more noticeable on the streets than ever before, and include new pedal-powered delivery services.

Another successful bidder is Ludhiana, in the state of Punjab. This city is home to 1,500 factories making bicycle parts and employing 250,000 people. More than 10m bicycles are made in Ludhiana every year, and it's the home of Hero Cycles. The city produces more than half of India's bicycles. Yet it ranks high in per capita automobile ownership, accident rates and air pollution. Ludhiana is now bringing its manufacturing strength to bear, in the service of sustainable urban mobility.

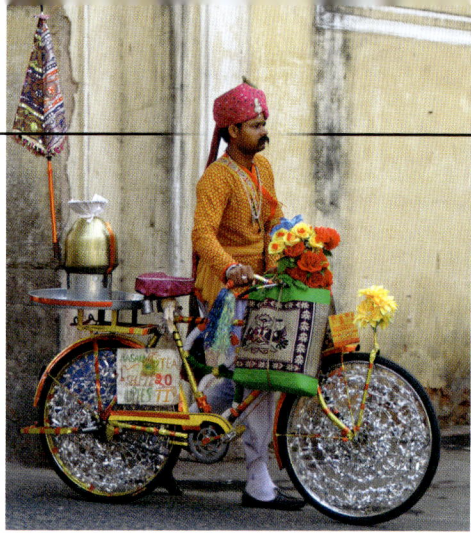

▲ A tea seller in Jaipur. A basic bicycle can be fundamental to the owner's living. Photo: Jakub Halun. Wiki Commons.

▼ An itinerant locksmith. Photo: Paul Jeurissen.

▲ An image from the past in India but spotted recently. Photo: Paul Jeurissen.

Ranchi shows that cycling is still strong in smaller Indian cities. Photo: Chartered Bike, Ranchi. ▼

Singapore goes strong on bikes

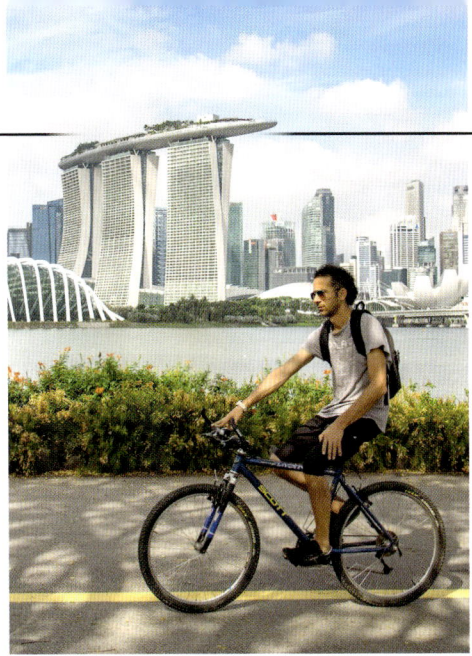
Great riverside path, questionable architecture.

Singapore, a city state of more than five million people, claims to be Asia's top cycling destination. It's certainly an unusual one, being a high population island approximately 40km by 20km in size, with over 800km of cycling paths, expanding to 1,300km by 2030.

On-road bike lanes are well maintained, and motor traffic generally gives a wide berth. Bus drivers give a polite double-toot when approaching cyclists. The authorities are strict about speed limits for cyclists, on and off the cycle paths. Don't be surprised to see speed-gun-wielding enforcement officers keeping riders in check.

The Park Connector Network provides linear green corridors linking major parks and nature areas across Singapore. It's a 300km tangle of cycle paths, taking cyclists alongside rivers and canals, and over many of the delightful bridges for which Singapore is famous. There's also the 24km Rail Corridor, a continuous green passage for cyclists, pedestrians and wildlife (and not lit at night to benefit wildlife).

800km of cycle path and more on the way.

Alongside this, Singapore has launched the Friendly Streets initiative, encouraging pedestrian safety, public transport and active mobility. Safe school zones are being created, along with 'silver zones' emphasising the active travel needs of older citizens.

Singapore is a small island state which has chosen its direction and has the means and public support to make things happen. However, Singaporeans do not have much choice in choosing their government. It's a de facto one party state. It has low corruption and high government efficiency, but human rights and personal freedom are limited. This does not detract from their cycling achievements. Such a densely populated and urbanised island needs more bicycles than most other places.

Images: Singapore Tourism.

An artist's impression showing Singapore's concept of Corridors for All connecting parts of the city through cycling 'trunk routes', bus lanes and pedestrian paths.

Memories of Myanmar

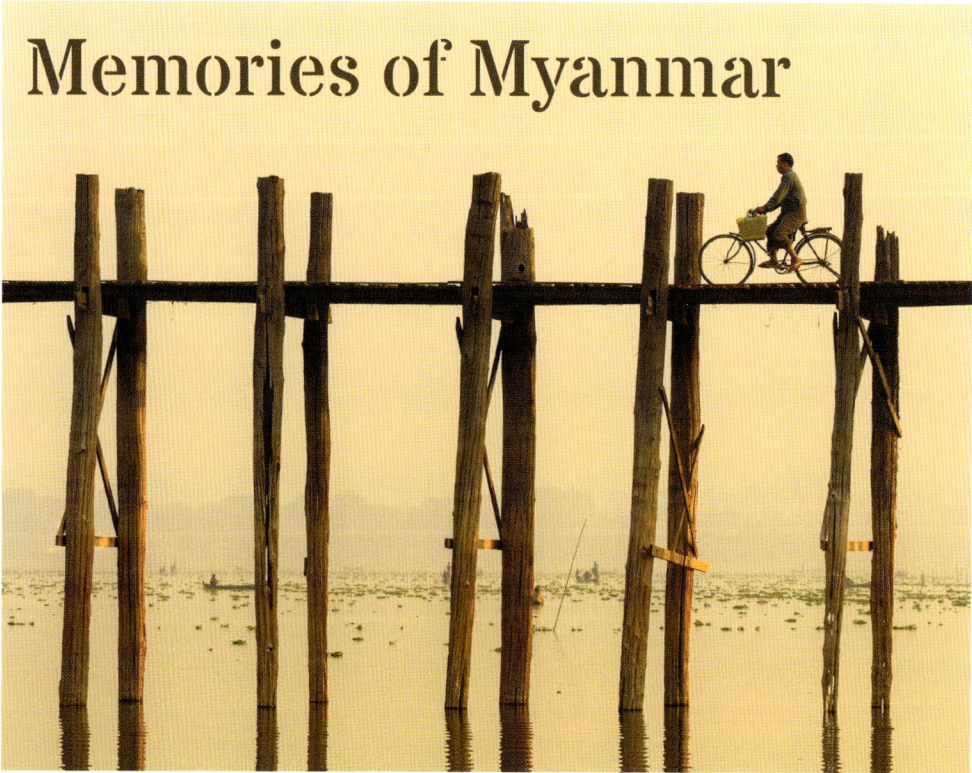

Slightly damaged in the earthquake was the U Bein Bridge which crosses the Taungthaman Lake in Amarapura. It's the longest teakwood bridge in the world. Photo: Tawan Chaisom.

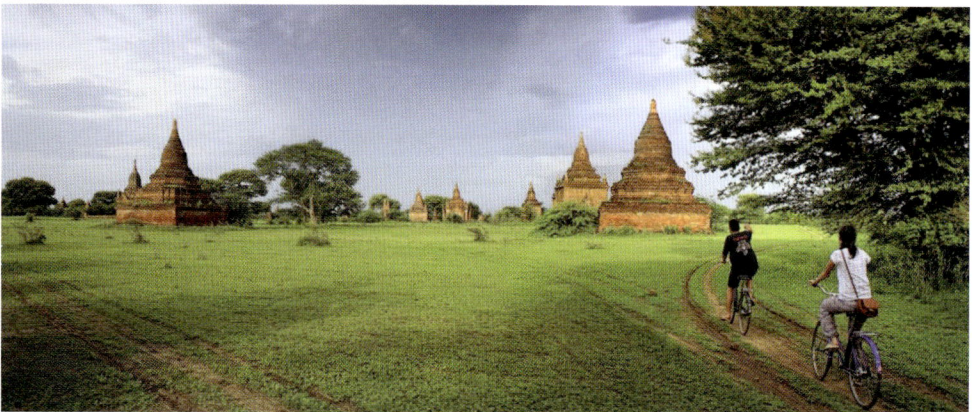

The historic temples of Bagan, a UNESCO World Heritage Site, were badly damaged by the earthquake and partially collapsed.

The Buddhist temples were primarily built between the 11th and 13th centuries. Marco Polo described Bagan as one of the finest sights in the world. Despite centuries of neglect, looting, erosion and regular earthquakes, this temple-studded plain remains a remarkably impressive and unforgettable vision. Bagan's kings commissioned more than 4000 temples. Photo and words: Ben Visbeek.

CHAPTER 3

How the Wonder Works

Understanding Frames

Cycles Victoire

A handmade steel frame by Cycles Victoire featuring S&S couplings to split the frame for portability.

The kingdom of steel

Some 95% of the world's bicycles are made from steel tube forming 'diamond' frames. It is cheap, easy to process, durable if well painted, and the hardest, stiffest, strongest, structural material available. It'll bend rather than break, but if you do somehow manage to break a steel frame, it's easy to weld back together..

Most steel frames are built for people who have no interest in their modulus of elasticity: that's the measure of its stiffness or resistance to bending. It's the same for all grades of steel in a bicycle frame, so don't believe anyone advertising that their super high strength tube-set will give a stiffer frame.

The most basic frames are made from thick-wall tubing that has been rolled from mild steel strip and electrically seam-welded. This produces a strong, stiff, low price, long-lasting and very heavy frame. Most of these frames are produced and used in China and India – or given to western children for Christmas.

Not much more expensive, but a lot better, is low carbon steel. This is often referred to as hi-ten by the cycle industry. It comes either seam-welded or cold-drawn and is the basis for most of the West's 'bread and butter' bikes. Where weight is not a major consideration it is a good choice. The money saved on the frame can be put into better components, giving you a more reliable bike.

However, the moment you start talking about performance, weight will start to matter. This means progressively higher tensile strengths. This allows the wall thickness to be reduced, keeping up the frame's strength but reducing weight and stiffness.

Virtually all of these specialised tube-sets and a lot of the chromo come in 'double-butted' form. That is, the last 50mm or so at the end or ends of each tube is some 50 per cent thicker than the centre section. This is not because the stress is higher at the ends but to allow for a possible loss of strength caused by the joining process.

Aluminium alloy

Although only a small percentage in global terms, aluminium frames are a big part of the performance scene. Aluminium has a lower tensile strength than steel, and a considerably lower modulus. It is much more prone to fatigue if badly used but it is a third the weight of steel. This is why it is what most aeroplanes are made of today – although not in tubular form.

All structural aluminium is alloyed with small percentages of other elements, in the same way as the high-grade steels. It is designated into groups that share a similar main additive. They run from the 1000 series, which is pure, to 8000 which has lithium as the main addition. Higher numbers are not necessarily better and grades of one series can be stronger or weaker than those of other series.

Basic steel framed bikes – strong, cheap and easily repaired. They are the versatile workhorses of the world, transporting hundreds of millions, plus heavy cargoes and even extra passengers. Photo: Jorge Royan, Wiki Commons.

using a 'low alloy' steel, usually referred to as chrome moly, or 4130, which is its aviation industry specification. Indeed, it was developed for aircraft structures, but that was in the days of biplanes. It is still very useful for cycles, and most of the world's 'affordable' performance bikes are built from it.

Chrome moly is not so commonly used by the many small frame-builders around the world. They spend a lot of time building a frame. The material cost is less important than their labour, which is much the same for crafting regular 'chromo' as it is for a range of more expensive tubes known by fancy numbers. At one time the only number a cyclist needed to know was 531. It was the universal tube for touring and racing cyclists worldwide. Not so today. Reynolds, the British producers, have been phasing out 531 in favour of differently numbered tubes with other qualities. Columbus in Italy have a similar range, and there are French, Japanese and American products to choose from. They all tend to offer similar types of steel alloy giving

"...but is it science, Pythagoras?"

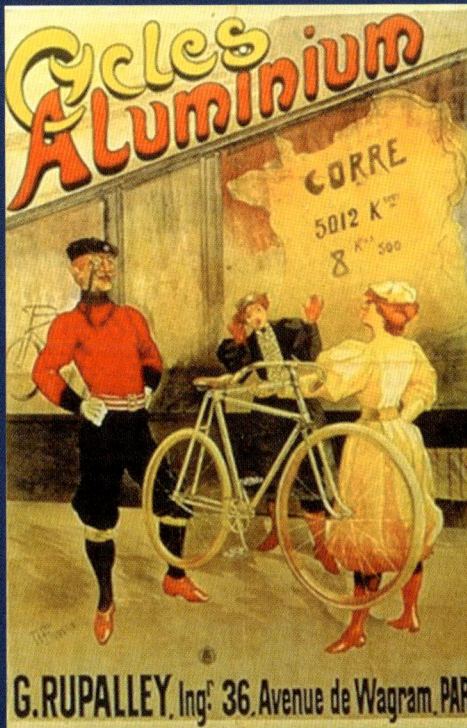

Cycles Aluminium

CORRE
5012 Kms
8 Kms 500

G. RUPALLEY, Ingr 36, Avenue de Wagram, PAR

The material's much lower modulus of stiffness means that it is essential to increase the diameter of the tubing, and in practice the wall thickness as well. Fortunately, aluminium being only one third the weight of the steel, the resulting tube is still both lighter and stiffer. This is due to a combination both of the properties and the nature of the mechanics of tubing – for each time you double the diameter of a tube its weight doubles but its stiffness quadruples, whereas doubling the wall thickness simply doubles weight and stiffness.

This factor would give aluminium an enormous advantage over steel, except that aluminium, even when correctly welded and heat-treated has a fatigue problem. This means that if the frame were allowed to flex as much as a steel one, it would crack sooner rather than later. For this reason all good aluminium frames tend to be over-built making them even stiffer than basic function would require. This is why most aluminium frames have a rather unforgiving feel to them. They are, however, very efficient at transferring power to the wheels, especially for more powerful riders.

However, this additional stiffness does not mean a harder ride, despite what you will have read in the bike magazines. The reason for this is that the diamond frame is in effect a two dimensional structure. It has a height and a length, but its width is a function of the tube from which it is built. And it is the height-to-length ratio that has the greatest effect on the vertical compliance or comfort of a frame – not that it is ever very much.

The tubing size, wall thickness or even the material itself, has the greatest effect on the torsional or twisting strength. This, unlike the vertical movement, can be noticed, especially when sprinting or riding a well-loaded tourer. The confusion in this area probably arises from the undeniable fact that our bodies are not well calibrated – unlike dial gauges and micrometers designed to measure things that we were not designed to measure. It is not so much that we cannot detect anything. Rather, we tend to jumble up the various sensory inputs, and so a frame that is 'whippy' is assumed to be comfortable.

Titanium

This is an interesting metal (more exactly, it's a metal alloy). It's around half the weight of a steel tube of the same tensile strength. It's less dense than steel so a frameset can be lighter while still having thicker-walled tubes. Titanium is easily repairable like steel and it's even more corrosion-resistant than aluminium. On the other hand titanium tubing is a lot more difficult for framebuilders to work with than steel or aluminium, which increases the price. It's the most expensive metal option.

Triangles and diamonds

The combination of steel tube and diamond frame has endured, although many cycles have 'compromised' diamonds, with squashed or missing main triangles, made possible by design compensation which also increases weight. This is becoming fairly typical for 'Dutch style' multi-purpose bikes, especially electric cycles, which are increasingly seen as unisex items.

The well established diamond frame gives anyone setting out to design a better (rigid safety) bike a bit of a problem. Bikes are unlike many other mechanical devices – cars, foodmixers and the like – where there are numerous design variations and opportunities for improvement. With the bicycle there is just one absolute and totally defined shape handed down to us by generations of frame-builders. And not only the shape, but even the size of the tubes, has been institutionalised.

Tuning the diamond

Whilst diamonds are trumps there is room for subtle variation, depending on the frame's intended use and the material of which the tubes are made. There is greater specialisation of design, with many designs becoming less universal. For example, the trend towards more compact frames is not ideal for touring bikes as the smaller rear triangle makes pannier mounting a problem. Other small changes can include ovalisation of tube in some areas. A more significant example is what happened when the mountain bike first appeared. It clearly needed a much stronger frame than the traditional road bike, so in came wider diameter tubing. Early off-roaders were heavy, but soon the usual pressures to produce lighter frames came into effect. Today, at least on top-end race models, these developments have caused little increase in weight over equivalent road frames – thanks to improved tubing – meaning thinner walls and tougher alloys.

However, there is still much 'oversizing' of the tubes. This might seem logical but is it really? What a mountain bike needs is more strength and the logical way to add strength is by increasing wall thickness. Increasing the diameter adds stiffness more than strength, leading to a more 'brittle' frame. This is definitely not a good thing for off-road use. The stiffness required is more to do with the rider's power input rather than the terrain the bike is ridden over.

There will always be a minimum desirable frame stiffness needed to prevent shimmy (lateral vibration). And the heavier wheels of the mountain bike, like the loaded panniers of the tourist or shopper, dictate a stiffer frame. But the best use of oversize thin wall tubing would be for the track sprinter who uses a lot of power over a short distance on a smooth surface. As they do this not very often, frame fatigue would be a minimal problem.

Alternatives to the diamond

Although the manufacturers of the 1890s had clearly got the diamond frame right, this has not stopped hundreds of people from trying to change it. But in all this time there have only been a few variations that might be called successful.

One is Alex Moulton's concept of small wheels with suspension, using (firstly) monolithic cruciform and (later) multi-tube geodesic frame construction.

Many subsequent small-wheel designs stem from Alex Moulton's 1960s original. That most of these derivatives are quite dreadful bicycles is not the fault of Alex Moulton or his design. It is still, if not a better bicycle, at least a viable alternative offering some real advantages over the traditional format. (The Moulton bicycle is featured on page 214)

Sticking to upright bikes, another alternative is the moulded monocoque racing design (shown below). It offers the racing cyclist at least some advantage over 'iron sticks'. It's easy to see why all the others failed. They were trying to radically improve the diamond frame bicycle when it is already virtually perfect.

Recumbents in all their multiplicity are, of course, another matter. Some make partial use of the diamond frame, but others don't. For more on recumbents see page 175.

Our exploration of bike frames is based on the writings of Mike Burrows, who sadly passed away in 2022. His insights into bike technology are found, among other fascinating subjects, in 'Bicycle Design, an Illustrated History' by Tony Hadland and Hans-Erhard Lessing.

Frame Suspension

Suspension is a feature of all cycles, one way or another. When your bike hits a rough patch various parts of it take their turn in protecting you from the jolts: the tyres, the spokes, the frame, the saddle, the grips, and more. But many cycles these days have one or more primary–purpose suspension systems. These are mostly found on mountain bikes, but are becoming common on hybrid cycles, on some city bikes, and on many smaller wheeled cycles to compensate for the rigidity which comes with those small wheels.

Front suspension is the most common, and cycles with this are called 'hard-tails'. Cycles with suspension both front and rear are known as 'full suspension' bikes. Rear suspension alone is not common on conventional cycles, but comes as a bonus when it is built into many folding bikes as part of the fold.

Giving a comfortable ride, either on potholed streets or off-road, is not the only advantage of suspension systems. When they are 'pushed' by a bump they absorb it, with little discomfort for the rider, then they spring back down on the other side of the bump, with minimal jarring. This smoothness can allow the rider to go faster over difficult terrain, but it also increases traction and safety in that it helps keep one or both wheels in contact with the ground.

Front suspension forks are usually 'telescopic' with the distance they move up and down (known as the 'travel') being set by the strength of the spring or springs. On higher-end systems, travel can be adjusted to suit the terrain.

Suspension seatposts can also help. The most basic are piston-style, with the post sliding up and down under spring pressure. Parallelogram suspension seatposts use dual linked bars that connect the saddle clamp to the post. There are many variations but all operate in an arcing motion.

The suspension on this Canyon gravel bike is not as massive as typical mountain bike suspension.

The effectiveness of any suspension around the saddle or seatpost depends on the rider applying their weight on the saddle, so it's more often seen on more upright varieties of bicycle, where the rider spends most of the time seated. Seatpost suspension is especially good for bikes with no other form of suspension.

Mountain bike suspension technology is very diverse and highly developed. If you want to immerse yourself in what works best for which purpose, visit the Wikipedia page on bicycle suspension.

❝ *It takes at least a year to become a suspension expert, and another two to realise that you don't have a clue.* ❞ Mike Burrows.

◀ *Seatpost suspension by Safort.*

Understanding Bicycle Wheels

Quella Bikes

The grace and glory of a bicycle lie in its light, elegant and immensely strong wheels. Your bike wheels can hold about 400 times their own weight on a regular basis and they won't collapse until subject to roughly 700 times their own weight, which makes them one of the strongest man-made structures on the planet (Paolo Salvagione). Skilled off-road riders, jumping from high obstacles, subject their wheels to forces of more than a quarter of a ton.

How do bicycle wheels achieve their unusual strength? The quick explanation lies in strength through tension, aided by advances in component materials. The detailed explanation is complex,

fascinating, and not for here. Read *The Bicycle Wheel* by Jobst Brandt to discover the wonderful world of static forces, three types of dynamic forces, pushing spokes and pulling spokes, flange diameter and flange spacing…

The bicycle wheel started its development journey when wheelwrights applied a hot-forged iron band to the rims of the wooden-spoked wheel of running machines. What they made was little different from horse-drawn cartwheels. As the band cooled it contracted, squeezing the wooden components into functional shape and strength. The iron band was known as the tyer – the word we use today for the very different pneumatic item which adorns our wheels, with no tying function. Since then human ingenuity has given us wheels different in almost every respect, although they remain circular for practical reasons.

We can compare cycle wheels with car wheels. Cars' wheels typically take a much larger load and with tyres at relatively low pressures, giving suspension. But on a bicycle it's mainly the tensioned spokes which provide the suspension by distributing the load. Cyclists go for low weight and good rolling resistance, so tend towards larger diameter wheels and narrower tyres than found on cars.

The hub

The obvious function of the hub is to cradle the turning wheel and be part of the spoke tensioning process. Some hubs do this and little more, and other hubs can be really busy items. They can incorporate a freewheel to let your legs rest, or one of four or five types of brake and/or a dynamo. They can host multiple gearing systems: either internally (hub gears) or externally (derailleur gears).

Spokes

Here quality really counts. A spoke is tensioned by turning the nipple by the rim using a special tool. When you ride each tensioned spoke is required to compress then stretch with each rotation of the wheel. Each must cope with all sorts of road surfaces, rider styles, and overall cargo weight. Most wheels are given extra strength by being 'laced' so that each spoke crosses three or four other spokes. On the other hand a typical high performance road bike will have radial spoking: so no spoke crosses another. This gives a stiffer, lighter wheel, but not as strong. 'Double-butted' spokes are thinner over the centre section to make them lighter, more elastic, and more aerodynamic. 'Single-butted' spokes are thicker at the hub and then taper to a thinner section all the way to the threads at the rim.

Spokes come in gauges. A 15 gauge might be found on a light road bike, a 14 gauge on a touring bike designed to carry loads in rough conditions, and a 13 gauge on a tandem, cargo bike or BMX.

A good bicycle wheel can hold up to 400 times its own weight and won't collapse until about 700 times its weight.

Bicycles balance on their journey so their wheels experience low lateral (sideways) forces, as opposed to the wheels of tricycles, quadricycles and cars, which do not have that luxury. The wheels on these vehicles need to be built strong and so tend to be smaller. Another variable is the number of spokes. The more the stronger, at the expense of weight and cost.

Spokes break when they have become fatigued. Rear wheel spokes fail more often. This is because rear wheels carry more weight, receive more stress from the rigidity of the rear frame triangle, and most of all, carry more of their load on the spokes of the right side. This is because they are built asymmetrically, to make room for a multi-sprocket gear cluster. This asymmetry makes spokes on the right side at least twice as tight as the ones on the left. The load by each side of the wheel is in direct proportion to the spoke tension, so a 36-spoke rear wheel with a ten-speed gear cluster is, in effect, hardly more than an 18-spoke wheel. The greater the 'dish' or asymmetry, the weaker the wheel and the sooner the spokes will break from fatigue. In contrast, road shocks encountered by the front wheel are cushioned by the elasticity of the fork and by the toptube and downtube that absorb these forces by bending. Together, the frame and the rider's arms absorb most of the peak loads on the front wheel. Suspension forks also help. *(Parts of the above are adapted from Jobst Brandt's book, The Bicycle Wheel.)*

The rim

The worst are cheap, heavy steel rims, prone to rust, especially round the nipples which makes truing the wheel difficult. In many countries, including the UK, steel rims were fitted to the majority of bikes until the 1980s. Rims are now normally made of aluminium alloy.

Most serious bike wheels have chunky box-section rims, often double-walled for stiffness. Good rims are reinforced with either single eyelets or double eyelets to distribute the stress of the spoke. A single eyelet reinforces the spoke hole much like a hollow rivet. A double eyelet is a cup that is riveted into both walls of a double-walled rim.

Artisan or robot?

That expensive bike in your local bike shop almost certainly has wheels built by a computer-controlled machine so sophisticated that it can match or outstrip the skills of the human wheel-builder, and in around 15 minutes per wheel which would take a skilled human an hour. During all wheel-building the turning of one spoke nipple causes multiple changes elsewhere. However, a wheel-building computer can calculate precisely and be more accurate in the turning of the nipple. The robot is given a 'recipe' for the wheel needed and can be set to refine and stabilise the wheel once, twice, or whatever.

There will always be an essential role for small scale cycle makers to build their own wheels, in particular specialised wheels, and every good bike shop needs to know how to build or rebuild wheels for customers.

Double Archway by Mark Grieve and Llana Spector. Glendale Public Art.

Annular Pneumatic Suspension

The pneumatic tyre helped make the bicycle a universal product, but the type of tyre you fit makes a big difference to you and your ride.

Quality varies. Pay more and you get firmer, faster, safer, longer-lasting tyres, with more protective layers.

For urban and touring best choose a tyre with some tread but not a lot of it. Don't choose too narrow a cross-section. Most modern street tyres have a good quality light carcass and a fat tyre gives a lot of security. Needless to say, big fat cheap tyres are not nice.

With off-road tyres rolling resistance is only one small factor. And even that does not always make sense. For example, a narrow tyre will generally have a lower rolling resistance than a larger cross-section of similar construction. This is because you can get more pressure into the smaller tyre, meaning less flat bit on the bottom. But if your tyres are very much on the fat side they will take more pressure than you would ever want to use. So the larger cross-section can have a lower rolling resistance on any surface.

Cars need tread, or grooves, in the tyre to prevent them hydroplaning above a certain speed. Bicycle tyres are much narrower than car tyres so there's rarely a problem getting excess water out from underneath. The amount of grip depends on the area in contact with the road, which is greater for tyres without much tread. Even in the wet a smoother tread will mean more grip on the road than a deep tread or knobbles. This is why high-performance road cyclists ride on 'slicks' – nice smooth rubber, dry or wet, with lots of grip. You could aquaplane with slicks, but you would need to be doing some serious speed. One problem with slicks is that they wear out more quickly than other tyres of comparable quality.

Off-road you do need tread, because the surface you are riding on is often softer than the tyre.

In wet and serious mud open tread knobblies are the only thing. Less mud sticks to them, so there is less added weight. Much defies analysis but, at the end of the day, there is a lot of security in a pair of fat knobblies off-road.

Avoid solid (non-pneumatic) tyres unless you don't care about comfort, handling and riding efficiency.

Going tubeless

Tubeless tyres are becoming common on mid-range to high-end mountain bikes and gravel bikes, and becoming more popular for performance road bikes. These tyres require specialised rims, making an airtight seal. Part of the deal is that you use sealant, which helps plug any small leaks while you ride.

Tubeless tyres give fewer punctures, but the main advantage is for off-road riders using lower tyre pressures to maximise grip. But this can make any tyre bottom out on tree roots and the like. With tubed tyres this invites an impact puncture, as the inner tube is squashed against the rim. This cannot happen with tubeless. There are disadvantages with tubeless. If you puncture them they can be messy. There are special plug kits for small holes, and you can squirt in more sealant, but neither can help with larger holes and rips. These are rare, and virtually impossible to repair during a ride. Converting tubed to tubeless means two expensive new wheels. Tubeless tyres cost more than tubed, and there's the sealant cost: it gradually dries out so you need to squirt more in every couple of months. Finally, tubeless tyres need to be pumped up more often than tubed tyres.

Is it all worth it? For mountain bikes: probably. For gravel bikes maybe, but only if you actually ride off-tarmac. For performance road bikes: perhaps. For other cycles it is questionable.

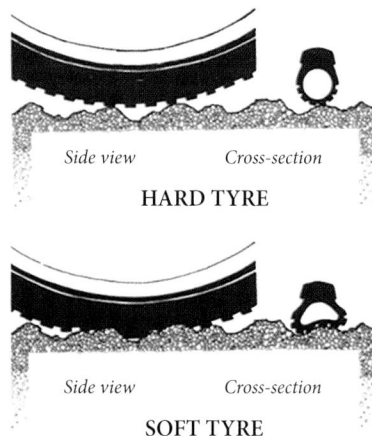

Side view   Cross-section
HARD TYRE

Side view   Cross-section
SOFT TYRE

Small Wheels Talk Big

Photo Gunnar Fehlau.

Through thick, thin and science the diameter of the bicycle wheel changed little from the day the first diamond frame rolled out of its maker's shed. But smaller wheels are making their claims heard.

The developers of diamond framed bicycles hit on the magic wheel measurement of 700c for the best balance of comfort and rolling resistance. It also worked well because it was the biggest size of wheel that could conveniently be accommodated in the robust, uncomplicated and easy-to-manufacture diamond frame.

Oddly, wheel sizes other than 700c are defined in Anglo-Saxon inches! Going down from 700c the common sizes are 26″ 24″ 20″ and 16″. For adult bikes we generally talk of 20″ and 16″ as being 'small wheels'.

The inventiveness of cycle designers has now taken us into new realms, including folding bikes, adult tricycles and HPVs (Human Powered Vehicles). Almost all benefit from smaller wheels.

A bigger diameter wheel rolls more easily than a smaller one, presuming they both have the same tyre construction, cross-section, tyre pressure, load to carry and road surface to ride on. In an unsprung frame the bigger wheel also gives a more comfortable ride. This is because it falls less deeply into small depressions in the road surface. Also, on hitting bumps, a larger wheel rises and falls more slowly. Make the wheel any bigger and you compromise the ease of mounting and dismounting that gave the 'safety bicycle' its name.

But over the years, some powerful advocates have argued for smaller wheels for regular bicycles. The small wheel was championed by the eminent French cycle-tourist Paul de Vivie (also known as Velocio) and, since the 1960s, by Alex Moulton. De Vivie was blunt:

66 *That universal agreement has fixed on 70 centimetres as the proper size for wheels does not in any way prove that this diameter is best; it simply proves that cyclists follow each other like sheep.* 99

He advocated balloon tyres up to a cross-section of 2.25" (57mm) on 20" (50cm) rims, giving an overall wheel diameter of about 22". He reached his conclusions cycling the equivalent of fifteen times round the world. This makes sense, as the volume of air and pressure remains the same, while a wider cross-section compensates for the harsher ride of the small wheels.

But what about the rolling resistance? For a given tyre pressure and load the contact patch area is constant, regardless of tyre's diameter (you can show this by taking the length of a tyre's contact print with the road, and dividing it by the inflated tyre radius: as long as your tyre is subjected to a known weight). With the Velocio approach the contact patch is wider but shorter, compensating for the otherwise higher rolling resistance.

Compensation, though, depends on a superior lightweight tyre carcass because the larger the cross-section, the stronger the carcass must be – difficult and expensive in Velocio's day. Thankfully there are now strong and efficient tyres in formats not far removed from Velocio's, many of them spin-offs from BMX and HPV developments.

What then of Alex Moulton? His background included steam power, aeronautical engineering, automotive suspension and rubber technology – his great-grandfather introduced Goodyear's rubber vulcanising process to the UK.

Moulton demonstrated in the 1960s that 16" x 1⅜" (ISO 37-349) tyres inflated to 50psi (3.44 bars) could match the rolling resistance of standard lower-pressure roadster tyres. Importantly, he did not use 'juvenile' tyres, but tyres which he had made to his own specification. To eliminate the rough ride, he added suspension, giving a

Frenchman Paul de Vivie (1853 to 1930) rode the equivalent of fifteen times round the world.

smoother ride than a conventional bike and reducing momentum loss.

Over the decades the Moulton formula has performed well in time trials, solo and four-man pursuit, criterium, ultra-marathon, triathlon, Audax and HPV races. The flying 200 metres solo HPV record (normal riding position) has been held by a fully-faired Moulton since 1985.

In 1964, Moulton, with Dunlop, produced a robust, wired-on high-pressure tyre: the unique Moulton 17" x 1¼" format (ISO 32-369). On smooth surfaces its rolling resistance matches a high quality 700c high pressure touring tyre. Since then other high quality small wheel tyres have become available.

It is true that for fixed conditions big wheels still have lower rolling resistance – but such conditions may not exist. With careful attention to tyre pressures and carcass design, small wheels are stronger, lighter, stiffer, more compact, have lower wind resistance and offer more design options. They enable faster acceleration and more responsive handling. Combined with suspension and supple, high-pressure tyres, they excel.

The above is adapted from the writings of Tony Hadland, author of several books on small-wheeled cycles.

◄

Charline Skovgaard and her twin daughters in Copenhagen. The 24″ wheel Jopo was introduced in the 60s by the Finnish company Helkama and has become an icon of cycling chic in northern Europe. Photo: charlisblog.com

◄

Spanish company Orbea promote their 20″ wheel Katu as a compact commuter cycle. They claim it is also 'democratising' by accommodating riders of different sizes, making it ideal for family sharing. Photo: Ecomove, Bristol.

◄

Small wheels allow all kinds of experimentation. This Lean Bike was made in the 1990s by Norbert Nattefort in Germany. Aerodynamic disc wheels can give problems on conventional cycles due to side winds, but this is less of a consideration with smaller wheels.

▶ Canadians Vik and Sharon after a 100km randonneur event on their small-wheeled Bike Friday.

▶ The Bambuk tandem trike recumbent from Germany, with 24″ wheels. Small-wheeled tandems make riding together less daunting, and in this case more comfortable.

▶ Small wheels can better stand up to the sideways forces applied when trikes and quadricycles change direction. This is the Poney4 by a consortium of German and Czech manufacturers.

Understanding Gears

Stepping down from our penny farthings was a defining moment in our evolution. The new 'safety' bicycle of 1885 used different sized sprockets connected by a chain, allowing a usable gear without the dangerously high wheel. Thanks to multiple gearing we can now match our limited power output to widely varying 'pedal outcomes', and we want transmissions which are clean, lightweight, user-friendly, indestructible and wide-geared.

There aren't very many options when it comes to gear systems. You can use the chain running over multiple sprockets and then make it 'derail' from one sprocket to the next. Or you have an enclosed gearbox inside the rear hub itself. Neither system is new. And each type has settled down to a comfortable middle age.

Hub or derailleur gears: which is a better choice? Derailleur systems tend to be used by high performance cycles and hub gears by everyone else. This is a gross simplification (and leaves aside the fact that most bikes in the world are single-speed).

How many gears and how wide the range?

For decades the three-speed hub gear was standard, but now there are hub systems ranging from two to fourteen gears. What that means in real life depends on the size of the chainwheel and the rear sprocket which your chain is linking together.

Most modern derailleurs have a single chainwheel, combining with multiple sprockets at the back. Systems with double chainrings relating to multiple sprockets at the back are more complicated in their gearing, and there is often near duplication of some combinations. With the larger front chainwheel directed to the smallest rear sprocket you get the 'hardest,' highest gear. Smaller front to largest rear gives you the lowest gear.

Whatever your system it's better to get the low gears right. You can choose to freewheel down the

hills but you always have to pedal up them: or get off and push.

Which is heavier?

Hub gears tend to be heavier, but not by much. Despite their clean lines and internal magnificence they are still a lump of steel in the middle of your back wheel.

Which type is more efficient?

The derailleur has the edge in efficiency. In good condition and going at speed it can be better than 96% efficient. Hub gears can give you an efficiency close to that, but only when your chain is in direct drive, so not engaging any of the other sprockets inside the hub. If you engage your lowest or highest hub gear you can expect efficiency losses of about 5% to 7%. With both systems' efficiency rapidly rises as the pressure is piled on.

Which type is more reliable?

Hub gears are very compact mechanical wonders, with cogs engaging with cogs in ingenious ways.

Derailleurs are relatively exposed and susceptible to damage. Hub gears have everything packaged away inside your rear wheel, shielded from the elements, and they need very little maintenance. There is also the matter of chain kindness. With a hub gear the chain is always correctly aligned. Your chain will certainly last longer than one being constantly twisted and derailled across a barrage of pointy metal teeth. Single-speed (1/8″) chains are intrinsically stronger anyway. On the downside hub gears can make a rear wheel puncture harder to fix.

Which is easier to use?

Both types are indexed, so click positively into place, usually in response to a twist-grip or trigger on the handlebar. For a derailleur gear change you keep pedalling – but ease off on the pedal pressure. For hub gears you freewheel for a second to change gear. With hub gears you don't have to worry about cross-chaining. This happens where derailleurs have multiple chainrings, giving you combinations to avoid. Derailleur systems now usually have a single front chainwheel and a genuine, simple and wide choice of sprockets by the rear wheel. An astonishing development!

With derailleurs, if you try to shift when you're stopped, you'll set off with a crunch and a lurch, and possibly do some damage. Ideally you should move into a low starting gear before you stop. But with hub gears you can change when stopped and move off smoothly in the new gear. It's no problem to stop in eighth and move off in first.

Can you retro-fit?

To change from one system to another is a massive, expensive job. Probably better to sell your bike and buy one with the system you want. However, you can fairly easily upgrade, simplify or otherwise alter the gearing on an existing derailleur system. You can also change the size of the single rear sprocket on your existing hub-geared bike.

Implications for the rear wheel

Derailleur systems need heavily-dished rear wheels to make room for the ever-growing numbers of rear sprockets. Dishing involves the spokes on the sprocket side coming down to a

Derailleur gears: the rider shifts the chain from sprocket to sprocket while pedalling.

Hub gears: The workings are all inside, protected from the weather. You don't have to be pedalling to change gear.

position closer to the centre of the wheel, while the rim remains centred in the frame. A dished wheel has reduced strength and is particularly vulnerable to sideways loading. Heavily loaded touring bikes can experience spoke breakages on the dished side. Hub gears do not have this problem and can be built into strong wheels, which is one reason why some serious touring cyclists go for hub gears such as Rohloffs.

Great moments of discovery: the conception of hub gears. By David Eccles.

Which are the main makes?

There are several hub gear options available but the most common are from Shimano, Sturmey-Archer and Rohloff. Makers of derailleur systems include Shimano, SRAM and Campagnolo.

Since very few people install their own hub gear systems few bike shops stock them. With derailleur systems you get a 'groupset' in line with the purpose and the overall price point of the cycle you are buying. Take advice from an expert dealer.

Latest developments

There is some interesting recent technology being applied to transmission systems. One is electronic as opposed to indexed manual gear changing. This is also known as Di2. Another is continuous variable transmission: so there are no steps between the gears, as with automatic cars.

A further development is the positioning of a gearbox low and central to the cycle's frame. This is mainly for serious off-road and expedition touring

bikes. The Pinion system has a fully enclosed oil-bath shell housing an array of sprockets and a camshaft which shifts through unique consecutive positions, cleverly aligning the two sprocket groups. The Pinion keeps a straight 'chainline', - in fact they use not a chain but a carbon belt. All gears are evenly spaced, and electronic shifting is available. You can change gear when stopped (but not change under load). Also, the 12-speed Pinion gearbox, probably the most common, gives a huge 600% gear range, compared to the 520% offered by the Rohloff Speedhub.

Disadvantages: Pinion transmission is expensive, especially since you have to buy the whole bike built around it. It's also more than 1.3kg heavier than a high performance derailleur system.

These gearboxes are situated exactly where higher quality electric bikes have their motor, which restricts Pinion's place in the e-bike market, but they do market an own brand cycle with a rear hub electric motor.

Pinions are being fitted mainly to high end mountain bikes but lovers of expedition touring are finding them perfect for their needs. They are only rarely found on other types of bike. It's a development which cannot be ignored: it's not clear yet whether Pinions will, in time, become cheaper and lighter so as to serve a wider market.

The Pinion system: heavier than other options, expensive and requiring a specially made frame. It's reported to be very reliable.

Chains and Belts

The derailleur chain is a work of wonder. It lives with the friction caused by around 40,000 articulations per minute yet stays over 97 per cent efficient – presuming it's clean and lightly oiled. This all explains why almost all cycles transmit your power through a chain. However unless you enclose a chain in a chaincase oil bath it will eventually, inevitably, wear out.

Efficiency drops by around 3% if your chain is contaminated with wet mud, and by 5% if that mud has dried on. Chains without lubrication, running metal to metal, give drive efficiency as low as 90% (Friction Facts, USA).

There are two main types of chain. The wider 1/8″ chain is used with single and hub gears. It keeps one straight line as it travels round your sprockets and chainwheel. The width of a derailleur chain can vary depending on the number of rear sprockets on the bike, but the nominal width is 3/32″. These chains are designed to be regularly shifted from one sprocket to another.

Belt drive is the main alternative. A half-inch wide belt made from carbon fibre and polyurethane marries with a similarly thick chainring. The belt is extremely strong, knows no rust, won't stretch over time, needs no lube, doesn't get your clothes dirty, and the whole system is lighter than a standard drivetrain. However, a belt can't be part of a derailleur system. Unlike traditional chains, belts cannot be split to fit onto a bike. So bike frame rear triangles must be specially designed to incorporate a joint to pass the belt through.

Gates belt drive combined with hub gearing. Photo: Canyon Bikes.

❝ *I still feel that variable gears are only for people over forty-five. Isn't it better to triumph by the strength of your muscles than by the artifice of a derailleur? We are getting soft... As for me, give me a fixed gear!* ❞

Henri Desgrange, founder of the Tour de France

The Technology of Stopping

Putting on the brakes is a necessity, not an option, so it's important to understand the technology.

Disc brakes

These have become lighter, more reliable and more affordable. We see them on more and more new cycles, and even on some children's bikes.

There are two main kinds. Mechanical disc brakes use a normal lever connected to the brake caliper by a cable. They tend to be much cheaper as they're less complicated but they aren't as powerful as hydraulic disc brakes and they also need to be adjusted for cable stretch and pad wear. Hydraulic disc brakes use a lever connected to the pistons (or caliper) by a hose containing incompressible fluid, which makes them more powerful.

Disc brakes provide controllable and predictable stopping power, and transmit more mechanical force. Because they use a metal rotor attached to the hub rather than a braking surface on the rim, they don't wear out as quickly and allow you to use lighter weight, disc-specific rims.

Hydraulic brakes also compensate automatically for pad wear, so the only maintenance needed is an occasional change of the brake fluid and new pads.

Hub brakes/roller brakes

Hub brakes are also known as drum brakes and more modern versions are known as roller brakes. They are housed in the centre of the wheel, often in combination with hub gears if that's the transmission system used. Curved brake shoes expand outwards to press against the shell's inner wall. You can't see what's happening, but it's all protected from the weather and road debris.

Hub brakes function even when the wheel itself is buckled, whereas rim brakes jam against untrue rims. In extreme conditions heat builds up in hub brakes just as with rim brakes, but causes less harm, being away from the tyre and inner tube.

These brakes come close to being maintenance-free, but the time eventually comes when they need a strip-down for brake pad renewal.

There is another form of hub brake: the coaster brake, also known as the back-pedal brake, operated by back-pressure on the pedals. The coaster brake is highly reliable, since it transmits power through the chain as opposed to a cable or tube. Coasters are common throughout Europe, with the exception of the UK.

Rim brakes

V Brakes are the most prominent type of rim brake. They revolutionised rim braking performance for off-road bikes, tourers and hybrid bikes. They have two long arms which lever onto the rim when the brake cable pulls.

Cantilever brakes are mounted much like V-brakes, but with a straddle cable between them, which is pulled vertically to actuate the brakes. They offer near V-brake levels of performance, without getting clogged up with mud.

Caliper brakes mostly attach via a single bolt through the fork crown. Good aluminium alloy caliper brakes are found on touring and racing bikes, whereas flexible pressed-steel side-pulls are typically found on cheap bikes of all kinds. 'Side-pulls' lose much of their bite in wet weather. They are even worse in the wet when combined with steel rims, as opposed to the aluminium alloy rims now standard on quality bikes.

All forms of rim brake are dropping in popularity thanks to the march of the disc brake.

For fixed-wheel braking see overleaf.

Catch me if you can!

Brakes played no great role in the cycling exploits of Laurie Lee's mother. In his book, *Cider with Rosie* he describes some of her alternative techniques:

❝ Happy enough when the thing was in motion, it was stopping and starting that puzzled her. She had to be launched on her way by running parties of villagers; and to stop she rode into a hedge. With the Stroud Co-op Stores, where she was a regular customer, she had come to a special arrangement. This depended for its success upon a quick ear and timing, and was a beautiful operation to watch. As she coasted downhill towards the shop's main entrance she would let out one of her screams; an assistant, specially briefed, would tear through the shop, out the side door, and catch her in his arms. He has to be both young and nimble, for if he missed her she piled up by the police station. ❞

Single-Speeds and Fixies

With single-speed cycling you have one gear and nothing else. It gives you simplicity, reliability, easy maintenance and cost savings. It's as cheap and efficient as it possibly could be. It's also used by the majority of cyclists worldwide: people in developing countries who use their bikes day in day out as primary transport and for load carrying.

'Single-speed' usually refers to a cycle which freewheels when you stop pedalling. 'Fixies' are single-speeds, too, but with no freewheel. So when you're moving, you're pedalling. You can't take a rest, so fixed-gear riding gives you a certain intimacy with your bike. Fixed wheel cycles are as old as cycling itself. The high bicycle (penny farthing) was a fixie.

You can slow down on a fixie by applying backwards force to the pedals. The force goes through the chain to the spinning wheel. That's a lot of kinetic energy to fight against, and it takes time, which is why a separate hand-operated brake is needed to keep you safe and legal for road use. Or you can put two rim brakes on a fixie, as shown by the image above. You can, of course, have a freewheel single-speed with a back-pedal brake.

Don't confuse back-pedal brakes with fixed-wheel stopping. They both need back-pressure through the chain to the rear hub but back-pedal brakes apply real and almost immediate mechanical braking force.

Creative Commons.

Photo: Richard Masoner.

Most complete fixed-gear bikes come with a 'flip-flop' rear wheel. If you put it in one way the gear is fixed, but if you turn it around you get a single-speed with freewheel.

Drawbacks? Fixed-gear riding causes extra stresses, so frames are usually made of heavier tubing: meaning steel or 'overbuilt' alloy. Also, you'll often find that your single gear ratio is not always the one you need at any given time. Fixies are at home in urban environments. They appeal to lovers of the minimal, and are here to stay.

Fixed Wheel Freestyle

Not so long ago, virtually overnight, everyone and their sibling took to riding around on fixed wheels. Inevitably some began fooling around on them. Street BMX riding requires an unusually high level of skill, but doing stunts on a regular fixed wheel bike is another kettle of fish. Skids were one thing, but grinding street furniture was asking for trouble. And, even if the humans were up to the job, the skinny-assed track bikes they were abusing were definitely not. So the people who breed bicycles herded two of them up, threw them together in a field, and we politely averted our gaze as rough-and-ready street BMX got jiggy with refined and elegant track bike. The snarling mongrels which emerged from the sordid encounter looked like track bikes in suits of BMX chromoly armour. You'd have to be a loony to ride one.

Mick Allan

CHAPTER 4

Bike Love: the Practicals

The Power and the Comfort

This section is about you and the bike you choose to ride. You make the music together, so here's how to ride in tune.

Get Cycling CIC.

Yours is the power

Your bike may be in great order, but what about its power source, presuming that's just you? It's motivating to think that your bio-chemical machine, unlike any mechanical device, becomes stronger and more efficient the more it's used. And when it needs repair it can usually fix itself or find a work-around. You outclass your bike in so many ways. The sophistication of your bones puts the best frame tubing to shame. The flexibility and efficiency of your joints, balanced and stabilised by co-ordinated muscles, outperform the most precise bearings in a bicycle. As you ride your body constantly regulates energy expenditure, heart rate, and oxygen uptake, and you process your complex fuel supply with astonishing efficiency.

Your body functions as a fuel cell. More precisely the mitochondria in each cell do the job as part of a process which breaks food down into energy through chemical reactions. During a demanding ride energy is first produced in the muscles themselves but then more complex fuel supply kicks in, as glucose is summoned from various sources.

Further into a hard ride your body switches to a longer-term metabolism as it begins to draw on aerobic (oxygen-based) energy. Here you experience that feeling of really 'getting going' during a ride.

When you hit maximum power adrenaline gives a further energy rush, as your heart pumps around five times as much blood as normal, and with 90% going to your muscles – all while you are taking in around 250 litres of air per minute to aerate that blood.

Your ride is coming to an end but the metabolic increase continues as it digests food and redistributes the reserves of energy around your body. You feel good. Your cycling has increased your general stamina, given you better lung function, lowered your risk of cancer and heart disease, helped with weight control, stabilised your levels of body fat and cholesterol, increased your muscle mass and strength, and helped protect from stress and depression. You have probably also experienced a high from endocannabinoids, a class of brain chemicals mimicked by cannabis.

Your bike may be special, but its power source is beyond compare.

Photo: Irankis, Wiki Commons.

Choosing your bike

Whether for children or adults a cheap bike is never exactly that, as quality components fail and disappoint. US cycle designer Keith Bontrager famously said: 'Strong. Light. Cheap. Pick Two'.

You can certainly pay more for better materials, more numerous and more complex manufacturing processes and for the research and development which brings better performance, less weight and more durability. But the familiar mantra, 'buy the best that you can afford', doesn't always serve well. You need to understand what you get at different price points. You can compare two bikes from the same manufacturer, right next to each other in the range, and discover that they have few components in common. Add only a little to a retail price point and sometimes everything changes: a slightly better bar, a slightly better saddle, one-step-up bearings with tighter seals, one more rear sprocket, better quality tyres and so on. Your local bike shop is there to explain and should welcome a host of questions from you. Few bike shops sell low quality bikes. They know that cheap bikes spend much of their short, brutal lives out of action, but worst of all, cheap bikes discourage people from cycling, because they reinforce the false notion, at every turn of the pedals, that cycling is inherently unpleasant.

Finding your positions

Regular bikes are generally available in three to five sizes. They give you a triangle of contact points: saddle, pedals and handlebars. Presuming your cycle is not completely wrong for you the 'contacts triangle' can be adjusted for your comfort, usually with just an allen key or two. And it's worth getting the set-up just right, even adjusting the position of the brake levers. The trouble is most people don't do this and so don't know what a well fitted bike is supposed to feel like. They contort their bodies and spend their days riding with the saddle too low and the bars too far away. Then they wonder why their bike is so uncomfortable.

A saddle at just the right height maximises the power your legs can create. The well-tried method for working out the saddle-to-pedal distance for an upright bike rider is to sit on the bike with the instep of your foot on the pedal, at which point your leg should be fully extended. This will give a slight bend at the knee when the ball of the foot is on the pedal. This is as close as any guidelines will bring you to an optimum position: you will have to do the fine tuning yourself. Less confident cyclists often keep a low saddle so as to get one or both feet on the ground on stopping. If that gives the sense of security you need, fair enough, but the trade-off is inefficient pedalling and the strain of pushing with bent knees can lead to pain and injury.

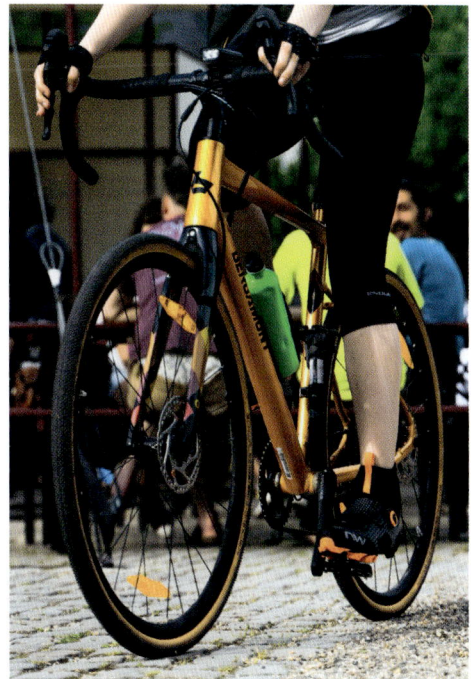

Photo by Maxime on Unsplash.

Reaching for the bars

Crucial to your comfort and body health is the position of the seat in relationship to the handlebars. The seat can slide forwards and back along its runners, giving about 9cm of adjustment either way. The position of the saddle is determined by the length of your thigh bone. Most advice points to the back of your kneecap being directly above the pedal spindle when the pedal is at its furthest forward position.

So much for the generalities of adjustment. But comfort relates to what kind of cycle you have, or want. If your bike was designed for upright riding (a town or city bike) it should have a well sprung or padded saddle and handlebars which are pretty much in the right position when you reach for them.

Whatever your type of handlebar your arms should not lock out, and not have a significant bend in them. There is usually some handlebar adjustability available: up, down, fore, aft and rotational. On modern mountain and performance road bikes the almost universal adoption of the 'threadless' headset system means that handlebar stem adjustment is very limited or even impossible. This makes relocating the bars a matter of completely changing the stem for one with a different length or rise.

Riding 'sit-up-and-beg' means all your weight bears down on the saddle, which can become uncomfortable after just a few kilometres, even with the best of saddles. This is no fun if you are committed to a long ride. The other extreme is the

▲ *Pivoting forwards at the hips and avoiding a curved back. This rider's hands are on the tops of the drop bars, leaving the option of 'going down on the drops' for a more aerodynamic position. Photo: Jason Patient.*

A bike giving an upright riding position: back is straight, head is up, arms relaxed. These are the built-in comfort features for city riding. Photo: João Pimentel Ferreira. Wikimedia.

sport-orientated high performance cycle, with drop bars and a long stretch.

Drop handlebars bring their own ergonomic issues. The most common mistake is having them set too low. This can be compounded by the way dropped bars are usually set in stems which extend forwards more than on other bikes. The vast majority of urban, day-ride and touring cyclists with dropped bars rarely go down to the dropped position. True, going down on the drops can give better aerodynamics: at 20mph/30kph 80% of your effort is used simply to overcome wind resistance. But how many of us reckon on keeping up that sort of speed? And how many can tolerate the long stretch and head-down position that goes with it?

Mountain bikes have a whole new set of targets. Control has a high priority, so the saddle can be lowered a little further than you might on other types of cycle – you don't sit on it much anyway. And mountain bikes don't use over-long stems or over-steep angles, else you end up pitching over the bars. Mountain bikes also have wider handlebars to give you more leverage when you steer over rough terrain.

Brake and gear levers can all be adjusted. It's all just nuts and bolts, so go ahead and adjust them to suit the angle of your wrists and your own preferences. Brake levers on flat or riser bars should be in line with your arms when you are sitting on the bike. Brakes on dropped bars have that nice place at the top for your hands to rest, between thumb and forefinger. But applying the brakes from that position is not ergonomic. Going 'down on the drops' gives better leverage on the brakes, but most people find it less comfortable riding that way for any distance.

Whatever your choice in bars you'll need comfortable grips to cushion shock. This can mean grips on the bar-ends for straight or almost straight bars, and, on multi-position bars, it means covering all likely hand positions with either bar tape or cycling-specific foam-based material. Padded cycle mitts also help.

Cyclists wanting a bit more performance and long distance comfort than is offered by the upright position find a moderate, forward leaning position suits better, with an easy, natural reach. This means the arms and handlebars share some of the weight which would otherwise all go straight down to the saddle. Osteopaths say it's better to hinge forward from the hip joint while in the saddle, and not through the middle of your back. Collapsing the back to give a C-curve restricts rib movement and breathing. Another frequent problem with dropped bars, often for older riders, is the need to lift back your head to see where you are going. It can become a literal pain in the neck, as the head is not in line with the spine.

Finding your perfect reach is ultimately a personal thing, and depends on sex, age, budget, cycling ambitions, and more. It also depends on try-out opportunities, and having someone to carry out quick adjustments for you. That's why they invented bike shops.

Wide bars give more control, especially off-road, but limit some of your options in traffic and other situations. Photo: pedalnorth.com.

A comfortable reach, with no curve to the back. A child's knee should never rise higher than the handlebars. Photo: Frog Cycles.

Stepping Through

The Germans take easy step-over seriously. These cycles from Excelsior show two approaches.

The Pagoba (above left) is a low cost three-speed with a steel frame. The strength of steel allows a graceful curve.

The Excelsior Easy Step has a less graceful curve as the use of lighter aluminium alloy necessitates extra bracing down below. It has the chainwheel positioned further back than normal to create more space for you to step through. The downtube under the saddle has to slope back so that you are not sitting directly over the pedals. This way you still have a natural riding position and lose no pedalling efficiency. Shown here is the electric-assist version. A mid-drive motor is not possible due to the already low frame so power has to come from the back of the bike to the front wheel motor, through cables within the frame.

Easy step-through tricycles are available at many quality levels.

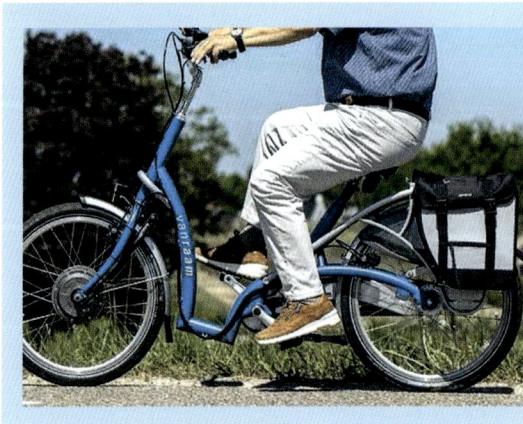

The Balance Bike from van Raam is particularly low and also has the seat set back in relation to the chainwheel. This has the added advantage of enabling you to get both feet on the ground at the same time when you stop. This gives reassurance and meets the needs of older or disabled riders. If you are on a conventional bike and can get both feet (or toes) on the ground at once, then your saddle is too low so you'll be pedalling inefficiently and in danger of knee damage.

Photo: Fat Lads on Unsplash.

Bikes for Women

The 'shrink it and pink it' approach is long gone, but there are still open-framed 'ladies' bikes, sometimes seen sporting a fetching basket. These cycles, usually with practical features and traditional styling, can be just the job for anyone, male or female, with limited mobility or who just wants to be able to dismount fast, in heavy traffic for example. Stepping 'through' the frame is important if you have a child in a child seat behind you.

With leisure and sports cycles women have some choices. Taller women have the option of a women's saddle on a unisex bike. This can work well and gives more model options.

The leading manufacturers of quality cycles do biometric research, mainly through their shop fitting services. Specialized, for example, have access to huge amounts of rider data which informs them that when it comes to body proportions and fit geometry there is likely more difference between two male cyclists than a male and female. Don't make a difference, they say, where there isn't one. They find that the biggest measurable variance between men and women is in sit bone width and subsequent saddle selection for width and shape. Specialized no longer make women-specific bikes, but use the body dimension data from women riders to evolve a unisex design approach.

Several brands now stick to a unisex frame philosophy with specific versions for women sitting within the brand's main range. They have many of the same parts as other cycles, but, usually, narrower bars, smaller brake levers (most women have a weaker squeeze than men) and, crucially, a women-specific saddle.

There are also bikes completely designed for women: geometry, parts, and build kit. There aren't many brands doing this, but by far the biggest is Liv Cycling, with frames made by Giant Bicycles.

Design decisions in women's cycles are taking somewhat different routes but largely converge in the creation of better and more appropriate cycles.

Saddle Comfort

Comfort on a bike is something you deserve and should expect. Too many new cyclists are put off for life by difficult saddle experiences. Manufacturers specify a saddle likely to suit you. This may work, once your bike dealer has set up your bike for you, but many saddles need to be changed. Some bike manufacturers actually seem to expect this. Also, our anatomy changes shape over time and new needs can be accommodated by features such as more or less padding, a flatter or more curved shape, a cut-out, or simply a change in the position and orientation of the saddle.

Sit bone widths vary across genders: it's not 'wide for women and narrow for men'. Most people's sit bone width is between 90mm and 120mm.

Saddles are generally made wider or narrower depending on their relationship to your handlebars and the geometry of the bike. This is because your saddle needs to give you the right amount of support for the riding position you choose, and that riding position causes your pelvis to move and shift, and your sit bone width

Photo: Mikael Colville-Andersen.

Somerville.

to change. So, in general, the more upright you are the wider the saddle should be. Conversely, as bars get lower and you lean further forward, saddles should become narrower. In other words, if you ride a 'sit up and beg' your position will be at your widest, requiring a wide saddle. On your fast or touring bike you reach forward, and the position of your pelvis changes, so you'll need a differently shaped saddle.

Sit bone width isn't the sole indicator of saddle size, as this is typically taken from an upright position. Next time you sit on your saddle, think about where you're feeling the most pressure.

Saddle fitting expert Jenni Gwiazdowski says:

66 *Women need to know if their vulva is an 'innie' or an 'outie'. When you squat down, does your vulva stick out? Outies will likely need a saddle with a channel or a cut-out for their soft tissue, but even these vary depending on your body. Similarly, perineal discomfort can also be solved by a channel or cut-out.* 99

A well padded saddle with springs will normally be found on city bikes. ▼

▲ *Hand-crafted leather saddles shape to your bottom and last decades if looked after. This is the shorter nose version of the B17 Brooks, made for women and smaller riders.*

▲ *A general purpose saddle, well padded at the back but unsprung. Generally found on touring and off-road cycles.*

People who reach some way to the bars, will usually benefit from a narrower saddle shape, but not always. Those sitting more upright are usually happy with a traditionally wider saddle shape.

The padded material in a bike saddle cushion will either be gel or memory foam. Gel is softer and more comfortable, so it's more popular with recreational cyclists. Foam, on the other hand, is firmer and more supportive, is preferred by people who spend more time in the saddle and it's also helpful for people who have sit bone pain.

Saddles for performance cycles and distance riding don't have much padding as they are usually designed to be used with padded shorts. Good-quality shorts will last for years, if you look after them. You probably won't be bothered with special clothing for rides of only a few kilometres

or miles. For longer rides don't be tempted to wear underpants, which can introduce friction.

When experimenting with saddle position, start with your saddle in the middle of the rails and keep it level. Use the spirit level on your phone.

A nose-up saddle puts pressure on soft tissue and makes your pelvis rotate backwards in an effort to get some weight on the sit bones. It also makes the bars seem too far away. You then cannot push hard on the pedals for fear of sliding off the back of the saddle.

A saddle which slopes down makes the pelvis constantly slide forwards. To compensate you push your body weight back off the bars and pedals. This set up puts more weight on the hands, creating numbness. It's really easy to mess up an otherwise perfectly good set-up just by having the saddle a couple of degrees out.

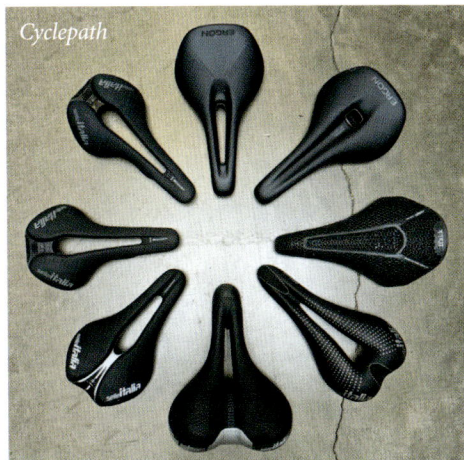

Cyclepath

This advice is provided by bike mechanic and saddle expert Jenni Gwiazdowski, whose blog, Spanner in the Works, gives: "Everyday bike maintenance for everyday people, brought to you by a female mechanic that is tired of the cycle industry's BS".

Cyclepath, a dealer in Portland, Oregon, who runs cycle maintenance classes for women and saddle-fitting services. In exchange for a deposit and a fee you can take away a saddle to try on your bike. This way you can experiment with various comfort positions. You bring the saddle back within a week and can buy the same saddle if it has worked for you, or try another one until you find the right fit.

The Great Helmet Debate

The subject of cycle helmets – particularly the idea of making them compulsory – is not as straightforward as many people believe.

Their effectiveness at preventing injury is often presumed as automatic. However, cycle helmets – which have to be much lighter than motorbike helmets, for obvious reasons – are flimsy things. They can only be designed, essentially, to cope with falling off a stationary bike onto a hard surface.

For children learning to cycle, or for adults in icy conditions, there are fair reasons for recommending them. Mountain bikers, liable to be struck on the head by jutting branches or prone to tumbling on rocks during tight slow turns, almost all use them. Racing cyclists, who can be dislodged in a cramped peloton and crack their head on a hard road, universally do. (Cycling event organisers often require their use for insurance reasons.)

Road 'accidents' are different. Moving impacts, especially with a motor vehicle, are so far beyond the design spec that helmets provide no guaranteed head protection. For the everyday, utility or easygoing cyclist, the minimal and unlikely potential benefit may not be enough to justify the discomfort or hassle of a helmet for short trips.

A trope of the debate is the 'helmet-saved-my-life' fallacy. Some people will proudly tell you how their helmet was trashed when they came off their bike at speed, citing it as 'proof' that it 'saved their life'. (The more such accidents they've had, the more they seem to feel this makes them a safety role model.)

Unfortunately, a helmet which has split likely hasn't worked properly at all. What's supposed to happen is that the polycarbonate plastic shell flexes to spread the impact, which is absorbed by the expanded polystyrene collapsing underneath. If the polystyrene layer hasn't flattened, the helmet absorbed virtually none of the impact. It was your skull that saved your life.

Problems arise when lawmakers, perhaps under pressure from manufacturers or bereaved individual campaigners, are tempted to make helmets compulsory. It happened in Australia and New Zealand a few decades ago, and general opinion is that it has not resulted in any public health benefit. Requiring helmets means far fewer people cycle; that means more people get ill, resulting in a net increase in bad health and premature deaths. Only a handful of countries in the world require their use for adults, and the safest places to cycle – notably the Netherlands and Denmark – have very low helmet use.

Cycling advocacy groups, such as Cycling UK, have clear views on helmet use. Typically they recommend their use but stress it should be a personal choice, definitely not required by law. Helmets are not even in the top ten things that make cycling safer. That's the view of Chris Boardman, Commissioner of Active Travel England. What matters far more is good infrastructure that keeps cyclists separate from traffic – and good driver behaviour when they can't be. That often depends on cultural attitudes to cycling; something that's very difficult to change.

Rob Ainsley

Be Good at being Traffic

Experienced cyclists have learned a lot about riding as part of traffic. Here are some tips to help you build up confidence and stay safe. You still need to make your own decisions, as no two sets of circumstances are the same.

▶ Practise riding your bike until it's second nature: starting, stopping, signalling, looking behind, gear changing and emergency stops.

▶ Anticipate problems. Assume that pedestrians, motor vehicles and other cyclists will do something strange.

▶ Don't stick to the very edge of the road where the road surface is generally poor and when motorists might try to overtake when they shouldn't. Take the road space you deserve if it's feasible. You can always move closer to the side if you feel under pressure.

▶ If you are going at the same speed as the rest of the traffic consider 'holding your lane' to stop the driver behind from trying to overtake pointlessly and squeezing you to the side.

▶ Keep a distance from parked vehicles in case of carelessly opened doors.

▶ In general, position yourself so as to be better seen by drivers. Sight lines are important.

▶ Move positively and communicate clearly, especially before you change road position or making manoeuvres.

▶ If possible look back often so that you have a picture of what is approaching from behind. Consider fitting a mirror.

▶ Look out for local cycle maps, showing quieter and cycle-friendly routes.

▶ Ride a quality bike so you can put on speed when you need it for safety. And it'll have better brakes.

▶ Keep your brakes in top condition and practise emergency stops, keeping your weight back on the saddle.

▶ Keep your tyres pumped up. You'll have better speed and control, along with fewer punctures.

▶ Change down to your start-off gear before you stop. You can also change after you've stopped if you have hub gears.

▶ Bright clothes make you more visible, but also show the dirt. This just shows you are serious about cycling.

▶ Some choose to always wear a helmet when cycling, and some wear one in specific circumstances.

▶ You need to access all of your senses, so don't cycle wearing headphones.

▶ Respect pedestrians. They are an even higher life form than cyclists. What feels a perfectly safe manoeuvre to you can seem reckless or threatening to walking humans.

▶ Appreciate modern bike lights: they are compact, light, and can be fitted and removed in seconds. They are rechargeable like your smartphone and their LEDs mean a charge lasts ages.

▶ Ride happy. If you want to engage with a poor driver it's better to ask a question than to make a statement. *"Did you know you just…"* is usually well received. If a driver has really gone too far then have some practised lines, to use as you see fit. The aim is to help them agree with you so that they can improve their future behaviour. Some cyclists have a helmet-mounted camera to record evidence. You can also photograph the number plate and report to the police.

Think ahead and plan. Don't get into dangerous situations.

Find It, Fix It

You're on the verge of committing to a used bike or maybe you need to know what's up with your current bike. Here's what to do.

Jenni Gwiazdowski of Spanner in the Works.

Buying your bike from a dealer usually means that you more or less get what you pay for, you have more choice, expert professional advice and (hopefully) some aftersales support. On the other hand taking on and fixing a used bike can be massively satisfying and empowering. But beware! If you discover that you need to need to replace one major part, such as a wheel, or a tyre, it may take a big chunk out of you project budget, and any serious work needed on the transmission alone can cost more than you paid for the whole machine. You will certainly make mistakes but be philosophical about it. It's how you build up an understanding of how bikes work and how to fix and repair them: skills for the rest of your life. Here are some tips to help you along.

General condition

Look for any external clues. Is the bike looking cared-for or rusty? Are the tyres bald and cracked or in good condition? Is the paint scuffed and the frame dented, or are there just the one or two honourable scars of a hard-worked but looked-after machine? Is there useful equipment fitted, such as a rear rack, panniers, pump, lock, mudguards? Are the wheels 'quick-release'? That's more convenient for you but also for thieves.

Wheels

Steel rims, found generally on older, cheaper bikes, are heavy and may be rusty. These days most wheels have aluminium alloy rims. They will not be affected by rust and tend to be lighter than steel, but vary wildly in weight and quality. The weight of your wheels, and of your rims in particular, makes a huge difference to performance. Check that the rims are not showing wear or concavity from years of being squeezed by the brake blocks. Low quality rims wear down quickly, meaning you'll need new wheels. This is not a problem on bikes with disc brakes. With steel rims the spokes may be rusted-in, making it hard to re-tension the wheel so it runs true (straight). Are any of the spokes broken? Check at the hub end. If two or more have gone, then more may be on the way out. Are any spokes slack? This is not a good sign, so check the wheel for trueness. Even if the wheel seems true, grip the top of it. Can you wobble it from side to side? If so, there's possibly damage to the bearings. As the wheels pass through the forks front and back do they run closer to one side, or even touch the fork? If so, loosen the wheel in the frame and re-adjust its position. Or maybe the wheel needs to be trued: this is probably a bike shop job. Very few cyclists can true their own wheels.

Brakes

Are the brakes operated by a steel cable (fairly easy to adjust) or through hydraulic pressure via a tube (bike shop visit)? If it's a steel cable check there's plenty of rubber on the brake pads and that they are lined up with the rim, and close to it but not touching. If you can pull the brake levers all the way to the handlebars your brakes need adjusting. It may be enough to turn the little barrel adjuster if there is one. Pull the brake lever a little and check the cable hidden underneath it. Steel cables commonly fray at this point. Squirt some oil down the cable. Are they seized solid? Are the cables rusty and frayed, or looked-after, oiled, and finished with a cable end cap? If a brake is hydraulic, possibly operating onto a disc by the hub, then you probably have a higher quality bike, but any brake repairs probably need a visit to a bike shop.

Chain

Taking the chain at the frontmost point of the chainring, (the big cog by the pedals), can you pull a few links almost clear of the teeth, while their neighbours still sit on the teeth? If so the chain is worn and needs replacing. If it has rusted badly or has dry rust on it, it may have worn the sprockets down, too, which are expensive to replace. You can also try twisting a chainlink from side to side. If there's lots of movement that's another sign that the chain needs replacing. To oil your chain apply lube, one drop on each roller, at the bottom of the chain, not the top. This prevents oil from dripping onto the chainstay. Over-oiling will shorten the life of the chain. Spin the cranks backwards a few times to get the lube permeate inside the chain and then wipe, wipe, wipe until the chain comes clean.

Headset

This is the area where the forks and bars swivel in the frame. Do the forks revolve smoothly? Apply the front brake, and see if you can make the fork rock forwards and backwards within the frame. If so that's a loose headset and needs attention.

Chainwheel & sprockets

If teeth have a sharks-fin appearance the whole drivetrain will be much too worn, which is very expensive. A worn chain, if left too long, will devour all the other components it comes into contact with. Chains are 'consumables', so need to be replaced when they become too worn.

Bottom bracket

This is where two sets of ball bearings hold the main axle through the frame, so that your pedal and cranks can turn smoothly. Grip the cranks and try to rock the axle side to side. If there's play and maybe a clicking noise then the bearing needs adjustment or replacement. Check that the cranks rotate smoothly. Grab the pedals and push one clockwise and the other anticlockwise. If there is any give on one or both then the cranks may not be firmly bolted onto the ends of the bottom bracket axle. They will become worn beyond repair if not tightened on.

Pedals

Do they spin smoothly? Do they rattle loose on their spindles? You may feel a rolling sensation in the ankles, caused by bent pedal spindles or bent cranks. Riding with misaligned pedals can damage ankles and knees (which are really expensive to repair).

Maintaining or fixing your bike becomes easier if you use a bike repair stand. It lets you work standing up and you can tilt your bike this way and that. There's often an attachment to stop the front wheel from flopping. It's great to be able to walk round your bike to access every part. There are fold-up bike stands for using at home, but professional mechanics use heavy duty stands, especially if they're fixing an electric bike.

Gears

If you have hub gears, hidden in a shell at the centre of the back wheel, they may need a slight adjustment if slipping. Each make has a different adjustment method, so it's probably a bike shop job. If you have derailleur gears you can see a nest of multiple sprockets in the back wheel with a kind of pulley device which moves the chain from one of these sprockets to another. If there are problems these gears may need re-indexing and it may be a bike shop job.

Tyres

All tyres should be inflated hard: they should barely give when you squeeze them. Do the tyres show cracks and bumps? Do the valve types match? How is the tread looking? Is the inner tyre carcass showing through? Are the tyres right for your needs? Knobbly tyres may look grippy, but they soak up your energy on roads. Slick road tyres go faster but may struggle on difficult surfaces.

Frame & forks

Are there dents, creases or wrinkles in the paint, pointing to crash damage? Squat down to inspect from the front, then look down the bike to see if the frame twists between head tube and seat tube. Then stand at right angles to the front forks and check they have not been bent back in an accident.

Handlebars

Are they bent? Rusty? Is everything attached to them firmly? Look at the stem. If you can see the minimum insert mark then there's not enough stem left in the frame for safety (the same applies to the saddle pin). Stand in front of the bike with your knees squeezing the front wheel, and try to turn the bars. Make sure they don't swivel easily: there should be lots of resistance. You could loosen them off and see if they are seized: possibly rusted solid. If seized then it's a big job to raise or lower them if you need to. A seized saddle pin can also be a major problem. Moving your bars and saddle up and down is important – unless they happen to be stuck at just the right height for you (which is unlikely).

Racks, mudguards, ancillaries

Check everything is bolted on firmly. Distorted or cracked plastic mudguards should be replaced for safety. Racks attaching at four-points are far sturdier than those attached at three points. If lights are fitted, check that they work.

Aftercare

Budget to spend a bit more once you've got the bike, replacing the safety-critical parts that are subject to wear. Change rusty, sticky or frayed brake cables: run a little oil over them before installing. Make sure you get the right cable type. Cable outers need replacing if they are kinked or excessively rusty. Replace worn brake pads. Keep your chain well oiled. Some modern 'dry' lubricants don't attract dirt, but they are more expensive and not as waterproof.

Toolkit and basic maintenance

Modern bikes use metric nuts and bolts, and allen keys for fixings and adjustments. An allen key nest (with 2, 3, 4, 5, 6mm keys) should always travel with you. Purchase quality tools individually as you need them and you'll eventually have a complete kit which suits your bike and your skill level. Luckily, almost everything on a bike is totally visible and accessible. And remember there are brilliant fix-your-bike videos on YouTube. If in doubt, take it to a bike shop. And take the opportunity to sound them out on other aspects of your cycle. Be curious and learn from the experts.

Happy fixing!

> 66 *I relax by taking my bicycle apart and putting it back together again.* 99
>
> *Actress Michelle Pfeiffer.*

Beating the Flats

Riding on air makes it possible to cycle efficiently and comfortably. Some cyclists almost never have a puncture, usually due to the right tyres and techniques. Here are some tips to keep you inflated.

▶ Fit good tyres, possibly with anti-puncture reinforcement. You can also have anti-puncture sealant squirted into the inner tube through the valve, to immediately seal small holes from the inside as you ride along.

▶ Buy quality inner tubes: they are more resistant. In some cases (but not many) tubeless tyres may be right for you.

▶ Keep your tyres well pumped up, so that less tread surface touches the road. This can drastically improve your pedalling performance, but it also reduces wear, so saving you money. On top of that it avoids 'pinch-punctures' where the rim bottoms out on a bump. Also, a poorly inflated tyre can make you bike harder to control.

▶ You'll find the maximum tyre pressure displayed on the tyre wall. You may prefer to ride at slightly less than max on poor road surfaces or if you're going off road on a non-mountain bike.

▶ Buy a track pump: it's quick, easy to use, takes any valve type, and gives you the pressure reading as you pump.

▶ Replace tyres with worn tread, as less tread generally means less protection. But some tyres are made to be smooth, for extra grip and speed, so don't replace them too early.

▶ Check that the tyre sits evenly on the rim, with no bulges or side-wall damage. If you have brake blocks they should grab the rim-wall and not the tyre-wall.

▶ Check tyres for shards of glass, stones or thorns which could eventually work their way further in.

▶ If the puncture has already happened check the inside of the tyre: the offending item may still be sticking through, ready to strike again.

▶ Take a spare inner tube. You can fix the punctured tube at leisure later. Make sure your spare has the right valve for the size of the hole in you rim, and that your pump can connect to it.

▶ Watch one of the many good online videos on how to fix a puncture. Also look out for real-life demonstrations on puncture repair. These are often offered by local cycling organisations and progressive bike shops.

▶ Solid (non-pneumatic) tyres are not a good idea. Compared to riding on air solid tyres are much heavier, and extra weight around the wheel rim is deadening. Also solid tyres are uncomfortable. They don't cope well with uneven surfaces and can make your cycling effectively 10kph (6mph) slower. Finally they do not generally grip as well as pneumatics, so may slip from under you in the wet.

Illustration: Phil Somerville.

CHAPTER 5

Bikes for every Purpose

Bikes as Different as we are

Almost all bikes are wonderful whatever their looks and function. But over the last four or so decades a deeper bicycle culture has been developing amongst those who enjoy cycling mainly as a values-driven way of life rather than (or as well as) a sports or leisure activity. They see cycle design and technology cutting free from conventions so that pedal-power can become more inventive and useful as it enters more 'meaningful' parts of our lives. The diamond frame bike is, rightly, still queen but it leads a whole procession of new and exciting variants.

Sometimes this results in a classic bicycle design being taken to modern levels of refinement. Sometimes people just want fun rediscovering exotic or simply neglected bike types from the past, and sometimes a completely different configuration appears.

Cycles are now being designed to meet multiple needs – for going faster than a conventional bike, or being more portable, or transporting huge loads, or carrying children safely and efficiently, or making

cycling possible for people with disabilities. These are entirely practical aims and have little to do with being different for its own sake.

In general the new breed of cycles and cyclists are extending the options we have in our transport decisions. Many of us find it just natural to own a small menagerie of cycles for different purposes. Specialised cycles are still not mainstream, and many never will be, but others are knocking on the door. For example, until recently in UK cities it used to be rare to see children being taken to school on a box trike or longtail. Now these are becoming common in many places, alongside other ways of carrying children. However, there are still conservative neighbourhoods and communities where it takes courage to be associated with bicycles at all, never mind with something exotically practical.

The market for specialised bikes will grow as pedal-power ventures where it has never been before, gradually replacing millions of short distance car journeys for reasons of cost and sheer practicality.

Town and Around

The ideal short-journey bike is a multipurpose mobility tool suited to riding on reasonable surfaces, in variable weather, in whatever shoes and clothes you like, and occasionally carrying loads.

If your everyday bike is to be an all-rounder it needs to have fundamental high quality. But quality is a nuanced concept. Dutch city bikes have quality but they are generally heavy, partly because they are fitted with everything you are likely to need. They are great for immediate practicality and a feeling of relaxed yet stately elegance, but with that come sluggish acceleration and generally slow speeds. Not a problem on the flatness of rolling Dutch cycle paths and powered by well-developed Dutch legs, but a challenge for other mortals. Also, genuine Dutch-bikes don't often come in small sizes! The Dutch are amongst the tallest on earth.

There are other choices. Your ideal multi-purpose cycle might be relatively light. It might have a compromise riding position which tilts you forward so your hands and arms take a some pressure off your bottom. It might have 'straight' handlebars, with a quick-release adjustment lever for the height, reach and angle of the bars. It might have seven or eight speed low-maintenance hub gears hidden within the rear hub. A cycle like this can meet virtually all your urban needs but it can also invite you out for enjoyable day trips.

City cyclists want to arrive at their destination in the same condition as if they had come by car, which means, in many countries, mudguards and chainguards. Lighting needs to be straightforward and preferably built into your bike. How many motorists would be prepared to buy a car, and then have to buy a set of lights to fit themselves?

There's another type of bike which is not really intended for everyday use, but can do the job pretty well. Owners of touring bikes fitted with panniers find that they make pretty good multi-purpose cycles. They typically have drop bars but some also come with straights.

What you wear and what you ride can express your values and aspirations.

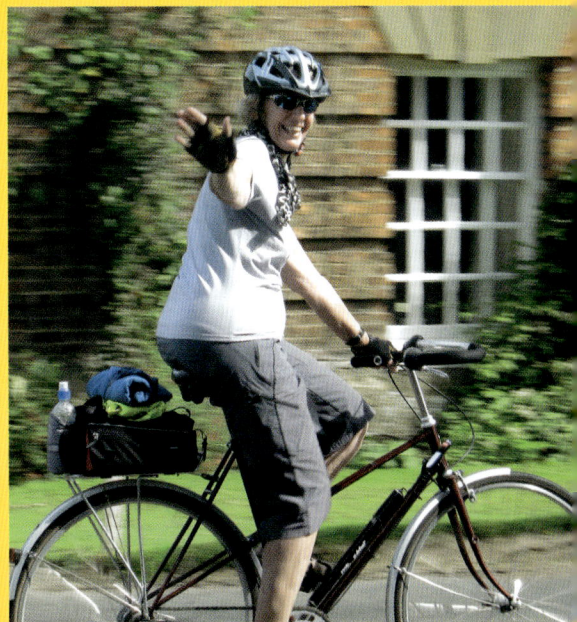

For many a beloved bike of quality can meet a gamut of needs: trips around town, country day rides and, in the case of this lady, cycling holidays.

127

Children on Board

Photo: Jason Patient.

There may be times for children to play video games in the back seat of the car, but cycling also has its pleasures and riding with children on board can be fun for everyone. There's the great feeling which comes with being active together as a family, with easy conversation about the world as it unfurls round about. You can stop any time for a picnic, or a play, or to explore whatever takes your fancy.

Riding with kids is not always birdsong and blossom. You have to build up to it, to make sure your children are happy on board and not going to scream or grump throughout your ride. Some things are not easily put right. For example very few family cycling options give all-weather cover, and we're not looking to produce a race of young spartans.

Cycling with young ones on board is for all stages of childhood thanks to an ever widening range of inventions and adaptations. Some may seem a touch pricey but that's what comes with quality, complexity and safety. There'll be plenty of opportunities for passing them on to another cycling family once your own children have grown into the next phase of their cycling lives.

Some configurations are solely for carrying children. Some are quite large and multi-purpose. Other fix in seconds onto a standard bike – you can take them off equally quickly to free up your beloved bike for solo riding. Whatever your solutions they will leave your children with positive attitudes about active travel, along with precious family memories.

Some manufacturers offer two-and three-wheel versions.

A top of the market Nihola from Denmark.

The simple **child seat** can work well if you are a confident cyclist and your bike is in top condition. You need a high quality rear rack and some find it helps to ride an open-frame bike so you can step easily through it when you stop, rather trying to lift a leg over your child's head. The child seat solution simplifies your life. You can take the seat off in seconds or leave it on as a cradle for your shopping. When buying the seat get the bike shop to fit it and to give your bike a safety check or service while they are at it.

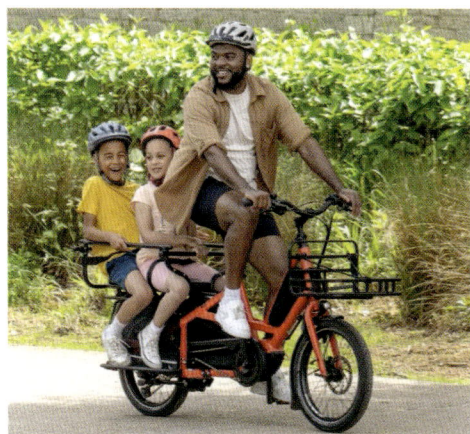

Child trailers are versatile. They carry your little ones but can also double up as general cargo carriers – drop your kids off at playschool and fill the trailer with shopping on the way back. Some have parent handles which make the trailer into a pushchair or jogging buggy. Trailers can be hard-shell, with a solid tray, or consist of fabric stretched over a tubular frame. Some are for one child and some for two. Your towing bike needs to have good brakes as you'll have more moving mass to slow down. For more on trailers see page 144.

Seen more and more on the streets are these **long-tail family cycles**, usually with electric assist. The small, robust wheels are fitted with fat tyres for a reassuring ride over difficult surfaces. Pictured is a compact version by Tern.

The **Co-Pilot 3** is a tandem trike with the pilot in the rear position, steering indirectly. This way you have full sight of your child pedalling in front of you. It's a big machine, but the front end detaches in seconds for easier storage. The writer rides a Co-Pilot 3 daily with his son (not pictured here).

▲ The recently introduced **Cube Trike Hybrid Family 750** gives full weather protection. It's another urban mobility product which takes full advantage of the improved electric-assist motors now available. Without the motor this would not be a bundle of fun to pedal.

▲ A *steer-from-the-rear-tandem* with the child also pedalling. These are common in the Netherlands – this one is made by van Raam. For stability purposes the rear rider needs to be considerably taller and heavier than the young passenger in front. There are also steer-from-rear tricycle tandems with the two wheels at the back or front.

▲ *Low-back tandems* for riding with children or small adults are simple, and readily available. If you are buying second-hand make sure the seatpost is not stuck in the frame: you will need to extend it as your child grows. As with all such conventional tandems the person steering needs to be taller and heavier than the stoker behind, for better control and safety.

▲ **Trailer bikes** connect to the seatpin of the towing bike or, as with this top of the range Burley, they clip onto a specialised rack. This solution works well with children aged four to six, and when they are too big for the trailer bike you'll find that the tail starts to wag the dog. If you think a tricyclised child trailer version may be the answer bear in mind that they use a universal joint connection, meaning they can tip, unless you ride conservatively.

A Dutch family go tandeming their way, probably in ▶ *the late 1940s. Photo: ANWB.*

The BellaBike from Denmark has rear-wheel steering which some find strange at first, but it give a tight turning circle and, as the cycle turns, the box keeps its position rather than swinging out. Owners become strong advocates.

▲ Three-wheel cargo trikes give you wobble-free road positioning and are less affected by winter road conditions. Most are steered by the whole box pivoting, as here, but more sophisticated ones have just the front wheels turning, as with a car. Cargo trikes can usually carry more children, or larger children, than two-wheeled versions. Both kinds have full all-weather hoods. The three-wheelers are not necessarily more difficult to store: they may be wider but they are also shorter than two-wheeled equivalents.

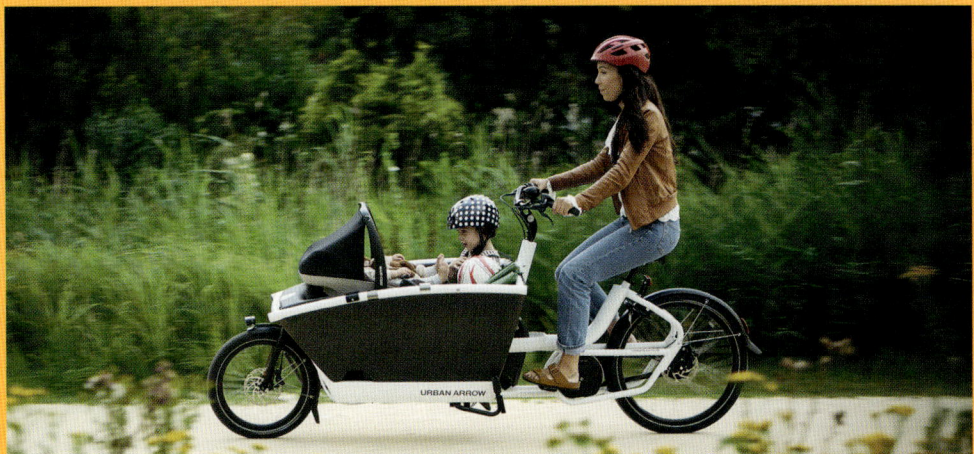

▲ A two-wheel cargo bike with childseats. The steering is indirect, through a rod running under the box. These family cycles also double as high-volume cargo bikes for shopping. Most cargo bikes and trikes sold these days have mid-drive motors.

Let the Children Ride

Jonathan Maus

There are limits to what many families can spend on cycles, but children often have to ride cheap and unpleasant bikes while their parents spend five times as much on really nice ones for themselves. Well, let's take the side of parents for a moment. Children are not always respectful or careful with their possessions. They might leave an expensive bike open to theft. They may just need something basic to knock about on with their mates. They may quickly grow out of any bike you buy for them. But if you want your child to get serious about cycling you need to buy them a decent bike at some stage, as even the most willing youngster can become exhausted and fed up during a longish ride on a heavy little single-speed.

That good quality costs can come as a shock to parents who expect the price of a child's bike to be proportionate to the size of the machine. Children's bikes can have just as many parts and require the same careful assembly as adult bikes. There are, of course, some very cheap bikes for very young children. Some use nylon bushings instead of ball bearings. This may be OK for a toy, but it will deteriorate very quickly and is unlikely to last more than a year or two.

The joys of pedal power can begin at a very early age and should be part of all children's play activities.

All children need the right and the freedom to cycle as part of their physical, mental and social development.

Children can begin their cycling life by scooting on a balance bike. This is a sensible alternative to fitting a pedal cycle with stabilisers (training wheels). These were always horrible devices: they stop children from learning to balance, do not work well on uneven ground and cause constant lurching from one side to another.

Robust children's bikes became widely available with the BMX craze. BMXs are generally strong, simple to maintain and fine for modest distances. As your child grows, and journeys get longer, the choice widens: there are fine children's cycles available from companies such as Frog in the UK and Puky in Germany.

Whereas adults' bikes are sized according to seat tube height, children's cycles are categorised according to wheel size. 16″ wheels are generally used for three to six year olds, 20″ for five to eight year olds, and 24″ for eight to twelve year olds. Good 24″ wheel bikes offer all the benefits of full-sized bikes in terms of frame design, transmission and braking. Whatever the size of wheel, the frame design and handlebar reach need to be natural for your child, without a long stretch.

If your child wants a decent bike they should also be keen to take on basic maintenance tasks, starting with lubricating the chain and pumping up the tyres. Mending the first puncture is a young person's rite of passage into a life of riding on air.

A team of young riders on a cycling holiday with parents. Photo: Jason Patient.

BMXs: strong, simple to maintain, and popular. Photo: Tribal Trap.

Children particularly enjoy recumbent trikes but their opportunities for riding them are limited.

Pleasure can be Portable

A Brompton folder and the oddly named but very reputable Halfway monoblade folder by Giant.

Standard bikes are great when they're carrying you along, but when the roles are reversed they are can become awkward things. The perfect portable bike has always been a challenge for bike designers. It has to be fun to ride, easy to fold, compact as a final package, light to carry, built to last, and easy on the eye. Each of these benefits is in creative tension with all the others. In fact, perfection is subjective, and customers choose according to their personal needs. There is a portable bike available for most of your cycling reasons: and

yes, there are folding tandems, folding trikes, and folding recumbent bikes – and trikes.

This fascinating sub-division of bike technology includes cycles designed to part-dismantle, as well as cycles designed to fold. Some models need a minute or two to take apart or fold down, others take seconds. Some are great for round town, others you could race on. Some have small wheels combined with suspension, others go down the other route; by running on fat tyres as an alternative to frame suspension. This can be a cop-out, or can be a serious design direction to take: tyre technology has come a long way of late. Some portables are high performance lightweights which come apart; others are virtually standard bikes with a single fold in the middle. Some models fold small enough to become hand-luggage on planes.

Some folders come with electric-assist, or folder-specific e-bike systems can be added (mostly managing to avoid making the fold more difficult). Beware of poor quality electric folders and retro-

▲ *The Joey, by Airnimal in the UK, is a high performance road bike which also folds. The 24" wheel size gives advantages in both the folding and the performance.*

The Flit, from the UK, is designed from first principles as an e-bike which folds. It is made from bonded aluminium in the company's own workshops. It weighs only 14.5kg (32lb) including battery and folds to just 797 x 600 x 305mm. The range is around 31 miles (50km).

fits at the cheap end of the market and remember that any electric-assist on a folder makes it heavier to lift and carry.

There is convenience in mixed-mode journeys: the litmus test for many is whether you can easily carry your folded cycle over a station platform bridge. In a congested, frenetic urban world there's a lot of pleasure and (smug?) satisfaction in taking a portable bike off a train and riding it past a queue of fellow travellers waiting for taxis and buses. You could be home well before them and you did it for free. People living in flats find folders especially convenient, and, whichever type you go for, security stops being a big deal – just fold your bike up and take it inside with you.

Many folders are bought by practically-minded people with little interest in 'cycling as lifestyle'. At the other extreme are folder enthusiasts with their own sub-culture, clubs and events. Owners' motivations vary, but there's little can beat the sheer practicality and flexibility which a portable bike brings you.

The Birdy folder from Germany. The suspension helps you keep up speed, and makes it possible to run the tyres at over 100psi yet still be comfortable. The basic Birdy weights less than 11kg (24lbs).

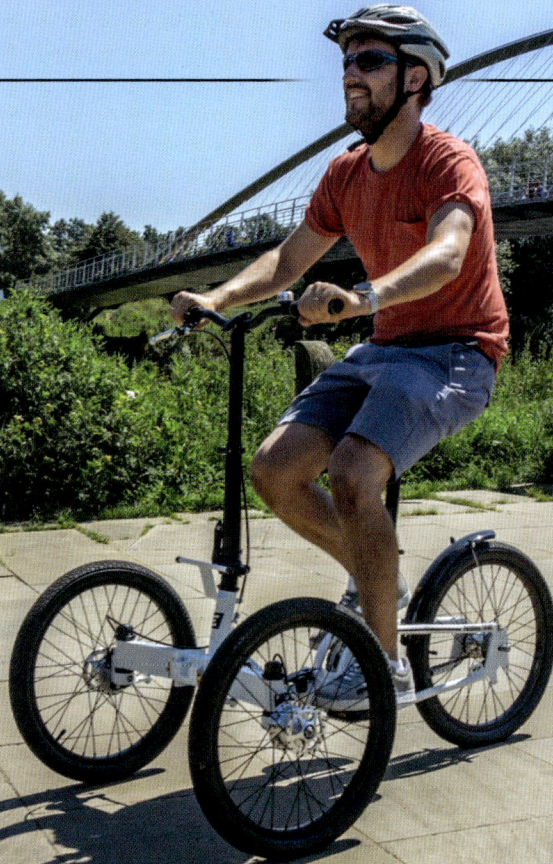

Three Wheels Good

The Etnnic folding trike.

Add an extra wheel and the potential of pedal power is transformed. Trikes are very little understood these days, and their image varies enormously from country to country. However they are generally experiencing a big revival. A trike gives stability, graceful low-speed manoeuvring and extra presence on the road. Some can also carry heavy loads and wriggling children. Certain trikes come close to replicating the functions and convenience of the family motor car and, of course, beat the car in many positive ways.

Not all trikes are designed primarily as cargo or people-carriers. Some are what people in many cultures naturally migrate to once they find they are not so great on two wheels anymore.

There are so many types of tricycle, each with its pros and cons. There are, for example, lightweight custom-built trikes for the thrill of hitting fast speeds and leaning into corners to counter centrifugal forces. Also, a high quality trike can make an interesting touring machine. Since you don't wobble at low speeds you can use fantastically low gears without falling off. And if

A delta format trike: the Tri-1 from Pashley in the UK.

you tire half way up a hill you just put the brakes on, stay onboard and rest a while.

Most trikes have two wheels at the back so they are known as 'delta trikes'. This gives a carrying space between the rear wheels and a familiar steering arrangement at the front. Most have transmission to only one rear wheel. Really good ones have differential transmission, meaning both wheels are powered simultaneously and you still have traction if one wheel lifts.

Other trikes have two wheels at the front and one at the back. These are knows as 'tadpole trikes' and sometimes have Ackermann steering. This is a form of steering found on cars as well as on higher quality tadpole tricycles. It ensures that, when you are cornering, the inside front wheel turns through a larger angle than the outside wheel. This greatly reduces scrubbing on the tyres and gives better road-holding.

The tadpole format usually gives you more stability and allows you to uses standard components for the rear of the trike, but it restricts your turning circle to some degree. Then there are recumbent trikes, tandem trikes, load-carrying box trikes, children's trikes, trikes for disabled riders. The list could go on.

Trike-riding is not as easy for the beginner as it looks, although if you've never ridden a bicycle you'll probably sail off on a trike with no problem at all. Tricycles usually require about half an hour of wobbling until the brain learns not to try to balance. You have to make yourself point the front wheel where you want to go and then relax. If you sense a severe camber in the road, or if you need to steer around a pothole, you make occasional slight and almost instinctive adjustments to your body position. Or go slower and go straight. Once you've got triking skills you keep them for life and can swap between bike and trike with equal but different skills for each.

Trikes do have some drawbacks: they weigh more and have higher rolling resistance than equivalent two-wheelers. They have three tracks instead of the bicycle's one and they don't generally allow you to squeeze past congested traffic. But trikes are stable and extra-visible on the road. They can greatly enhance your life and you might say they are a broadening experience.

Style also matters to Joseph.

Van Raam's Easy Rider. An attractive and inclusive trike in children's and adults' versions.

A recumbent trike by Hase Bikes in Germany. The low centre of gravity make these trikes extremely stable and fun to ride.

137

Twice the Power, Double the Fun

Windswept in the Netherlands. Whatever the weather traditional Dutch tandems seem to go on forever.

Some just love them, some worry about their relationship. Whatever your take on tandems they do have plenty of advantages. With legs in harmony tandemists zip along a fair bit faster than on a solo. That's because a tandem weighs a lot less than two bikes, and with just about the same rolling resistance and air drag as a solo. The extra momentum flattens out rolling roads and if one partner eases off for a while the other can put in what's missing. Two riders of unequal strength and range can comfortably ride together. The stronger rider can pile on the speed and the weaker can contribute with no chance of being left behind. A tandem enables a rider who wouldn't venture on the road alone to still experience all that cycling has to offer. Almost anyone can take to the back of a tandem, including those with impaired vision. Tandems are also great for transporting children to school or anywhere else.

Tandems make great taxis. Imagine you need to pick someone up from the station. You can ride a tandem there solo quite comfortably, and while everyone else is queuing for a taxi, or fumbling for their car keys, you and your visitor are winging through town without a care in the world.

A modular child-back tandem from UK company Circe Cycles.

A Circe tandem loaded for touring. The heavier person is at the front for stability.

Tandems are not just extended solo bikes – they are designed to cope with extra stresses and strains. There is a tremendous range in quality, design and purpose. Tandems crossbreed with many other forms of cycle: there are tandem tricycles, tandem recumbents, folding tandems, rear-steering tandems, city tandems, racing tandems, wheelchair tandems, child-back tandems and side-by-side sociable tandems.

The controls are usually in the hands of the person at the front (the 'pilot'). The person on the back (the 'stoker') must practise the art of not leaning to steer. It really helps if the pilot communicates well with the stoker about upcoming gear changes, rough road surfaces ahead, decision-making and anything else to increase enjoyment and reassurance.

The rear rider steers on this Pino by Hase Cycles.

As a rule the heavier rider should steer. Steering is harder work than on a solo and you need greater concentration to stop and start (and only the pilot should put an initial foot down). When riding, pilot and stoker are usually locked into pedalling together. The pilot is in charge, pedalling and freewheeling as he or she sees fit. The stoker must simply follow. However, some tandems have a kind of intermediate freewheel, which allows the stoker to do their own thing. Some say this spoils that whole sense of togetherness. Others see it as necessary independence. Tandem riding needs a bit of getting used to – you have to co-ordinate well in town traffic, and togetherness on the open road becomes a shared delight.

A steer-from-the-rear with disabled rider at the front.

Tandems can be bought off the peg with a low-back frame for smaller people.

A Co-Motion expedition tandem loaded up by Laura Massey-Pugh and Steven Massey for their ride around the world. They did it in 180 days, beating the existing record by 83 days. Laura published a book on their ride: 'Backseat Rider'.

A back to back tandem by Ostrad. Shorter than a conventional tandem, and having heads close together make for easy conversation. It requires a stoker with trust and strong nerves.

An Azub recumbent tandem.

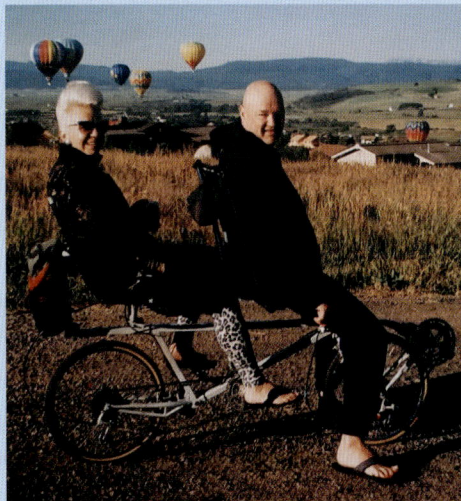

This American couple show there is no end to the ways that two people can share two wheels.

The cost of perfection

You can have a tandem custom-made which involves a serious consultation process. UK tandem-maker George Longstaff had some interesting perspectives:

66 *Couples can have very different ideas and personalities. I can't remember how many times we've had to make tandems with differently coloured front and back ends. Our enameller once had to paint a tandem with one side in red and the other in white. The couple only realised how eccentric this was when a neighbour asked them how it was that they set off in the mornings on a red tandem and returned on a white one!*

Quite a lot can happen in the three to five months that it takes to supply an order. Couples split up. We were once asked if we could re-unite a tandem sawn in two after a particular nasty divorce. Fortunately we got the other end from the other party and did the job. 99

Tandems go Large

A 2-Rider and a steer-from-rear Co-Pilot 3. Photo: Get Cycling CIC.

Tandem is Latin for 'at length' and it mainly applies to two wheels and two riders in line. But what about tandems which have also got wider? If it's a side-by-side format they are mostly called 'companion cycles'. If it's a three-wheeler with one rider in front of the other it's called, quite logically, a 'tandem tricycle'. Four wheels give you a 'quadricycle'. What all these cycles are called is not as important as what they do.

Multi-wheeled cycles for more than one person have all the advantages of stability, togetherness, easy onboard communication, equalised power output and enormous road presence.

Their disadvantages quite obviously include unsuitability for certain kinds of ride. There's another problem: the mechanical stresses caused by the cycle not being able to tilt like a two-wheeler mean that a lot more strength has to be built into the design, which generally means more weight. This why most riders these days go for electric-assist.

These cycles are ideal for passengers with learning or physical disabilities, and they are particularly good for people living with dementia. It's common for in-line tandem tricycles to place the pilot at

Fun on a side-by-side two-wheeler, sadly no longer produced.

the rear, controlling indirect steering to the front wheel. This way the pedalling passenger has no responsibility and a good view of the world, while the pilot behind can easily spot any problems the passenger is experiencing.

For many journeys these companion cycles and tandem trikes offer much the same functionality as a small family car. You can use them for getting children to school, for going shopping or giving people lifts. They can go places which cars can't, and parking is free. True, you are more exposed to the weather, but car passengers don't get the exercise, fresh air and fun.

A Gran Tour, by Dutch company Berg. Previously regarded as mere fun machines for holiday parks, they now have an e-assist option so become a potential local runabout for eco-friendly families. Berg products are well designed, robust and attractive, but use a lot of steel so they're also heavy. Only the rear seats have pedal positions.

A companion tricycle from Wulfhorst in Germany.

Cycle-lovers have always been inventive. This family quadricycle is probably from the 1890s.

This family six-seater in Merida, Mexico, was created by joining two conventional tandems together and extending the back end. There are commercially available kits for coupling conventional tandems and solo bikes together: for example Bluebird in the USA. Photo: Ian Morton.

Loads to Tow

Trailers are a simple way to extend the powers of almost any conventional cycle, giving you a flexible and affordable way of carrying children, large volumes of shopping, heavy touring luggage, or whatever loads you carry in life – which could quite easily be the tools of your trade or a canoe on its specialised trailer.

Your towing cycle needs to be up to the job, especially in the brakes department. In any case you need to give yourself plenty of stopping distance, and even more than that if you tow with the added momentum which an e-bike adds in its own right. And if you pull a trailer in hilly terrain you'll be grateful for a towing bike with mountain bike gearing.

Trailers come in many categories and varying quality levels. With heavy loads a low hitch connected to a point on the frame near the middle of the rear wheel will give better handling. This arrangement generally adds to the cost of the trailer.

The arrival of electric cycles makes towing a trailer even more feasible. Most e-bikes are restricted to 25kph (15.5mph) but the better quality motors have 'excess torque' available which can go towards hauling a trailer. Expect a loss of at least 30% on your range, but less loss with single-track trailers.

There are trailers specifically designed for electric bikes, often with a hitch compatible with the electric bike's frame. Or you can hitch a good upright trailer to the saddle pin.

Depending on your own pedalling contribution, and the terrain you are covering, your e-bike motor may come under stress if it delivers less than 70Nm of torque. So make sure yours has a high enough capacity. It's the same reason why professionals use high quality motors for large, e-assist cargo bikes.

Hubert van Ham had this woven basket custom-made to fit a Cyclone bike trailer. (Wiki Commons)

Basic boxes. These simply luggage boxes are cheap, relatively ▶ heavy and often without a rain cover. They usually come with a drawbar so you can also use them as handcarts. They connect to your saddle pin in seconds and some have a metal loop to lock the trailer to your bike. You get a lot of function for little cost and they might last you several years. As with most cycling products there are lighter and better made versions at higher price points.

◀ **Upright trailers.** These two-wheel trailers tend to be lightweight and stylish, with specially designed bags available. Uprights have the advantage of presenting a smaller footprint on the road (or in your hallway). Also, they can be easily pushed as a trolley when off the bike. Being upright they need to attach to the saddle pin but they are designed to minimise the effect on the handling of the bike, especially if the heavier part of the luggage is stowed low down. This example is by *Burley*.

Platform trailers. These are particularly useful ▶ for carrying camping equipment behind a touring bike, but also serve perfectly well as round-town cargo bikes. This *Cyclone* is a lightweight trailer by *Radical Design*. It connects to the rear hub, has lashing points for many shapes of cargo and folds up for storage.

◀ **Single-track trailers.** These can usually carry no more than about 30kg (65lbs), but they weigh less than two-wheeled trailers and 'track' well as they run in the wheel path of the towing bike. This makes them especially useful off-road, and in towns their narrow profile helps you squeeze through congested traffic. Their low fixing point and centre of gravity minimise any influence on the bike's performance. This *BOB (Beast of Burden)* trailer is one of the most popular, especially amongst touring cyclists.

Child trailers. For many families covered child-trailers serve ▶ multiple purposes in that they give you carrying space when you have no children on board. If you have no small children you can still use a child trailer for luggage carrying and you can pick them up cheaply secondhand. Go for one with a solid base.

For information on child trailers see the section on Family Cycling, page 128.

Leisure cargo.

German company Reacha offers trailers and adaptations for carrying canoes, dinghies and surfboards – but they are handy for other purposes, too.

Trailers for dogs.

Trailers primarily for dogs usually have a solid, flat surface so your canine passenger can travel comfortably. There will also be a leash hook to stop your dog escaping. *Photo: Hamax.*

A solar-powered Carla trailer in Freiburg, Germany. The solar panels are charging an onboard battery which powers the trailer's front wheel motor. The towing bike has no e-assist of its own.

Micro-campers.

Electric-assist cycling is creating new and ingenious possibilities for camping trailers. The B-Turtle, designed and made in Austria, is a smart cargo trailer which transforms into a comfortable two-person tent with windows. With a decent pump the whole setup takes up to 20 minutes.

The B-Turtle's aluminium frame helps keep the weight down to a very decent 29kg (64lbs). There is also 120 litres (4cu ft) of storage space in the solid aluminium tub underneath. It's ideal for tandem couples as they can put in double the pulling power to ease the load and then have accommodation to share.

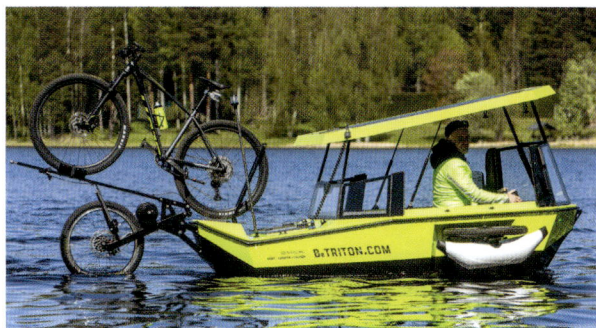

The strangest trailer ever?

The people at *Be Triton* in Latvia are renowned for their innovations. This is an electric-powered boat which is towed to water as a trailer. Then the bike hooks onto the rear rack and the journey continues over water. The Be Triton also functions as a camper.

Pedal back the Years

Photo: Centre for Aging Better (from Unsplash).

Regular cyclists, the UK's Chief medical Officer once confirmed, have on average the health of someone ten years younger – but the benefits never stop as researchers discover new information. For example, as we get older our immune systems naturally become weaker and produce fewer T-cells, which are important in the fight against diseases. However, a 2018 study suggests that the thymuses of older cyclists are generating as many T-cells as those of young people. Older male cyclists also keep higher levels of testosterone.

We also know that moderate physical activity reduces the risk for Alzheimer's disease by 29% and for cognitive decline by about 26%. But, unlike other fitness activities, such as gym exercise and swimming, cycling is integrated into your daily life: it keeps you fit while it gets you about.

Having the right bike (or bikes) is a way to enjoy continued mobility if walking becomes a problem: cycling is kinder on your legs and is four times more energy-efficient than walking. It's also a positive mobility option if you can no longer drive. It can be a major lifestyle change for the better and

a massive cost saving. If you need to start thinking about giving up your car it will help if you bring cycling into your life as early as possible, giving you time to understand your changing capabilities. For example, moving straight to electric-assist is not always a good step, as you could be missing out on several years of happy unassisted cycling.

You can ride in normal clothes but more specialised cycle clothing will keep you riding comfortably in poor weather and help avoid chaffing.

As we get older our brain function changes, and some become more anxious and risk averse. Also, it's common for older people to lose some sense of balance. An easy introduction, or reintroduction to cycling can help: with short, simple rides and some cycle training where it's offered. It's better to cycle, on two wheels or three, than not to cycle at all.

Getting the right bike

Certain types of bike can give you more reassurance than others. Your ideal bike may well have a relaxed frame geometry, giving you a better sense of control. It may even have the pedals situated slightly forward of the unusual position, making it easier for you to extend your legs for maximum pedal power while also making it easier for you to get a foot down when you stop. It may also have a fairly upright riding position. This reduces the pressures on tired hands and wrists, and it avoids a crick in the neck from an unnatural head position.

As we get older we may find it harder to look behind when cycling. It helps to practise swivelling the upper torso a little, as well as the head. Another solution is to use handlebar mirrors, or mirrors fitted to your helmet. Also consider the reassurance of a low step-over frame. This helps you, whatever your gender, to step on and off the bike easily and quickly by slipping your foot through the frame and not over it.

Think about your hand comfort, especially if arthritis is setting in. Experiment with the position of your brake levers. You can also ride with a back-pedal brake, as millions do around the world. You'll still need to have at least one handlebar brake fitted for legal reasons. Twist-grip gear changing is more ergonomic, allowing you to use your whole hand to change gears rather than individual fingers. Modern saddles (some featuring 'gel' inserts) can make a big difference, and various forms of bike suspension can help keep you comfortable. Some older cyclists are anxious about getting a puncture, so it's reassuring to ride on high quality puncture-resistant tyres.

There is virtually no age at which cycling stops being an option. There are multiple kinds of tricycle: most types are upright but some are semi-recumbent and with a seat not a saddle. Trikes are now being used by people of all ages for various practical purposes and are simply a natural progression for people of any age who need them. They give easy, low-speed manoeuvrability and you can drop into very low gears and go as slow as you like: at speeds which would cause you to loose balance on a two-wheeler. Add to this the tricycle's greater carrying capacity and you get a very useful all-round machine support an active lifestyle as the years advance. For more on trikes see page 136.

This couple were experienced tandemists for most of their lives together and found no reason to change in older age. Photo: Jason Patient.

A recumbent offers older people the comfort of a seat and can offer the reassurance of three wheels. These are ICE trikes from the UK.

The electric-assist Easyrider from van Raam.

Rediscovering the joy.

Electric with age – handle with care.

Electric-assist can give older cyclists a boost in both senses and can make life a lot easier and more fun. But it's a step you should think carefully about. An e-bike can be life-changing but it can also lower your exercise levels, as it can be hard to find the motivation to turn the motor input down or off.

There's another issue. Interesting research is coming out of the Netherlands, where very large numbers of older people have become early adopters. Virtually all will have been experienced and regular cyclists beforehand – such is Dutch culture. Thanks to the e-bike they are cycling to a much higher age, but it seems that injuries and fatalities affecting seniors on e-bikes are rising fast. The reasons are becoming clear. They are riding faster but some are not as alert as they used to be and reaction times are slower. The bike itself has more moving mass than non-electrics, making injuries more serious, especially since older people are physically more vulnerable. There are also instances of these heavier e-bikes injuring people as they simply get on or off, or they are getting injured once dismounted because they can't keep their heavy e-bike upright and it simply falls on them. The Dutch are introducing familiarisation and training courses for older citizens.

Risk increases with electric share-bikes, which are four times heavier than standard bikes, making injury so much worse in a crash or fall.

Access Bikes

A party of disabled cyclists and carers from York on a holiday in Münster, Germany, organised by Get Cycling. No two cycles are the same!

Cycles are built around the human body so designers and adapters can respond to specific details of need. If your body's not conventional cycle technology can be made to adapt and enable, making inclusion possible. Disabilities are immensely varied: on the one hand you can meet a professor with multiple sclerosis and, on the other, a child with profound learning disabilities. So inclusive cycling has to cover a very diverse range of complex needs – met by the work of dedicated designers and engineers, many disabled themselves. The spectrum contains fairly standard but lightly adapted bikes, easy-to-balance trikes, detachable wheelchair tandems and side-by-side companion cycles. At the other extreme are ultra-light racing recumbent trikes powered by hand and helped by a very wide range of gears.

Why do disabled people want to, or need to cycle? For the same reason as everyone else and then some! People without disabilities have no shortage of choice for activities in the great outdoors: rambling, running, climbing, to name a few. But only certain wheeled forms of recreation work for many with disabilities, and the chance of a good bike ride can give access to a whole new world of mobility.

There's also the health factor. Most disabled people die not of their disability but of degenerative or

The lever-driven Mountain Trike .

A Tomcat handcycle.

other diseases associated with their less active lifestyle. Swimming and 'wheeling' are limited in scope, but cycling combines exercise, pleasure, social inclusion and practicality.

Bikes for disabled people need to be extra-well designed and constructed. A problem which would be a minor irritation for most cyclists can become very limiting when even just getting on and off the machine may be difficult. And of course, the implications of your cycle breaking down in the middle of nowhere are inevitably more serious.

Inclusive cycles are produced in small runs and may need individual adaptation and the making of special parts. So they are generally not cheap, but their potential for changing the quality of the owner's life makes a well-chosen machine more than good value for money.

Some people with disabilities want to cycle regularly but find that ownership is not for them. They don't have storage space for these often large machines. Or they simply don't want the cost and responsibilities of ownership. To meet their needs the UK charity 'Wheels for All' provides regular social cycling sessions, all bikes provided. They run these in various parts of the UK, and there are also independent organisations offering similar.

Credit: Get Cycling CIC.

Members of BLESMA, the Limbless Veterans charity, on their annual bike ride in York.

Companion cycles are either one-before-the-other or side-by-side. Photo: Sustrans.

Electric-assist, specialised pedals and other adaptations got Sam Taylor cycling. Photo: Get Cycling CIC.

Handcycles usually feature a very wide range of gears to optimise arm-power. Photo: Get Cycling CIC.

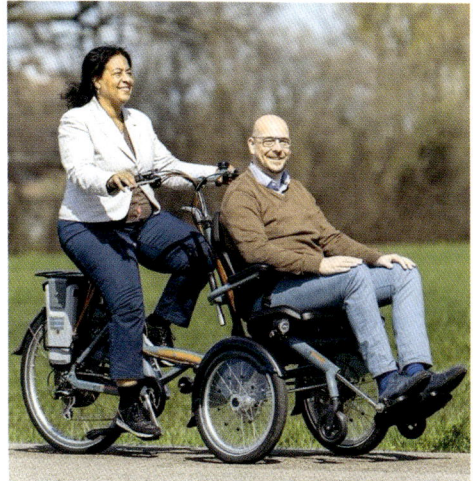

Handcycle attachments, with or without power-assist, can transform a wheelchair into a radically different vehicle. Making the attachment compatible with a specific wheelchair is a specialised job, given the multitude of different wheelchair types out there. Once the right connection is created the attachment will clip on and off in seconds. This one is by Team Hybrid in the UK.

A wheelchair tandem has the chair integral to the cycle, meaning the user has to transfer from their normal chair. The rear end detaches in seconds, leaving an independent wheelchair to be pushed by the person who had been cycling; these wheelchairs are not easy to self-propel. This one is by van Raam.

A wheelchair transporter is different from a wheelchair tandem. This one has a ramp and platform so users like Lucy can enjoy cycling without leaving their own wheelchair. Wheelchair transporters are ideal for multi-user environments. Photo: Get Cycling CIC.

The author, wife and son with an electric-assist steer-from-the-rear tandem tricycle. They are at Get Cycling CIC, the social enterprise they founded to support inclusive cycling. Get Cycling has been funded by the Motability Charity in the UK to research and launch 'Pathways to Pedals'. This is a programme to help people with disabilities, and especially those on low incomes, to access specialised cycles: through better try-out opportunities and support services and through bike loans, rental schemes and flexible leasing.

Handmade

The workshop at Mercian Cycles.

Aluminium, titanium and carbon-fibre composites can all be made into frames which are lighter than steel – thanks largely to mass production. The sheer volume coming off the production lines has driven prices down and this has driven steel out of most manufacturers' ranges. The last hold-out of steel bicycle frames was the very bottom of the pile – the cheapest brands, the supermarket bikes. Quality steel bikes had taken their last breath. Or so it seemed.

Mass production bikes can perform beautifully. They can be fast, light and durable. The trouble is that one Brand X top-of-the-range superbike is exactly the same as the next Brand X top-of-the-range superbike. Such is the nature of mass production. Many are not even made by real

people. The alternative to the Brand X superbike is a bespoke cycle, made in very high quality steel (and occasionally other metals).

The custom or handmade sector doesn't register on the radar of most bicycle buyers because it still represents a tiny fraction of the global cycle manufacturing industry. It might be the fastest growing sector but a fast-growing tiny thing is still a tiny thing.

At one time most framebuilders served mostly clients wanting a bespoke lightweight bike for amateur cycle sport or serious touring. Over the years certain framebuilders gained national reputations and some introduced unorthodox design concepts to distinguish their brand, such as ornate lugwork, curly frame tubes or radical frame configurations. But the basic requirements of the clientele did not change much.

These days clients' needs are less narrow. They want to spend good money on something special: a bike for life reflecting their tastes, personality and outlook on life. It could be for touring, racing, off-roading or city riding. It could be for a years-long world tour or it could be just for the pleasure of owning something unique and beautiful.

Somerville

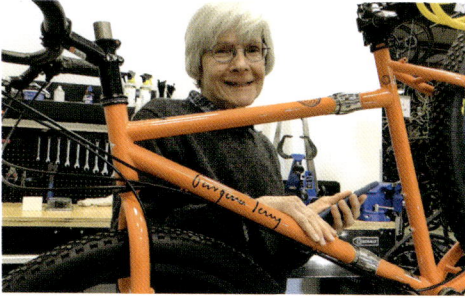

Celebrated for her saddle designs for women, Georgina Terry of the USA has now lent her expertise to the design of bespoke cycles for women. Here she demonstrates one of her cycles fitted with S&S couplings for enabling a frame to be separated for transportation.

This frame by Ironbridge Cycles, UK, incorporates a distinctive self-referential touch.

A custom bike is measured to fit like a bespoke suit, designed to meet your exact requirements and built to last you out. If you know what you are doing you can specify tyre clearance, chainstay length, wheelbase, handlebar shape, paint scheme and much more. You put your trust in the experience of your chosen builder. You are a client more than a customer. The modern framebuilder has to be confident and knowledgeable in genres of bike and be expert in component selection. He or she also needs to have a flair for aesthetics, including often complex paint schemes. The framebuilder needs to know how to customise, personalise and advise. The task can involve the best kind of reverential pastiche or can be born of sharing imaginative ideas with the client. Good framebuilders nurture and enjoy their relationships with their clients – who tend to be a very interesting bunch.

The resurgence in custom bikes tells us that cyclists haven't forgotten what an incredibly well developed material steel is for making bike frames. It might not make the lightest frames on the planet but it builds a bike which is lively, comfortable and durable. And when a complete bike weighs in at just 9kg to 11kg (20lbs to 25lbs) what's a pound or two between friends?

Prices for the very finest handmade bikes can seem astonishing, particularly if you're familiar only with the other end of the market. Some folk are happy to spend hundreds of thousands to have the very best car, motorbike, hi-fi, antiques or fine art, and no-one bats an eyelid. A bicycle might be 'a simple thing' but you really can have the best in the world – beautiful, unique and built just for you, reflecting who you are. It will cost more, but probably not much more, than a top of the range production bike. It will reflect who you are and remain a treasured part of your life.

Whatever the client wants… A special creation by LaFraise Cycles, in Roubaix, France.

Pechtregon Cycles of France offer the Luguru adventure bike, with folding frame and handlebars, an 'octopus' fork, bespoke bags and a camping burner fed by compressed gas in the downtube.

The Pathfinder is an 'adventure touring/gravel' cycle by Darron Sven Coppin, of Sven Cycles in the UK. The frame and forks are of extremely corrosion-resistant Reynolds 921 stainless tubing. Reynolds claim this is probably the highest strength cold-worked tubeset in the bicycle industry. Owners generally go for the naked steel look, but polish regularly. The Pathfinder can be built for compatibility with Gates Carbon Belt-drive or a Rohloff Speedhub, or with S&S Couplings so the frame can be split for transport. It can even be configured as a flat-bar super-commuter.

Also from Sven Cycles is the Forager. It was commissioned by Hugh Fernley-Whittingstall, celebrity chef, writer and organic food campaigner. He needed a cycle suitable for off-road food foraging. The interesting suspension in the front wheel is by Loop Wheels, who developed the technology for wheelchairs.

Two creations by master of many styles Ricky Feather of Feather Cycles near York. *Top:* A road bike built from Columbus Spirit HSS tubing, fillet brazed and filed into smooth transitions between each tube. Paint schemes involve creative consultation between the client and Feather Cycle's own painter Jack Kingston. *Above:* Details of an unorthodox but elegant 'retro-direct' cycle made by Feather for a client with very particular requirements. Everything on this bike is custom-made bar a handful of parts. Retro-direct is a gearing mechanism from the early 20th century which provides a second gear ratio when pedaled backwards. Another achievement is the one-piece handlebar combo incorporating stem, brake levers, light mount and bell mount.

Artist Terry Aaron paints bicycle frames as an enjoyable challenge but found that plenty of cyclists want him to apply his talents to their own bikes. Custom-painting a frame is not easy. You need to strip your bike down, have the frame sand-blasted to bare metal (or you can spend ages sanding down) and apply layers of primer paint. Then you get creative with epoxy paint, using either a spray can (with face mask) or a brush. You can mask off areas or create stencils for interesting effects. Finally you apply layers of transparent finishing coat. Allow lots of drying time at each stage. For a useful guide search 'livestrong painting a bike'.

Bespoke by other Means

Temple Cycles.

There are custom-builders who will meet almost every whim but there are other routes to owning a special kind of bike.

Some framebuilders and larger cycle dealers produce small batches of off-the-peg framesets in common configurations. They work with you on selecting the right frameset, components, accessories and paint scheme. Then they build your cycle and make sure it's correctly set up for you.

Other cycle businesses offer much the same degree of personalisation but have their frames made in batches by specialist companies in the Far East, or sometimes in Europe. Orders are typically placed for three to five different frame configurations to cover most clients' needs. These framesets are likely to be in aluminium alloy whereas traditional full-service custom builders mostly work in high-specification steel. An exception is Temple Cycles in Bristol who use high specification Reynolds steel tubing made into framesets by a Taiwanese factory in Vietnam which they have worked closely with for 11 years.

Whether frames are batch-made in-house or in a distant country the client gets a quality-controlled frame from a specialist business which has built up its brand on the service they provide and the essential quality of the bike.

Importing frames (or whole bikes for that matter) can come with risks for brand owners. Supply chain disruption is one of them and so some brand-owners are now having their frames made within the European Union: in Poland, Portugal and the Czech Republic for example. Sizeable orders need to be placed and payment is usually up-front, yet the stock may take a year or more to sell.

Whatever the business model the customer gets a bike which combines off-the-peg and some customisation at a price they can afford.

A bikebuilder at Temple Cycles in Bristol fits bespoke parts to a frame from a stock of frames ready to use. Temple are up-front about where parts and labour come from, setting it all out on their website. Design, frame-painting and leather saddles are from the UK; tubing is made in Taiwan under licence from Reynolds in the UK; frame-making is in Vietnam; gearing and bearing components come from Japan and alloy components from Taiwan.

Rakete in Berlin make frames to order, but produce small batches in five basic designs to meet common requests. This is their mixte frame, with twin tubing from headset to rear hub. You can buy one off the peg or have one made specially for you in your chosen colour and with the components and accessories you specify.

Quella in the UK are single-speed bike specialists. Their steel frames are made in the Far East to the company's specification. They stick to a single frame option in different sizes but customers can pay more to specify frame colours and for alternative components and accessories, including electric-assist and internal hub gears.

Duratec, in the Czech Republic, make aluminium alloy framesets for a wide range of cycles and yet add a high degree of personalisation. They engage with clients in multiple ways. You can visit them in person, or you can order and customise your bike online, sticking to one of their off the peg framesets or opting for fully-customised. Finally, you can visit one of their representative cycling experts in your country. In the UK, for example, you can go to Bikes by Design, who will order for you and who also have off-the-peg Duratecs such as this e-assist with Pinion gearing.

Condor in London have been a prestigious name in framebuilding for decades. But they also offer other brands off the peg, including specialist framesets made by third party builders. This is Condor's Galibier, created in the late 1940s in London and now made for Condor by a specialist framebuilder in Italy. The customer gets a distinctive classic with their personal choice of components.

Extra Energy

The advance of e-bikes

A Tern e-bike with a frame-fitting mid-drive motor to help power a serious load.

We've now had over a decade of serious e-bike development, giving us reliability and assurance, and we see big-name manufacturers continuing to pile in with ever better cycles.

E-bikes are a boon for the less fit, and have helped fit cyclists to travel even further. Many start to wonder whether they really need their car, or their second car. Electric-assist gives new mobility to people in hilly areas and to transport-poor rural districts. It also makes heavy cargoes possible: for distribution services, and for carrying shopping and/or children. And it's liberating people with disabilities whose often complex cycles are heavier than most.

You can buy e-bike kits to convert almost any bike. A retrofit motor can be placed within the front wheel or back wheel, or in a 'mid-drive' position, slightly under the existing bottom bracket. On some systems the motor senses the pressure you are putting through the pedals. It feels this torque and adds to the power you produce yourself. On others a cadence sensor activates the motor whenever the cranks are simply turning.

E-bikes have thrown up a few issues. Some riders (especially the older generation) have problems dealing with the bike's weight and speed. Conversely, some human-power cyclists can't understand why fit young people need e-power. A further issue is the illegal speeds made possible by tampering with the software. The legal limit for e-bikes is 15.5mph (25kph) in the UK and Europe. Another problem concerns the limited life-span of e-bikes, which may be, on average, around five years. This is related partly the rapid obsolescence of evolving technology, and to the unavailability of parts for models no longer produced, especially where the company is no longer trading. Then there is the high cost of replacement batteries, perhaps after five years. There's also the cost and inconvenience of regularly replacing the transmission chain on cycles with mid-drive motors. These chains must carry both human and motor-power combined. For information on battery fire hazards see over the page.

Types of Motor

▲ **Rear-wheel hub.** This is a popular place to put the motor. It's low down and much of the rider's weight is on the back wheel, so handling and road grip are not too much affected by the extra weight and power.

▲ **Mid-mounted.** This motor is fitted into specially made cycle frames, keeping the extra mass low down and central which gives you better handling. Mid-mounted motors are considerably more efficient that a motor in one of the wheels so use less battery power. This transmission system is becoming increasingly common and is generally found on higher quality cycles.

▲ **Front-wheel hub.** This works for most but can affect steering. Generally there's not as much weight on the front wheel so the action of the motor may cause you to lose some grip occasionally. It's often used for folding e-bikes and sometimes for hybrids.

▲ **Motor and battery combination.** This is a Zehus all-in-one motor and battery. Here it is fitted to a Quella bike, preserving the cycle's clean lines and low weight. There are no cables – just an app linking by Bluetooth to your phone and giving you power settings, ride data, GPS and an anti-theft rear wheel immobiliser. Quella estimate 60km (37.5 miles) from a charge.

▲ **Retrofit mounted on the disc brake.** The Scarper is a combined gear-drive-and-battery unit attached to the existing disc-brake, if there is one. It can convert a regular bike into an e-bike in minutes, leaving the frame and wheels unaffected. It clips on without tools and can be removed in seconds.

This **Ebco** is a good example of higher quality e-bikes. It has a mid-drive motor and the battery is 'hidden' within the frame of the bike. The powerful hydraulic disk brakes are especially important on e-bikes. Photo: Ebco Cycles.

Electric-assist has made the weight of the bike less significant for some. This has led to cycles with chunky, motor-bike styling and a high proportion of them for sale online in Europe and the UK are illegal in terms of power output, speed limit and the facility to power without pedalling. However, they may be getting people onto bikes who would not otherwise want to be seen on a bike. Unfortunately this sector of the e-bike market is prone to low quality, lack of dealer networks and poor after-sales service.

The **Eovolt Afternoon** is good example of current directions in electric folding bike development. It's an upmarket cycle with a Bafang rear motor. Bafang are a Chinese manufacturer with a big reputation for quality and reliability. The motor reacts to torque sensors, adding variable power in response to the pressure you are needing to apply to the pedals. This gives a better ride feel and improves your battery efficiency compared to cadence sensors that are found on lower spec bikes. There's an automatic two-speed gear change, which is probably all most people need when combined with the torque sensors. Other markers of modern

design include transmission through an oil-free Gates belt-drive, the battery in the seatpost, and auto locking hinges allowing an unfold in under 5 seconds. The Eovolt is manufactured in France.

The **GoCycle G4** e-bike is an unorthodox UK brand. The monocoque folding frame combines an aluminium front end with a carbon fibre central section and a magnesium-based transmission section. It's also monoblade, so the wheels are easily removed. The GoCycle is particularly light, at around 17.6kg (38.8lbs). It's no surprise that it has been designed and developed by a former McClaren motor racing engineer and has won many design prizes. A recent development is the GoCycle family cargo cycle.

Batteries on Charge

There is concern about lithium e-bike batteries catching fire under charge. The risk is very low for batteries from reputable brands which have not been damaged.

On the other hand cells in a poor quality battery are not individually monitored and so a faulty one can continue to take a charge and overheat. This can start a chemical chain reaction causing a fire which is hard to put out as it doesn't rely on oxygen in the air. This is one of several safety problems found with cheap, down-market e-bikes and, in particular, with low grade retro-fits, often used with incompatible chargers.

With batteries from leading up-market brands a cell will very rarely go bad, and if it does the Battery Management System is there to identify the problem in nanoseconds and switch the whole battery into non-functioning fault mode. Some manufacturers have gone one better and fit their batteries with large resistors which dump all voltage and energy from a 'bad' battery rendering it harmless.

Strong e-bike brands, and the kind of dealers who sell them, have reputations to keep, whereas most people selling kits online have little incentive for any sort of accountability. At the same time there are some on-line sellers of legal and reliable conversion kits.

Facts and some figures

Reports from the cycle industry give some reassurance and insights.

The Electric Bike Shop, with 25,000 e-bike sales through ten branches, reports not one e-bike fire incident. Giant Cycles, including all sub-brands internationally, also report zero incidents.

Joshua Hon, founder of one of the market's leading e-bike brands, Tern Bicycles, is a leading light in redefining product testing standards for e-bikes and cargo bikes. He confirms that Tern remains with a clean sheet:

66 We can say that we've manufactured, stored and sold many tens of thousands of Bosch systems since 2017. Our bikes are used on five continents in many different ways including commercial fleet applications where they tow trailers for up to 20,000km per year. We have not had any official reports of fires on any of our products, dating back to our initial launch of e-bikes in 2017. 99

Hon is not complacent. He advises that "no matter how well a lithium ion battery is designed and manufactured, whether for an e-bike or a car or a phone, they do need to be used and stored properly. Impacts that damage the case and/or internals (such as dropping the battery), or leaving it in temperatures that exceed the safe range (such as in direct sunlight on a hot day), or submerging it in water – these can all lead to accidents."

Cycling electric

Our report on battery safety is based on a much more detailed report, updated February 2025, by Mark Sutton of Cycling Electric Magazine.

The issue of e-bike battery safety is dogged by weak and unreliable information while research and product development get better all the time. Much of the information you are now reading will already be out of date. For current reports on battery developments and other use e-bike news we suggest you follow *cyclingelectric.com* magazine and newsletter.

Almost all cycles carrying their battery within the frame allow for easy key-release so you can remove the battery for charging. Pictured is the Momentum Transend.

Speed and Distance

Bikes for the long and open road

Participants in the White Rose Classic Sportive organised by Ilkley Cycling Club in Yorkshire. Photo: Ilkley CC.

Technology moves at pace in the world of cycle racing, which is good news for anyone who just likes the thrill of speed on an exciting lightweight bike. New materials are developed, and frame designs are constantly being tweaked to achieve that perfect blend of lightness, stiffness and aerodynamic efficiency. Somehow, for the professional road racing scene at least, this all has to be done within the strict confines of regulations laid down by the Union Cycliste Internationale (UCI). That's the international cycle sport governing body.

We can all now benefit from materials and technology refined by the racing cyclist: titanium and carbon fibre frames and components, integrated brake and gear levers and electronically controlled transmission systems of unparalleled precision. Campagnolo, SRAM and Shimano have spent years battling for supremacy in the racing-component market and the regular 'trickle down' means that even their mid-priced groupsets are fine pieces of equipment. In time-trialling high technology has come the way of the entry level racer and amateur: with aerobars, aerodynamic tubing and helmets, and tri-spoke or disc wheels.

Road racing is big business. It is also a mass participation sport, with thousands of road clubs worldwide running time-trials and races. The term 'road bike' covers a wide spectrum of specialist machines – different tools for different jobs – with time trial bikes at one end and touring bikes at the other. But no well-informed cyclist would include city bikes, even though these also live almost exclusively on the road.

York Rouleurs on one of their regular rides. This is about enjoying distance and speed, with a strong social aspect and a choice of rides for different abilities and preferences. Photo Victoria Harley. www.yorkrouleurs.co.uk.

Time trial bikes

These sit at the pinnacle of UCI-sanctioned competition. They are designed for the 'Race of Truth', against the clock, where competitors ride alone, with no hiding in the aerodynamic shadow of another rider. These bikes are twitchy and nervous. They require the rider to adopt a position which minimises the aerodynamic drag co-efficient of the body. There is no concession to comfort, and head-down time trialists don't always look where they are going. In a sport where every fraction of a second counts designers and engineers strive to remove every whisp and whirl of drag. Airflow is analysed in wind-tunnels so that wheels, frames and other components have only the most aerodynamically efficient shapes and profile.

Triathlon bikes

These don't have to comply with the UCI's restrictions on geometry and tube profiles so are usually more radical in appearance. Triathletes require a fast machine with good aerodynamics but with a riding position which, whilst minimising aero-drag, also eases the transition between the triathlon disciplines. Many triathletes run their bars a few millimetres higher than time trialists and the riding position may be a little more forgiving,

Road racing bikes

The bikes used in road races are a little more comfortable with slightly more relaxed geometry and with drop bars which allow several hand position options. These bikes run in packs: they are high-geared for powering along with the momentum of the group, lightweight to fly up the climbs, yet robust enough to cope with 60mph (96kph) descents and elbows-out sprint finishes. The bikes are shaped like this not because it is some sort of racing ideal, but because much of their geometry, shape, even their minimum weight, is decided by a UCI committee. Although innovation does improve the breed this remains 'formula' racing. Manufacturers vie to get their bikes under the shorts of the world's top teams, which is the mark of credibility for certain bike and equipment brands.

Slovenian time-triallist Janez Brajkovič shaped for speed at the 2012 London Olympics.

Randonneurs, Audax, Sportives

Over 1000 riders take part in the annual Tour de Môn Sportive on the Isle of Anglesey, Wales. Photo: sportpicturescymru.

Randonnée/Audax

These are usually a single or two-day personal challenge for serious amateur riders. They need to be self-sufficient and to pass through control points where route cards are stamped. General time limits are set but riders are not individually timed. It is non-competitive and participants are recognised equally whatever their finishing order. These are sociable events and impromptu pelotons often form. Riders typically complete routes which might be 200km/125 miles in a day or 1,200km/750 miles over several days.

The phenomenon is popular in France where it began and is known as randonneuring. It has a following in a score of countries, some of which, including the UK, use the term 'audax'. Confusingly, Audax UK recognises anyone who has completed a 200km event as a randonneur.

Audax/Randonneur riding is firmly franco-phone and is overseen by the Audax Club Parisien who work with other randonneuring organisations worldwide.

Sportives

These put more emphasis on (friendly) competition and tend to ride higher tech kit. Riders are looking to enjoy the day and be with friends but most are also keen to clock up a good finishing time. Also, distances are usually not as demanding as in an audax. A sportive has a whole support system which usually includes route marking, marshals, feeding stations, mechanic support and a broom wagon to rescue lagging riders. They are usually run on a commercial or semi-commercial basis by enthusiasts: there's a fee to take part but you usually get a lot for that.

There is little cross-over, with few participating in both sportives and randonneurs/audax. There's a witticism amongst cyclists that a sportive is a bunch of cyclists pretending to race, and an audax is bunch of cyclists pretending not to race. It has also been joked that audax riders don't ride sportives as they are too expensive, and sportive riders don't ride audax as they are too cheap. In reality the costs reflect the level of service.

Gravel Bike Adventures

Why 'gravel bike'? Blame the Americans. They have endless miles of gravel tracks whereas we don't really have them in Europe. The term 'adventure bike' would have been better.

The rise of the gravel bike is a major trend. It combines good performance on tarmac with steady handling on the rough stuff: and some find their gravel bike just perfect for commuting, especially over bad road surfaces.

Gravel/adventure bikes have similarities to road bikes but you do notice that the tyres are a lot bigger. Then there's plenty about gravel bikes which you may not notice straight off. They tend to have taller head tubes for a higher riding position, and the head tube angle will generally be slacker to keep the steering calm. Also helping with stability will be a lower bottom bracket and a longer wheelbase. A gravel bike will have extra frame clearance for the larger tyres and may have slightly smaller (and therefore stronger) wheels than the 700c of road bikes. As with touring bikes there will probably be mounts for mudguards and a rear pannier rack. Drop handlebars are normal but some gravellers go for straights.

Finally there's the groupset. Gravel bikes no longer come with transmission parts hijacked from other types of cycling. These days they are fitted with groupsets designed specifically for the purpose and you can also expect that your gravel bike's gearing will be lower than on a standard road bike.

Gravel biking in Saalbach-Hinterglemm, Austria. Photo: Saalbach Tourist Board.

A Topstone gravel bike by Cannondale.

A flat bar gravel bike by Genesis

Mountain Bikes

Passing from France to Italy at the Col de la Seigne. Photo: le ded Collection.

They have been mass-produced since the early 1980s and they've had a massive impact on cycling. With their light, strong, fat-tube frames, rock-resistant tyres and wheels, empowering gear ratios and sure handling, mountain bikes can appeal to almost all cyclists, at almost all levels of ability.

Mountain bikes (MTBs) have brought innovations to the mainstream, such as suspension forks and index gearing. They have influenced cycle design in general, leading to products like the 26″ wheeled expedition tourer and the commuter/leisure hybrid. Novice cyclists can feel safer taking to the city streets on a mountain bike, because of the more upright riding position, the assured steering, the effortless pothole cancellation and the powerful disk brakes. But the mountain bike's home territory is still off-road.

The variation in types is mind-boggling. There are virtually indestructible free-ride bikes, cross-country race bikes, fully rigid single-speeds, 4X, all-mountain, back country, hard-core hard-tail and dirt-jumpers. Then there are trail bikes, trials bikes, mud bikes, even dedicated snow bikes.

The diversity is impressive but the high octane marketing of mountain biking pushes potent themes, such as personal challenge, extreme power, breaking loose from the beaten track, powering through natural environments and the conquest of nature. The marketing is so persuasive that some are spending more dosh than they need to on serious duty, highly-specified bikes, and then never use them for the extreme off-roading they were designed for.

Some hi-end MTBs intended for trail riding are loaded with expensive technology, but don't seem to get any lighter. Thick-set machines at over 18kg/40lb are not unusual thanks to long-travel shock absorbers, tread-heavy reinforced tyres, burly forks, coil shocks, big brakes and possibly a telescopic dropper post so you can change the saddle height as you ride. All this extra mass may be fine going downhill but the expensive tech doesn't help much on the rest of the ride.

'Biking' was not a common term before the MTB came along, and the term has become associated with off-road riding. For cyclists less committed

This Merida Big Trail 500 is an example of a good, medium price MTB for off-road leisure cycling. It will typically give you an aluminium alloy frame, front suspension, disk brakes and very low gears. There'll be no front changer: the rear changer will give you up to 12 gears all on its own. The 29″ wheels are bigger than on most road bikes, and enlarged by the fat tyres.

to MTB culture it can mean glorious outings on designated, well defined paths and trails which you stick to. You need a good bike, but not one with exotic technology. A bike with front suspension only (a 'hardtail') is enough for most. Then there are forms of biking which imply skill-based adventure and perhaps crossing that mysterious, undefinable line which takes you into the realms of sport and all its multiple subcultures.

Very generally, people who self-define as bikers are usually less interested in broader cycling issues and some will rarely ride on roads – on any bike. Of course, many enjoy both forms of cycling – they are not opposites.

Mountain biking still carries controversy. Irresponsible or simply unskilled riding causes vegetation loss, soil compaction, erosion, mud creation and disruption to wildlife. This is far less of a problem on well constructed trails which offer low impact riding and no incentive for riders to create informal new trails. Riding off-track can damage soil surfaces by the compaction force from the weight of the rider and bike, and from the rotational shearing force from the turning rear wheel. It is when mountain bikes go uphill that they generate the greatest torque with soil-damaging slippage. Tread impact during downhill travel is generally less due to the lack of torque and lower ground pressures, unless poor control and braking are involved.

Mountain bikes have brought many benefits, and we all need adventure in our lives, but we do need to find ways of riding off-road without tearing up fragile eco-systems.

This alloy-frame Rocky Mountain Instinct, with serious suspension front and back, is for more demanding off-road riding. The technology is impressive, with vocabulary to match. We learn that the bike comes with suspension tuning to match a rider's size. The company dials in *"custom shock tunes for each frame size, aiming to ensure ideal small bump compliance, mid-stroke support and end-stroke progressiveness for riders big and small".*

Photo : Susanna Kosa for Merida.

The World before the Mountain Bike

Riding to Everest Base Camp, 1984.

Welding a broken crank, French Alps, 1973.

In the age of the high-tech mountain bike there is still a proud group of individuals who stick to more traditional values. For over seven decades the members of the Rough Stuff Fellowship, an English club known for preposterous challenges, have been taking their cycles into untravelled wildernesses.

They ride robust tourers, reinforced in several ways. They seek out the wild places, mainly in Britain and Europe. They sleep under canvas, in mountain huts, or out in the open – one of them even specialises in sleeping in caves.

When the going gets too tough they get off and push! They don't see this a defeat, but as a chance to enjoy a change of pace – a handy moment to take a drink, check the map, or just enjoy the view.

It all began in 1955 when around 40 men and women founded the RSF at a pub in Leominster. Members undertook expeditions abroad and reported back on their experiences and discoveries. They even made it to Everest Base Camp. The first expedition abroad, to Iceland, was in 1958, which meant three nights at sea. In their report we learn how they crossed the

Iceland, 1958.

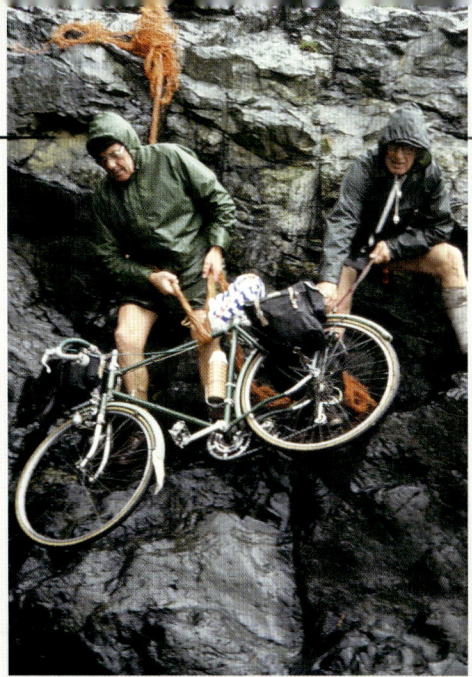

Isle of Mull, 1987.

glacial river of the Tungnaárjökull using a guide rope and a dinghy. They clearly travelled well equipped. We are also told about their version of the cyclist's power bar:

66 *We found, lying in the sand, some discarded dried fish (which) someone had cast away as unfit to eat. We fell upon this morsel, cooked some and devoured it with obvious relish.* 99

Many are now ageing, but the RSF is recruiting new members, mainly thanks to their website, www.rsf.org.uk, and to an emphasis on fighting for access rights. Newcomers, drawn from the mountainbiking generation, find something special in the powerful simplicity of the Fellowship's outlook and attitudes.

Switzerland 1969.

Ploughing on in a Scottish field, 1972.

Isle of Arran, 1978.

Bikepacking

The Llwybr Ucheldir Eryri, or Snowdonia Highland Trail, is a weekend loop around the mountains of Snowdonia. Photo: Jacob Martin.

Designing bags for bikepackers has become a specialism. Andrei Turro demonstrates his gear from Six Moon Design in the US.

Heike Pirngruber has been bikepacking round the world since 2011. Here she is in Oregon.

Bikepacking is about getting close to nature by being self-sufficient: by riding off-road and by overnighting outdoors. There's also the deep pleasure of having fun for free. It's an attitude, a set of values not a set of rules. Bikepackers can choose to make it a big challenge or decide to occasionally pass through towns to use some services.

Bikepackers tend to be freethinkers and not consumer orientated. They are interested in creating and sharing routes and less in what kind of bike you use. In fact practitioners point out you may not realise that you have the right bike already and, if not, you might want to invest in a cheap secondhand hard-tail (no rear suspension) MTB. It's more about how your bike carries your minimal necessities.

Specialised soft bags mean that bikepacking doesn't depend on a particular frame having eyelets for racks and panniers. In essence there are three staple bags: handlebar roll, saddle pack and frame bag. Most bikepacking bag manufacturers have matching sets but bikepackers are not looking to be stylish: they often mix and don't match. Not all bags fit all bikes and, clearly, the frame bag needs to fit the inner dimensions of your frame.

Of course, bikepacking describes what some individualistic cyclists have been doing for over a century but the idea has been developed, energised and popularised worldwide by (mostly American) enthusiasts, and in particular by the people at bikepacking.com.

Seats not Saddles

Photo: Laid-Back Cycles (USA).

Why has recumbent cycling become more popular over the last thirty years? Enthusiasts tell us it's about having a more relaxed ride, about the comfort of a seat rather than a saddle, about the riding position relieving your hands, wrists and elbows of the pressures they can come under with conventional bikes. Added to all these benefits are the technical advances, such as developments in suspension, made by manufacturers who will themselves be enthusiastic riders.

Recumbent riding is an experience everyone should try and, if possible, you should try both two-wheel and three-wheel formats. Two-wheelers give you all the above advantages but also the chance to hit some exceptional speeds and distances thanks partly to their aerodynamics, and with no sacrifice to comfort. Some types of two-wheelers can be a bit tricky in urban stop-start situations: it's not what they were designed for.

Three-wheeled recumbents are the 'same but different'. The balance problem obviously disappears, though very fast turns may need some leaning-in. Being lower down, you get a greater thrill of speed as the ground seems to disappear extra fast beneath your wheels. Conversely, you can go as slow as you like without ever falling off, and at the top of a demanding hill you can just pull over and maybe enjoy a comfortable snooze on your vehicle.

You can't 'honk' on a recumbent. That is, you can't rise up and put your weight above the pedals for extra speed as you can on a conventional bike. You use different muscles and in different ways. Hill climbing can be slower but your gearing will be incredibly low. The overall speed is still competitive if you include the downhill stretches, as recumbents are generally more aerodynamic than equivalent uprights.

Fast cornering on an Azub with underseat steering. Photo: Azub.eu.

A Sunseeker trike from the USA with steering above and not under the seat.

Recumbents vary just as much as uprights: there are recumbent trikes, tandems, tandem-trikes, load-carriers, racers, tourers, city-bikes, folders, e-bike versions and more.

Alongside the usual variations of components, suspension and frame materials comes the question of wheelbase. Two-wheel recumbents with front and back wheels close together are usually speedier and require more skill in handling. Longer wheelbase varieties are traditionally more popular for touring and are easier for beginners. Medium wheelbase recumbents meld the benefits of both styles.

Two-wheeled recumbents have to balance, of course, so higher ones are easier to handle than lower ones. Very low ones are correspondingly unstable and are meant as high performance racing or time-trialling machines. They find some stability only when up to speed. The opposite is true for three-wheelers. Low-recumbent trikes are more stable than high ones thanks to their low centre of gravity.

Both types come in more lying-back versions for speed and more upright versions for practicality. Also, as with tricycles generally, recumbent tricycles divide into two configurations: *tadpoles* (two wheels at the front and one behind) or *deltas* (one at the front and two behind).

Some say recumbents are hard for motorists to see. Well, experienced riders will explain that the rarity value of laid-back cycling attracts special attention from motorists – and specialised visibility flags are commonly fitted.

A tiller-steer by Nazca in the Netherlands.

The Delta TX 'E-Chopper for all Generations' by German company HP Velotechnik.

The world of recumbents is not uniform. North Europeans tend to go for under-the-seat steering with relatively short wheelbases, whereas Americans tend to go for longer wheelbases and above-seat 'easy-rider' steering. There are countries in northern Europe where two-wheel recumbents remain popular, whereas they seem to be less popular in the UK and USA. Then there are countries where recumbents are still seen as very weird. Give it time!

Colourbox

A handcycle built for speed, and a truly recumbent position.

Velomobiles

Velomobiles have full-body fairings. They come in various designs made from fiberglass, plastic, and carbon-fibre materials. They are all handmade and generally fitted and adjusted for each rider, with care being taken that the feet, knees or shoulders do not contact the shell while riding.

That velomobiles have a full-body fairing can be for several reasons. At one extreme are the aerodynamically refined speed machines for racing and record-breaking: on a bicycle, once you are moving faster than 20kph (12.5mph), 90% of your energy is spent pushing the air out of the way with only 10% accounting for the rolling resistance of the tyres.

At the other extreme are practical machines, such as the Leitra (above), produced in Denmark from 1980 to 2020 by Carl Georg Rasmussen. It's a multipurpose workhorse for commuting, shopping and other daily tasks. The fairing keeps you warm and dry, and it protects your luggage.

Leiba velomobiles are a well-established German company. The Leiba Classic (above in red) is for everyday and light touring use, with room for shopping and luggage. They also make the Hybrid electric-assist. Leiba bodies are in either glass-fibre reinforced plastic or in carbon fibre.

David Hembrow, a cycling refugee from England now living in the Netherlands, bought his velomobile so he could cycle 30km (20 miles) to work each day and back again. He now rides for leisure, enjoying how the aerodynamics take him up to high speeds on long rural bike paths, and protect him from the depths of Dutch weather. In the worst of winter his three wheels give him security over ice, and, with the canopy closed, his body heat creates a warm, microclimate, but with adjustable ventilation.

Bikes go Touring

Photo:
Ortlieb Panniers

You can't say you've really visited a country until you've cycled through it. What other form of transport lets you travel at 'look-at-that!' speeds and gives you the flexibility to just turn off and explore an enticing track or a destination you suddenly fancy? You are discovering the living heart of your host country rather than rushing through, and cycle tourists never cease to be amazed at the hospitality they receive. You travel lightly on the earth using fuel which is completely biodegradable, and there's no room on your bike or in your head for ostentatious consumption.

One way or another most tourers will experience the phenomenon that defies description. You're into the second or third day, spinning along the road when 'it' happens. The pedalling gets easier, the road slips by quicker, the climbs are less of a challenge, and the bike feels part of you. You can start your touring experiences at any level – perhaps with day rides into your local countryside.

Tim Walton and Linda Beilig showing how they loaded the cycles that took them from Europe to China. You'll find lots of touring tips and their photobook at pedallingtheplanet.wordpress.com.

Linda and Dirk are enthusiastic touring cyclists from Belgium. They have spent ten years riding different routes within Europe, more recently on their Santos bikes with pinion drive. They share their experiences at dilistuff.com. Photo: Linda and Dirk.

You'll soon find out what your comfortable distance is. So much depends on your choice of bike. If you are riding a touring bike it will probably have 'neutral geometry' with a longer rear triangle and wide tyre clearances. With that set-up you and your bike will cope with almost anything.

Some travel light, with just a change of clothes, a credit card and a fast bike. Some go for the half-luxury of carrying clothes but eating in cafés and restaurants and sleeping in hostels and hotels. Some take delight in carrying everything they need with them – tent, stove, sleeping bag, clothes, tools, spares, maps, books, eating irons: all stowed in carefully allocated spaces in panniers.

Another variant is bikepacking, a form of off-roading which emphasises self-reliance, discovering wilderness and, usually, camping out. Bikepackers usually ride mountain bikes and generally have little interest in style. See page 174.

Voices of experience

Canadians Stephen and Jane began cycletouring as newbies in 2013 and rode more than 15,000 miles in 22 countries. They have insights to share:

❝ *We met cyclists from all age groups, backgrounds, and budget levels. What we have in common is the deep desire to experience the world in ways not available to most tourists. Plus, bikes are commonplace around the world, giving you an instant connection with any person who has ever felt the childlike freedom of pedalling a bike. You'll meet people from all walks of life (and they'll all think you're crazy – in a good way).*

It can change you. Every day is a new physical challenge and builds your physical strength a little more. A demanding bike tour reveals your true character and builds emotional strength. Meditative hours in the saddle peel back all your layers. Though you can plan a tour that takes you mostly on quiet roads or cycle paths, it's very difficult to avoid busy roads entirely. There are also nights when you have to camp in an empty field or are the only guest in a creepy hotel. There is inherent risk in bike touring that doesn't exist if you go on a cruise or take a bus tour. You've gotta be OK with that to really enjoy yourself out there.

Your first smart move will be to get your bike properly fitted. When Stephen and I set out on our first bike tour we let the shop staff set our bikes up for us. We adjusted the seat height and that was about it. It wasn't until years later, when Stephen finally got a pro bike fitting, that we discovered all the things we should have done to prevent aches and pains on the trip. Learn to fix your bike! We've had tyres go flat in every conceivable circumstance. Chains have broken and cables snapped. At a bare minimum learn to fix your own flat tyre. I learned other basic repairs from YouTube while on the road. ❞

From: myfiveacres.com/cycle-touring.

Touring and Expedition Bikes

An expedition bike by Oxford Bike Works rests at the Ak-Baital Pass, on the Pamir Highway, Tajikistan.

Road touring bikes share a common ancestry with road racing bikes, but these days they share very little (apart from the diameter of their rims). A modern tourer will give you remarkable luggage-carrying capacity, relaxed handling and a comfortable ride. It will have racks designed to spread the luggage evenly. The handlebar will be broader than most. You'll have a wide spread of gears and the lowest will be particularly low. Wheels are built for strength and to accommodate wider tyres. Powerful disc brakes stop you and your load when you face the unexpected. The mark of a fine touring bike with a well-distributed load is that you can forget about it: nothing wobbles or rattles, so you can devote your whole attention to your travels.

Expedition touring bikes have all the features, bells, whistles and load carrying ability of road tourers but with even greater strength and durability. Often based around the 26″ mountain bike wheel standard rather than 700c, an expedition tourer can handle poor roads and off-road trails which a road touring bike would baulk at.

A Salsa Marrakesh road tourer ready for its panniers.

Long distance expeditions or weekend exploring – it's all adventure cycling and there are bikes and luggage systems to meet almost all needs.

CHAPTER 6
Creative & Ingenious

Photo: everybodyscycling.org.uk

Imagination Unbound

The bicycle is the product of many minds in many countries. Sometimes the technology was there but not the insights and sometimes the insights but not the technology. Four centuries before the Industrial Revolution Leonardo da Vinci was creating notebook sketches showing engineering concepts familiar to us today. (Claims that he drew a bicycle have been proven false.)

We can smile at some of the strange ideas of early inventors, but we have to admire their optimism.

66 *The inventor of the device which we present not only employs the hitherto wasted female power to oscillate a cradle, but at one and the same time to vibrate the dasher of a churn... the hands of the fair operator are left free for darning stockings, sewing, or other light work while the entire individual is completely utilised.* 99
Scientific American, 1873.

The arrival of cheap electricity and fossil fuels drove mass production which overpowered much homeworking. Some pedal or treadle devices such as the sewing machine continued. They were, like the bicycle, offspring of the Industrial Revolution.

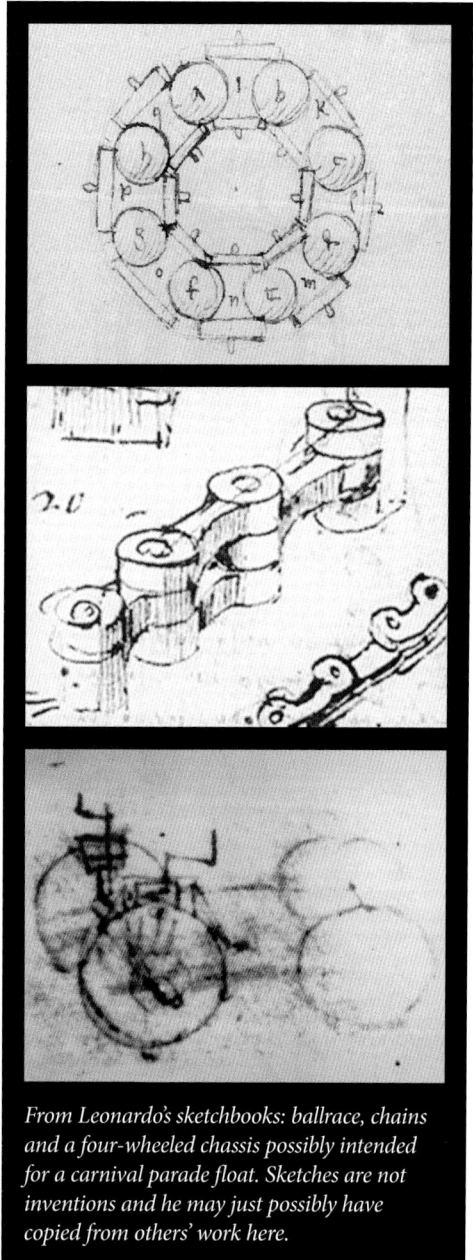

From Leonardo's sketchbooks: ballrace, chains and a four-wheeled chassis possibly intended for a carnival parade float. Sketches are not inventions and he may just possibly have copied from others' work here.

In the final quarter of the 19th Century inventors created all manner of mostly improbable pedal-powered vehicles, largely in a heady spirit of experimentation. They shared their thoughts and enthusiasms in the pages of periodicals such as *The Scientific American* and *The Amateur Mechanic*.

▲ A treadle-driven carriage built by Jackman of London. From about 1750 to 1880 human-powered vehicles were typically built in the manner of horse carriages but with a luckless footman bouncing on a cranked rear axle or pushing levers while his master sat in front to steer. These were gentlemen's pleasure carriages for private amusement on their estates.

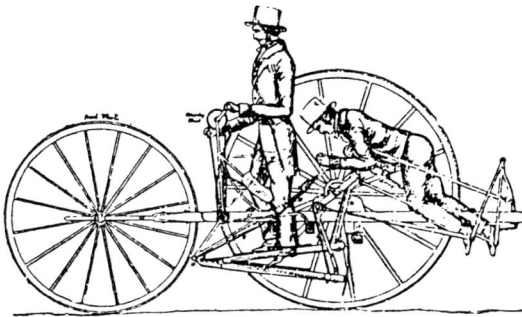

▲ In 1870 a Mr Ward of New York sought to maintain the perpendicular by fixing heavy weights below the axle of his unicycle. It has been calculated that in order to stay upright a rider of average weight would require about a quarter of an American ton (227kg) in weights down below.

▲ An American example of dog-power probably from the 1870s.

▲ What may have been the world's first tandem tricycle was invented by the Englishmen Bramley and Parker in 1830. We wonder whether the gentleman on the rear is enjoying the view.

A few professional craftsmen made commercially ▶ successful quadricycles. One such was Willard Sawyer of Dover. Between 1845 and 1868 he produced refined machines with wooden frames and wheels, and with treadle drive to a cranked axle.

▲ *Mr Najork's foot motor boat of 1895 had an alarmingly high centre of gravity.*

▲ *The Centre-Cycle, nicknamed the 'Hen and Chickens', was an unsuccessful experiment, in 1882, by the Post Office in Horsham, England.*

▲ *Barathon's propeller-driven life buoy of 1895 was presented at the Paris Exhibition by an English manufacturer. It featured an inflatable seat, simultaneous pedalling and hand-cranking, a sail, and a lamp for the attention of rescuers.*

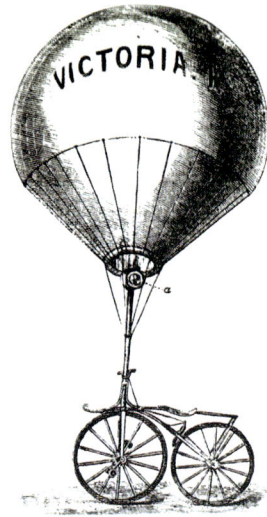

▲ **" Sir, I propose a hot air balloon velocipede. My object is to secure the perpendicularity of the machine by a balloon just large enough for that purpose, thereby securing confidence in the rider. At the same time it will assist the machine in climbing hills and passing over rough roads. There is an oil lamp to supply the balloon with hot air. The opinion of some brother correspondents on the merits of the balloon will interest me. "**
W. T. Trindon

▲ *The Pedespeed was an American invention of 1870.*

▲ *An 'Improved Airship' was patented by Mr John Holmes of Kansass in 1889.*

The Big Wheel

▲ A Chinese porter pushing a sail-assisted wheelbarrow, drawn around 1880. Records go back to the second century of Chinese handcarts with a large central wheel.

▲ That large wheels pass better over poor surfaces added to the comfort of the high wheel bicycle riders of the 1870 and 1880s – something also recognised by the Japanese many years before. This drawing from Thomas Stevens' 1887 book, Around the World on a Bicycle, shows him traversing Japan and behind him is a jinrikisha with equally large wheels.

Monocycles, defined as wheels which enclose the rider, proved to be hard to manage and very difficult to stop.

▲ Big wheeled carts were common in China until recently. They could carry people as well as goods, as shown in this image from 1901.

The 'Swing Bicycle' ▶
by Nathan Ward of Kansas in 1887.

Bikes on the Job
Ideas and Inspirations

Groni are pedal-powered painters and decorators operating in York and other Yorkshire cities. As you'd expect, their paints and materials are all eco-friendly.

In the 1920s, in hilly Halifax, England, there was a pedal-powered fish and chip shop complete with hot fat fryers. In 1905 the Automobile Club employed its first cycling scouts to patrol the roads of Britain to warn motorists of police speed traps. In 1896 youths in Paris made a living pushing aristocratic female cyclists up hills. In the USA the telephone companies put inspectors and lineboys on bicycles to patrol the overhead cable networks. In cities worldwide, wherever cycling had permeated, hundreds of thousands of delivery and messenger cyclists, usually young boys, were thronging the streets on two or three wheels.

In the world as a whole the working bike never went away. But pedal-power is now working its way back to where it once thrived: in the towns and cities of the industrialised world. Some traditional services based on bicycles have continued in specific local forms. You can still find pedal-powered knife-grinders in the countries of southern Europe, blowing a whistle to announce their presence.

Self-employed entrepreneurs are everywhere working on new business models around pedal-power. The creative thinking behind their ideas gives them a more efficient, more resilient enterprise, a strong local profile and ethical credentials, which in turn bring clients and customers.

These entrepreneurs are enabled by new formats of working cycles designed and built often by businesses of the same size as their customers. It becomes a symbiotic relationship.

A window cleaners' tandem tricycle in Antwerp, Belgium, probably 1930s.

The cycling chef

Morten Kryger Wulff is known in Copenhagen as *Cykelkokken* (The Cycling Chef) and he offers a unique concept in tourism. He takes groups on cycle tours of Copenhagen's historic streets, waterfronts and oases of green, but he does all this on a cargo bike functioning as a mobile kitchen. As you'd expect, Morten is a highly experienced professional chef. At five carefully selected 'hotspots' during the ride he serves an outdoor gourmet dining experience. The dishes and beverages are selected to reflect the character of the various corners of Copenhagen which are visited. The menu emphasises local, seasonal and organic ingredients from local suppliers who share Morten's values and outlook.

Eco-laundry

Oxwash provide a linen wash and rental service for the businesses of Oxford. Collection is largely by pedal-power and they use highly sustainable techniques for the washing process that was developed from PhD research by the social enterprise's founder.

Riding clean

E-Cargo Bikes were a perfect solution for London company Ride Clean. Their employees can transport their cleaning and maintenance tools and equipment from job to job across the city, without the time, cost and stress which come from parking, congestion and emission charges. They enjoy keeping fit and healthy as they cycle between jobs.

Eco ice-cream

An old style Italian ice cream vending trike operated by Pinolo in Portland, Oregon. Stylish ice cream trikes enhance the buying experience, promising ices as classy as the cycle, and the buying experience is far pleasanter than standing amongst the noise and smell which come from diesel ice cream vans.

Modern ice cream trikes can benefit from solar panels to keep their cargo refrigerated for longer. Some vendors have set up their cycles so they can pedal when static to charge the freezer battery. Or customers can be invited to pedal for their ices.

Attention, please

James Allen replaces the kind of draughty sash windows found in the Regency houses of Bath, England. He carries his materials in this eco-friendly way which also advertises his business to the whole city. The leaf-sprung trailer has a solar panel roof supplying a charge to a battery inside which assists James's pedalling. Few fail to notice this classy and unusual vehicle.

Info and Promo-Cycles

An info-cycle and a promo-cycle both adapted by Get Cycling in York. These cycles are both from the same standard cargo trike base. The info-cycle can access pedestrian zones, parks and local fêtes taking the client's message where motor vehicles cannot go. The branding and message boards can be swapped out. The promo-cycle can also venture into pedestrian areas and elsewhere. The one pictured can be rented out to social enterprises who use volunteers to ride it where it will be seen.

Journalism by bike

❝ Is there any other way to cover a climate protest? ❞ asks BBC news reporter Anna Holligan. She's based in the Netherlands and is seen here working at a climate protest in the Hague. After online criticism from trolls she had to point out that it's her personal bike and cost the BBC nothing.

Compost by bike

The Compost Courier is a service provided by Community Compost, a social enterprise in Nelson, New Zealand. Food waste is collected from local households and businesses and compost is distributed. It shows what can be done with a simple trailer pulled by a conventional bike.

The business of coffee

Claudia Brose has taken on a coffee bike franchise in the Berlin area, operating at events and fixed sites. She appreciates the way she can cycle to her regular sites so easily from her front door, and enjoys chatting to her regular clientele. She came across the concept at a street festival and became an accomplished barista after completing the training course at the Coffee-Bike Academy.

Jobs well done

The French not-for-profit 'Cyclick' have created a mobile 'dry toilet' which they transport on a specialised trailer to outdoor public events. 'Dry' because only sawdust and enzyme-rich biomass is used. The plexiglas roof lets in natural light and the solar panel charges a battery for night use, when the toilet puts on a bit of a light show to advertise itself as well as lighting up the interior. There is plentiful ventilation to remove any odours the sawdust does not deal with. The tank is pedalled away to be emptied for long-term composting.

Plombike

Thomas Olivier is a plumber and heating specialist working by bike to serve the city of Rouen in Normandy. He finds he can get to jobs quicker and more efficiently than by motor vehicle.

Handyman services

Man Maid deliver their handyman expertise in the London Borough of Hammersmith and Fulham by using a fleet of box trikes. Founder Mungo Morgan claims that their choice of transport makes them ten times quicker then using a van.

Cargo bikes help recruitment

Dutch company ESNW has 60 vans delivering heating and ventilation maintenance around North Holland. In the town of Alkmaar their technicians travel by cargo bike. This is partly to do with speed, efficiency and good PR, but it also opens up new recruitment opportunities. It is a means of attracting and enthusing new technicians who don't have or want a driving licence.

Entertainer on wheels

Australian entertainer Shannon McGurgan uses
cargo trikes for his various acts: some for transport
and others as an intrinsic part of the show.

▲ **Mobile stage**

This *Kulturrad* ('Culture Cycle') portable stage
takes music to venues around its home city of
Hanover in Germany and travels to neighbouring
towns and cities. The rear box can alternatively
seat two musicians sideways so they can perform
while being pedalled around.

▲ *Theatre in a box*

Stanley Youngman transports his comedy street
theatre full of 'absurd and utter nonsense' in a
Nihola box trike. It gets him right into city centres.

Last journeys ▶

Le Ciel et la Terre (Heaven and Earth) is an ecologically sensitive undertaker business run by Isabelle
Plumereau and providing funerals in and around
Paris. Isabelle created a pedal-powered hearse so that
those who believe in living lightly on the Earth can go
on their final journey in a fitting and respectful way.

Going Loaded

The mainstay of cargo bike design is the two-wheeled big-box format with indirect steering. Photo: London Cycling Campaign.

Several happy developments are coming together. Reliable electric motors are making larger, specialised bikes more feasible, and a growing eco-system is linking operators, cycle manufacturers, software suppliers, rider training companies, maintenance providers, consultants and big name clients.

There are reasons why cargo cycle freight is the solution for urban logistics. E-cargo cycles are generally faster than motors in cities and can safely navigate and bypass congestion, bringing huge time and money savings. Their overall annual running costs are 19% of that of a small van and cumulative time and cost savings make them 30% more efficient. E-cargo cycles are also future-proof – we are moving to a low carbon economy and motor traffic is being phased out of city centres.

Logistics software helps operators maximise efficiency, giving information, for example, on riders' location and distances travelled. One software supplier claims to monitor and measure over 30 variables.

▲ *Some small businesses pedal their own deliveries. Here Freddie of Freddie's Flowers in London transports his daily sales.*

◀ *A cargo trike in the service of a local community group. The Alecs is made by Pashley in the UK. The rider section tilts, giving the handling characteristics of a bicycle, while the load platform remains stable. Its design allows for easy storage and parking – five of these cargo trikes fit in the footprint of a standard car parking space.*

Photo: Dutch Cycling Embassy.

The annual World Cargo Bike Festival brings together inventors, makers, professional practitioners and enthusiasts.

It's not all rosy. Recently the UK's largest e-cargo bike delivery company, operating in nine cities, went into administration, and a similar sized Dutch company had to restructure and now offers only letterbox-sized deliveries.

Rich Pleeth, an entrepreneur in sustainable logistics, says:

❝ *Sustainability has a price, and it's a price that needs to be valued and prioritised by both consumers and brands. The race to the absolute bottom on price, with sustainability as a mere afterthought, is a self-defeating cycle. We need a fundamental shift in mindset.* ❞

Ethical employers operating in the last-mile delivery space have higher labour costs yet compete on price against outfits involved in modern slavery and tax avoidance enabled by the gig economy. A solution is to stand out from the others by providing services with better efficiency, reliability and refinements. None or this is easy.

Almost everywhere there is goodwill towards shifting cargo to specialised pedal-power. The public is more ambivalent about the meal delivery couriers working for the likes of Deliveroo and Uber Eats. These riders are not generally so highly invested in cycling as a lifestyle choice, and some (not all) would just as happily, or more happily, used a motor bike or a car if they had one and could drive.

The demand for 'messages' to be cycled quickly across cities has dropped as so much can now be sent electronically. A few couriers (known as messengers in some countries) still ply cities, carrying light goods on fast, lightweight bikes. They are not well paid, and work within the gig economy. Still, they have a job they probably enjoy, which allows a flexible lifestyle and gives opportunity and purpose to the rider's love of cycling. Some can hardly believe that they can get paid just for riding their bike. Actually, they get paid for that and for good customer service both ends of each journey.

Pedal-Me in London operate standard cargo bikes with a maximum load capacity of 150kg. This becomes a total load of 300kg with a Carla trailer attached.

The Challenge of Size

This is the ePack4, reckoned to be the largest cargo cycle within the regulatory frameworks of the EU and UK. These new forms of cargo cycle are testing the limits of cycling infrastructure and legislation. Most of the larger commercial e-bikes have pedals only as a legal formality. The human engine is putting in only about 75W, while the e-bike dominates with around 175W. There are now regulatory 'edge cases' such as electric-assisted cargo cycles (like the ePack4) where the 250W power limit is applied to more than one motor, each controlled by chain-free 'digital drive'. Electric-assisted trailers have also appeared.

Not being treated as motor vehicles means that very large cargo e-bikes, can use cycle lanes and they require no vehicle registration, insurance or a driving licence.

There are currently no legal limits in the UK or the EU on the number of wheels, nor on the weight and size of cargo bikes or trailers. However, discussions at EU level are exploring possible regulation. A final position is not yet agreed, although it seems likely that the dividing line may well be based on the highest gross vehicle weight covered by the upcoming European Cargo Bikes Standard of 600kg. Until changes to EU regulations are in place some individual countries are looking at setting their own limits for cargo bikes, and some have already set width limits to make them acceptable for travelling on cycle paths.

There are those who argue that a different kind of cycle path is needed: wide enough to accommodate friction-free all forms of slow-moving soft energy vehicles, from bicycles to substantial cargo bikes.

The Icai by Veleon. A semi-recumbent position does not allow the rider to apply more power by shifting bodyweight to above the pedals. This problem is largely solved by almost all large cargo cycles having electric-assist.

The Vok from Estonia.

DB Schenker Norway operate their Armadillo electric cargo bike with semi-trailer in all the larger Norwegian cities.

Couriers in the Netherlands moving 'city containers' from a trailer to Cubicycle cargo cycles.

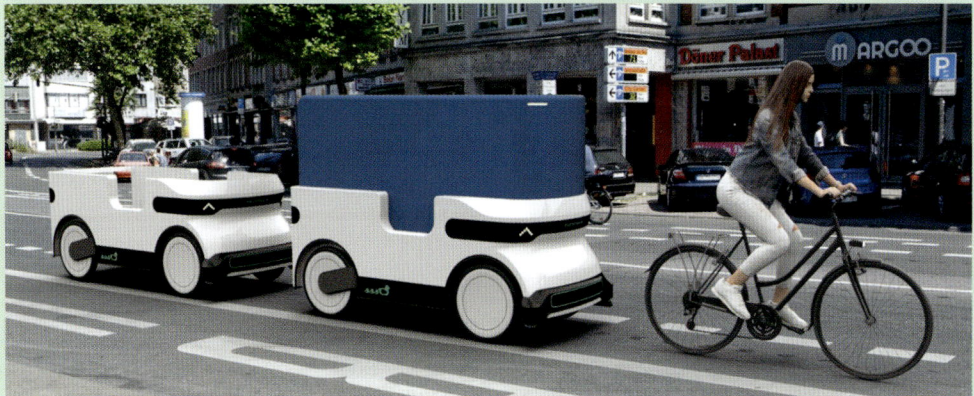

The experimental Trailerduck by DroidDrive in Germany, using follow-me technology. (This image is computer-generated.)

Moving People

The Quicab from Sweden operates in some major cities around the world – here at work in Paris. It easily carries two passengers and their luggage and offers comfort, weather protection and privacy. An intercom connects passengers and driver. It operates legally on most cycle paths, although it doesn't leave much room on narrower paths for other users.

Velotaxi, pedicab, cycle rickshaw, trishaw, pedal taxi – many names, many types. Whatever their format pedal-assist people-movers, boosted by the arrival of reliable electric motors, are changing the way we can be transported around our city centres. Velotaxis don't have the overheads of motor taxis and can often get places quicker and at about half the cost of a diesel-powered taxi fare. They are common in many developing countries but the industrialised world is catching up. For example, 850 licensed velocabs operate in New York City, mostly serving the tourist trade, and with regulated fares.

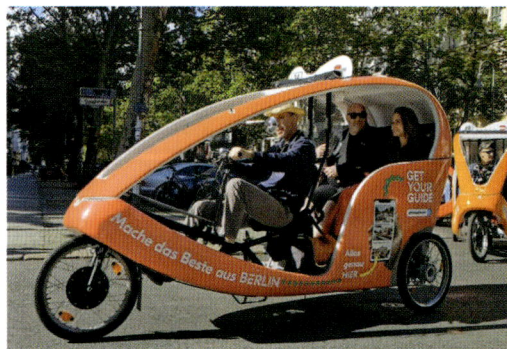

One very successful variant of velotaxi shelters passengers in a cab open on both sides. These vehicles, generally known as 'velocabs', originated in Berlin and are found worldwide. Large numbers still operate in Berlin and are here seen being used for guided sight-seeing tours. Velocabs are now manufactured in the Czech Republic and there are Chinese copies.

'We are Amsterdam' take groups on 75-minute social rides with 20 litres of beer as part of the deal. The operators give reassurance that the driver/guide is always sober. A variant of this is the Cyclo-Café in Paris, offering good food en route rather than beer.

There are always issues: taxi drivers feel threatened and complain to the licensing authorities, car drivers can be impatient behind a slower moving velotaxi, access to pedestrian zones is not always given, longer distances are uneconomic, and battery life is restrictive unless there's a chance for a battery swap.

The Pedal-Me taxi service in London.

Cycling without age

Ole Kassow, a resident of Copenhagen, wanted to help older citizens with limited mobility get back to cycling. His solution was a cycle rickshaw and in 2012 he offered free rides to residents of a nearby nursing home. He was soon supported by social inclusion consultant Dorthe Pedersen and with city council support they bought five cycle rickshaws. This was the beginning of Cycling Without Age, a movement now in 50 countries, strengthened by cycle manufacturers pitching in by developing the highly specialised cycles needed.

The Chat by van Raam for Cycling without Age.

Photo: Bergen City Bikes/Vilde Bang Foss.

Bike-Sharing

Bike-share systems now operate in around 3,000 cities worldwide. They are largely the work of large international 'micromobility' companies bidding for partnerships with the public sector, which almost always means in big cities with dense population centres.

There are two common formats. One uses docking systems, which keep everything tidy and secure, especially with CCTV in play. Some docking systems involve employees travelling round to swap out low-charge e-bike batteries with full ones. Becoming more common and manageable is direct charging at the docking stations. Docking systems are expensive to install and there need to be a lot of them sited fairly close together. A cheaper, more flexible option is to go dockless but it's open to pointless theft and vandalism (docking stations can also suffer from vandalism). Dockless facilities are prone to inconsiderate parking – sometimes in the nearest river. Providers are learning lessons and improving their systems. With both systems the bikes are located and released through an app, so you have to have a smartphone. With dockless systems the app identifies the nearest available bike left at a random location by the previous user.

Docking system operators need a strong relationship with the host city, due to the cost and the need for long term assurance of revenue, whereas a provider of a dockless system losing money can, once out of contract, simply pick up their bikes and move to another city.

In Taipei, capital of Taiwan, share-bikes are outside all metro stations. About 55% of metro users take one of these bikes to get to or from the metro. The public bike share scheme in Paris, Vélib, has 20,000 bikes and 1,400 parking stations spread across 450km². Its popularity is linked to significant improvements in the city's cycling infrastructure.

A scheme's charging policy is critical. Users often enjoy 30 free minutes each trip, which can cover most journeys. Many schemes charge an increasing fee past that first half-hour, creating a strong disincentive to take the bicycles out of the city centre.

Share-bike activity creates data and users volunteer additional information. This is revealing that some users of share bikes and scooters have simply switched from walking or public transport, and that fewer car journeys than expected have been replaced. Analysis is complicated in that the public sector also encourages more private bike use, which can also cause people to switch from walking and public transport. These are all issues which active travel professionals all over the world have to grapple with – along with analyses of the additional carbon emissions caused by bike-share facilities and operations. (See page 369.)

Bike-sharing will grow as it becomes a natural part of people's daily life. Transport planners learn best practice from each other, systems improve and alternatives to share bike travel become less attractive. It's still new to many but is already a significant part of urban life.

App-based e-cargo cycle-sharing schemes are available in several cities worldwide.

Santander bikes in London ▲

This publicly-owned facility has more than 12,000 bikes and around 800 docking stations.

Bublr bikes in Milwaukee ▲

These people do bike-sharing in their own inspiring way. They are a not-for-profit organisation operating over 100 bike stations across Greater Milwaukee in the USA. Being community-based helps Bublr run initiatives such as their Youth Workforce Development Program providing young people with the skills and opportunities to work in the bike industry. There's also an Access Pass Program, which offers affordable rides for individuals on low incomes, and Bublr offer Savvy Cycling Courses teaching how to navigate the Bublr system, how to keep safe on the road and how to get the best out of your cycling experiences. There's also a scheme in which groups wanting to go on a ride together can have the cycles delivered to their home or workplace. Bublr are funded through government and non-government grants, sponsorships, individual donations, membership fees and usage fees.

Dott bikes in Frankfurt ▲

This city does it dockless and includes electric bikes and scooters.

Stadtbikes in Hamburg ▶

This city's Stadtbike scheme, with half a million subscribers, has over 3,500 bikes at 290 docking stations. The scheme has been helped by the new cycling infrastructure brought in at the same time. Share-bikes won't get used if the rides are not seen as safe.

Musical Rides

Pedal-power can take music anywhere – carrying player and instrument into the heart of shopping centres and public squares, schools and parks. In many cases the instrument of travel and the instrument of music complement each other. The music can be about cycling, but the combination can simply say something eloquent about self-expression, freedom of travel choice and a planet-friendly lifestyle.

Pedalling pianist

Eric Rich is a roofer, carpenter, and visual artist from Salt Lake City, Utah. He's also a self-taught pianist and composer inspired by American minimalism and post-rock. He fell in love with the piano after teaching himself to play in his early 20s. He wanted to take his piano on the road but in an ecologically sustainable way. Hence his fascination with creating the perfect pianobike. He aimed to create a unique, eyecatching but functional design and has achieved this partly by cantilevering the rider out over the front wheel. Eric takes this combination of old and new technology on occasional tours of the USA. *Photo by Elizabeth Wilhelmsen.*

Innertuba

Jon Hodkin, tuba player and cyclist, alliterates his priorities and pleasures: his Tuba, his Tricycle, his Trailer – and his Travels with all three of them. He even calls himself a Triking Tubadour. He delights in connecting with people, as happened on his InnerTuba Tour of the Mississippi (above): 3000 miles (4828km) in 150 days, performing with local amateur musicians in towns and cities along the way.

Dom Whiting
Drum'n'Base

Until 2020, Dom Whiting was a regular DJ playing in UK clubs. When entertainment venues closed during Covid he decided to start livestreaming outdoor Drum'n'Base sets on Facebook. The first two were stationary, but in September 2020 he built a special rickshaw with a DJ deck at the back where he played his electronic music as a passenger. Later that year he built a new trike that allowed him to play and pedal at the same time. The popularity of Whiting's livestreams grew quickly on social media and other cyclists began to join his rides, turning them into massive bike-raves of several thousand people. In 2022 Whiting's rides expanded beyond the UK, taking place in Belgium, Germany. Spain and elsewhere. *Photo: Genaro.com.*

Dutch bike orchestras

The Dutch have this thing about making music on bikes. Here the Crescendo Bicycle Orchestra performs one of its synchronised routines.

A different technique is practised by the Fietsorkest ('Bicycle Orchestra') of Brabant in the Netherlands. It features two saxophones, a bass drum, a tuba, a trumpet, an accordion, a bicycle bell, and cymbals for the pilot. Their repertoire includes jazz, ragtime and circus music – with not a little slapstick. *Photo: Mikael Colville-Andersen.*

Cycles go to War

British paratroopers with folding bikes board their D-Day glider.

Going into The Great War (1914-18) soldiers on bikes were seen as the progressive vanguard of the 20th century. The major European powers had organised bicycle corps used for scouting ahead, message-carrying and fast-response. Cycles were used less by the military in World War Two but civilians everywhere resorted to cycling as petrol was rationed and public transport often damaged.

The Dutch and Danes have not forgotten the millions of bicycles stolen by the Germans during the war. On Dolle Dinsdag, or Mad Tuesday, German troops panicked when the BBC announced that Allied troops had crossed the Dutch border (they hadn't, in fact). German soldiers stole bikes from the public and rode out of Holland, with whatever else they could loot. So a common Dutch taunt of Germans after the war was *"Geef mij mijn fiets terug!"* ('Give me my bike back!')

Hubris was in the air. British army engineers rode this experimental cycle around Aldershot, pulling a trailer full of equipment.

During the Boer War Australian forces constructed rail cycles. They could travel at up to 30mph (50kph) searching for Boer commandos and demolition charges. They could also tow a machine gun trailer and carry wounded comrades on a stretcher between the bike frames.

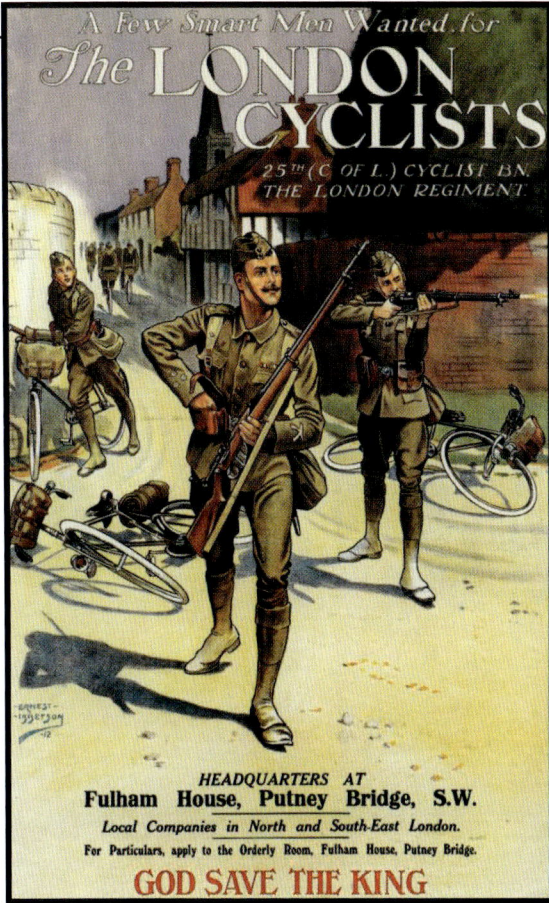

A First World War British army recruitment poster.

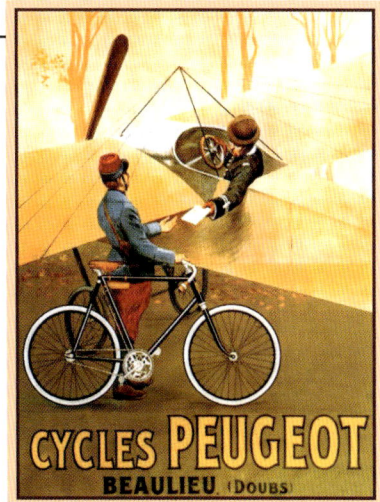

Cycles Peugeot associated their cycles with patriotism, military efficiency and aviation.

The Zouaves were a class of light infantry in the French Army. This image is from 1912.

Young teenagers of the Volkssturm militia ride with rocket propelled grenades towards the approaching Red Army. Photo: campfire.com.

Steven C. Price, Creative Commons.

Pack bikes

That the 'pack bike' could win wars was first demonstrated by the Viet Minh army. During the Indochina War of 1946 to 1954 they expelled the French from what had been the colonial territories of Vietnam, Laos, and Cambodia. Pack bike porters overcame very difficult terrain to supply the soldiers facing the French army, resulting in the insurgents' conclusive victory at the Battle of Dien Bien Phu. It was perhaps fitting that their bicycles were mostly French Peugeots. The wheels were reinforced, the frames buttressed, racks added and a steering pole plus steadying pole attached. Each cycle could transport more than 200kg of cargo.

The pack bike became equally significant in the Vietnam War which followed. The trucks supplied by the Soviet Union often got stuck and became easy targets for American aviation. But bicycles were more difficult to spot and could be pushed around crater edges. Porters would camouflage their bikes during the day and move at night to escape detection. Refinements to the bicycle design doubled the cycles' load capacity to around 400kg and the heaviest pack bikes needed two porters to push them. There were over 200,000 bike porters available.

In 1967, before the US Senate Foreign Relations Committee, an exasperated Senator Fulbright demanded to know why the US Air Force was not bombing the bicycles instead of the bridges. Was

the Pentagon aware of this issue? Apparently the room erupted in laughter at the idea of bombers hunting down bicycles.

Shown top right is a worker in the village of Bat Trang in 2005. He's transporting ceramics using the same two-stick technique as had been used during the times of war.

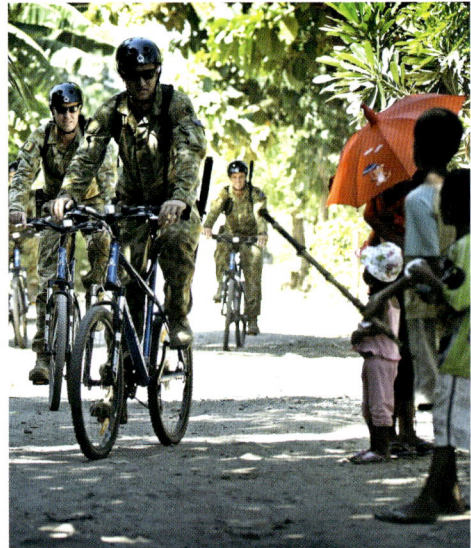

Australian soldiers on street patrol in East Timor, a situation made possible by the country's stable security situation. Cycle patrols could cover a lot of ground and still engage easily with members of the community. (Photo: LSPH Paul Berry.)

The Swiss Army Bike

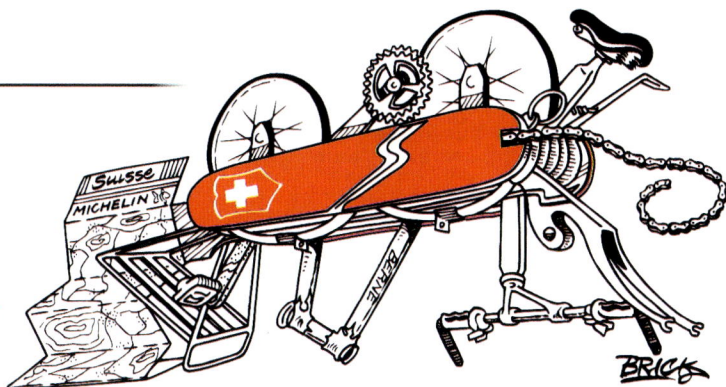

The Swiss are famous for maintaining an elite front-line bicycle regiment into the 21st century. Right up till 1993 they used a single-speed cycle introduced in 1905 and weighing 22kg (49lbs). This monster of a bike was replaced in 1993 by the *Militärrrad 93*, a modernised version with derailleur gears. Only the fittest applicants were accepted. Training included a 200km (124 mile) forced 'pedal march' including alpine passes, while carrying a pack of 75kg (165lbs).

Switzerland hasn't been truly at war since 1798. It's a naturally defensible country and the bicycle regiments were expected to quickly and quietly move across countryside and urban areas to ambush motorised invading armies.

The cycling regiments were disbanded in 2003. Bike Commander Julian Voeffray described the move as stupid:

❝ Over short distances we are very fast, much faster than the motorised units. We can be very discreet, we are well armed and we perform well against tanks. ❞

The story continues. In 2012 the Swiss Ministry of Defence ordered 4,100 new bicycles, the MO-12, generally known as the *'vélo zwölf'*. It was built by the Swiss company Simpel and features a reliable, eight-speed, internally-geared hub, front and rear disc brakes, mudguards and cargo racks. This sounds like a pretty good commuter bike and that's more or less what it is. It's used by all ranks for getting about when on duty.

The original 1905 Swiss Army Bike design, but enhanced with a drum brake post WW2.

Crossing a gorge with full equipment.

The modernised version of 1993.

Riding on Water

It's off-road cycling but not as we know it. Cycle on water opens up a whole new set of freedoms and adventures. There are two main ways to do it: you can convert your cycle to become a catamaran or you can pedal a kayak.

A good example of the catamaran option is the Shuttle Bike kit, made in Italy. Steve Holard (pictured) used one of these to give a new twist to the classic British travel challenge: from Land's End to John O'Groats. He completed it on cycle paths, inland waterways, lakes, lochs and bays, all on the same bike. Strapped to the back of his cycle was the Shuttle Bike kit. As soon as he ran out of dry land it was out with the boat and onto the water. Steve achieved this on his recumbent, though virtually any standard bike can be used.

Steve Holard. Photo: Simon Levermore.

Hobie pedal-powered tandem kayaks are designed for maximum efficiency and stability through the water, enhanced by 'kick-up-fins' that retract on impact. The rudder also retracts for beaching and convenience. Hobie are a US company with outlets in various countries.

Another form of pedalling on water is hydrofoiling, which means getting your hull above the surface tension of the water – an activity for the very fit. Various versions are available online.

Photo: Hobie Kayaks.

In 1883 William Terry rode his tricycle from London to Dover before converting it into a rowing boat and crossing the English Channel. The only parts specific to the boat, so not 'recycled' tricycle, were a couple of airbags and lengths of wood for bracing and to form a keel. On arriving in France he was detained on suspicion of smuggling.

Pedals Take Off

Human-powered flight has long been a dream of mankind but the engineering and endurance issues are almost overwhelming. Over recent decades the best brains at Massachusetts Institute of Technology and NASA have worked on the challenges. One massive achievement was in 1979, when Bryan Allen flew the Gossamer Albatross from England to France: a straight distance of 35.82km in two hours 49 minutes. This won the machine's creator Paul MacCready the second Kremer prize of £100,000.

Research and experimentation go on but it's incremental and depends on the limited power outputs of the human body. However, drone technology is now showing what can be done with small, light motors, and we may see new developments in flight combining human power with electric-assist. Perhaps we'll soon see pedal-powered flight for lesser mortals than the record breaking athletes who have conquered the air so far.

▲ *Current human-powered aircraft are huge, fragile and limited to flying low and calm weather. They also need a superbly athletic pilot. The FlyCycle, on the other hand, is a pedal-powered microlight with electric-assist for both road and flight modes, making it an unorthodox form of mixed mode travel. According to designer, Bill Brooks, who has a PhD from Cranfield in aircraft design, the FlyCycle can give 30 to 40 minutes of flight powered by a lithiumion pack, and up to 10% more with pedal-assist. Of course, level flight is not what microlights are made for, and the FlyCycle can certainly soar unpowered once aloft. Bill offers plans for the aircraft and may consider production in future.*

Bryan Allen sets off from the English coast to France. Headwinds endangered the flight, and with the coast of France still unseen, Allen was about to give up. However, he tried going a little higher and, to his surprise, picked up a layer of useful air turbulence and so managed to continue, touching down in France. ▶

Multicycles:
Spectacularly Social

▲ *A Dutch bike bus, with just one parent steering, and seated centrally to supervise the young team.*

If people can ride together on a bus why not also on a multicycle? Well, there are lots of reasons why, and some why-nots, including weather, incompatibility with certain traffic situations, and basic transport logistics. But, for the situations when a multicycle becomes just right, it give everyone a whole lot of fun, exercise and sociability.

▲ *The four-seater ZEM was made in Switzerland and is sadly no longer in production.*

▲ *Members of the inventive Bicycle Forest in Canada ride their own design of quadricycle. The back-to-back arrangement gives great efficiency, and there's easy communication between all four riders.*

▲ Cyclofan in Italy make robust quadricycles to carry two, four or six riders, not counting two small children seated forwards of the front riders. Their main market has been leisure parks, open air attractions, seaside promenades and the like. The addition of drum brakes to all four wheels, combined with e-assist, now gives these cycles potential as people movers in other situations, including public roads. Cyclofans are happy, sociable fun machines for short distances, with the drawback that seat heights can't be adjusted.

▲ The seven-seater 'Conference Bike' (sometimes called the 'CircleCycle' in the UK) has become a big hit in many countries. It is used for sight-seeing tours, community-building and sometimes even business conferences. The driver (here far left) communicates easily with their human power units, and their vehicle moved in the direction they are facing. The two riders far right pedal in a normal direction but travel backwards, which can be alarming on a first ride.

▲ This 'Rudderrenner' ('Row-Runner') quadricycle was extremely fast, and competed in human-powered vehicle races. It was conceived and master-minded by engineering student Andreas Baumüller in the late 1970s with the help of co-workers who are also the riders. Forward leg-pushes send power to the rear to be converted to circular motion. Riders need to draw on a great deal of leg, arm and stomach muscles, which cannot be kept up for long. It was admired by experts but appears to have never been replicated.

Eckhard Möller, Irre Fahrradtypen, Bauverlag, 1984.

◀ Members of the Dutch national cycling federation in around 1882, with only four wheels for four riders.

209

Bike Trains

Lukas Külling, Thuner Trampelwurm, Switzerland.

Bike trains are fun and sociable but also have some specific applications. For example they can put large numbers of riders under the control of one cycle tour guide.

You have to get many things right. The driver needs to be able to communicate quickly with all passengers, including the people at the very end of the train. Braking needs to be co-ordinated, helped by overrun brakes in the hitch mechanisms, as used on trailers behind cars. When the lead unit brakes, the forward shunting of the others activates all the brakes. Radio-controlled braking is a possible solution. There's also the question of how a driver can operate an underpopulated bike train, or get an empty one back to base. An electric motor can, or course, help, but may not add enough power. There are hurdles to overcome but also plenty of opportunities for brave entrepreneurs.

As the family of Methodist minister David Warnock grew, so did their form of transport.

An extendable bike train with overrun brake, by van Raam, disability cycling specialists in the Netherlands.

Students at Perkins School for the Blind in the USA ride together, around 1892, steered by one sighted man. The Royal Normal School for the Blind in the UK had a similar machine.

Monorail Cycling

Conceived as an experimental transport system of the future, the Shweeb monorail in Rotorua's Velocity Valley in New Zealand carries riders around a 200m track. Enclosed in pedal-powered pods riders see scenic farmlands whizz by as they power through three laps of the course, experiencing 60 degree angles on the bends. Riders can race family and friends, or the clock, and maybe challenge the world Shweebing record.

Back in 2010 Google invested US$1 million in funding for research and development. They and the makers envisaged a system with junctions where Shweebs can switch lines at high speeds.

Monorail pod-riding may well have potential, and speeds of 45kph (28mph) were planned for a fully developed system built over existing urban infra-structure and rural areas without affecting what's on the ground. However, as yet there has been no rollout of the Shweeb system outside of Velocity Valley.

As with all forms of rail-bound cycling certain design challenges don't go away. Where and how do riders get on and off? What do you do with empty ones getting in the way? How do you overtake slower users ahead of you? These are some of the issues which may be holding back the concept of pedal-powered monorails.

The suspension 'railway' at the Royal Panarmonion Gardens, London, around 1834.

The Hotchkiss bicycle railroad, 1892, ran 2.9km (1.8 miles) from Mount Holly to Smithville, New Jersey. It had a complicated route, crossing the same creek ten times, and was mainly intended to help workers get to their factory more easily.

The Pedersen Exception

" Perhaps the most remarkable design of machine in the long history of the bicycle. "

That's how celebrated bike designer Alex Moulton described the original Pedersen bicycle. Its unique feature is the use of small diameter thin-walled tubes in a lightweight triangulated structure supporting the comfortable hammock saddle.

Mikael Pedersen was a Danish engineer who came to England and spent much of his working life at Dursley in Gloucestershire. He filed the first British patent for his 'improved bicycle' in 1893 and went on to make thousands of beautifully finished Dursley Pedersens.

Pedersens have the stately feel of a long wheelbase roadster, but they can also be high performance machines. The unpaced record for riding London to Brighton and back was broken on a Pedersen.

A Pedersen in bronze with inlaid wood mudguards (fenders). Photo: Umberto Brayj.

Mr and Mrs Pedersen in 1898.

A Pedersen interpretation by cycle-maker Michael Kemper in Germany.

An electric-assist Pedersen by Utopia Cycles in Germany.

Production stopped in 1917 but in recent decades the special merits of the Pedersen are being rediscovered. The hammock saddle has a very different feel to a conventional seat. Pedersen explained that he designed it mainly for comfort, but also to save weight – conventional saddles at the time had some very heavy steel-work underneath. The hammock saddle was, and is, appreciated by cyclists who cannot come to terms with conventional saddles. The pedalling action on a Pedersen causes a very slight sideways swing in the saddle position but this is a small price to pay for the added comfort. Some claim that the upright riding position coupled with the hammock saddle is a therapeutic configuration for riders with back problems. It can be the only option for other reasons. This was the case for German entrepreneur Kalle Kalkhoff. He was an above-the-knee amputee, and the Pedersen hammock made cycling possible for him. He liked it so much that he became a leading advocate and manufacturer. He was largely responsible, in the 1990s, for the Pedersen revival in Germany, and then internationally.

The Moulton

The Moulton bicycle broke the design conventions set by the diamond frame bicycle. Its key features are small wheels, suspension, stiff unisex frame, adaptability to a variety of uses, and innovation in design, engineering and manufacture.

Being small, Moulton wheels are immensely strong. Their lower moment of inertia allows faster acceleration and more responsive steering. Small wheels also reduce the overall length of the bicycle, making it easier to transport. High pressure tyres have always been fundamental to the Moulton design, giving lower rolling resistance and less aerodynamic drag. But small wheels and high-pressure tyres need to be combined with effective suspension and Alex Moulton was a specialist in this: he had designed the suspension system for the Mini car.

The Moulton had considerable success in bike racing until small wheels were banned by the UCI. Since then it has continued its competitive successes in long distance events. It did well in the 1988 Race Across America in which a Moulton rider completed the 3,037 miles (4,888km) in 10 days, 15 hours and one minute.

The early Moultons were a big hit in 1960s Britain, leading to Raleigh buying the manufacturing rights. They failed to develop the brand so Moulton

Alex Moulton in 2010. Photo: Dan Farrell, Moulton Bicycle Company.

took manufacturing back under his own roof. The result was the spaceframe Moulton: lighter, stiffer, faster and more comfortable than early versions.

Alex Moulton died in 2012, but his bicycles remain internationally famous and are still built by hand in Bradford-on-Avon by a loyal team of engineers, technicians and craftsmen. There's an enthusiastic Moulton Bicycle Club which publishes *The Moultoneer*.

The Anerley Bicycle Club in South London race on early F-frame Moultons, much-loved predecessors of the spaceframe Moulton.

The spaceframe Moulton.

The Brompton

Wait a while at any major railway station and sooner or later a Brompton will be wheeled past, then folded and lifted onto a train. Its ultra-compact fold makes it easy to stash on public transport or under an office desk.

The Brompton, manufactured in London, is a world-famous success story – over a million have been sold. Brompton have essentially only one product, which they have improved and developed incrementally. However, one significant innovation has been the use of titanium parts on some models. It's also relatively light, which is a factor when the cycle is carried as well as when it's ridden.

Another variation has been the Brompton G Line. It's a multi-terrain cycle with new frame geometry, larger 20″ wheels and fatter tyres. However, some owners point out they are still waiting for Brompton to make it easier to fix a rear wheel puncture!

It's now nearly four decades since Andrew Ritchie invented the Brompton. He struggled in the early days after being ignored by the bicycle industry. However, investors finally appeared and Brompton have developed beyond anyone's imagination,

The electric-assist version of the Brompton.

while remaining an independent company. The company is innovative with its marketing and owner services. They offer hire contracts and security lockers. There's Brompton Renewed, a programme offering lightly-used, refurbished bikes at discounts of up to 20%. There are also get-togethers of Brompton owners in many parts of the world, and the company itself organises the Brompton World Championships.

A standard 16″ wheel Brompton.

The recently introduced multi-terrain G Line Brompton with 20″ wheels

Carry Me

Transport experts talk of mixed-mode transport and micromobility. One of the simplest solutions is a cycle which you can fold in seconds to take on any public transport, and betweentimes you can wheel it along when it's folded.

The aluminium-alloy CarryMe is designed to do all this. It may look a touch delicate but it's robust and has been enjoyed by fans for decades. It weighs only 8.5kg (19lbs): partly due to its small wheels, but the downside of small wheels can be felt over poor surfaces. Its four-step fold takes around 15 seconds.

The CarryMe is designed and manufactured by Taiwanese manufacturer Pacific Cycles led by George Lin, who has a long history of successful cycle creations. Pacific are also consultants and manufacturers for some high-end brands of specialised cycles in Europe and the USA.

The CarryMe is sold all over the world but it's most popular in Asia, especially in Japan and Taiwan where it has become something of a 'travel lifestyle cult' for many. Riders share their mixed-mode journeys and adventures on social media. The CarryMe's travel case trailer is often part of these activities.

Pacific also produce a tricycle version, the CarryAll, aimed at people with balance problems, or disabilities.

Bicymple Novo

The aim is minimalism: direct-drive with a freewheel – a concept around in the late 1880s but improved by modern technology. It's fundamental to the Bicymple, developed by a couple of cycling entrepreneurs in the USA. It's more than a concept bike and is fun to ride, as long as you are ready, like the 'penny farthing' riders before you, to let your legs and feet swivel in the direction you are turning the wheel. It's a one-size-fits-most cycle, with enough adjustability for riders from 1.6m to 2m (5′3″ to 6′5″). The single-speed version, with dual hydraulic disc brakes, takes you to speeds of around 10 mph (16kph). The other version has a two-speed hub which gets you up to 15mph (24kph), so you can keep up with your friends.

Sandwichbike

There's flat-pack furniture so why not a flat-pack bike sent to you by post in a box? The Sandwichbike, brainchild of Bleijh, a Dutch industrial design studio, is engineered as a 'sandwich' of two highly weather-resistant sections of layered plywood. Using what are essentially two wooden plates gives the freedom of printing and cutting techniques. Once you have had the satisfaction of putting your sandwich bike together you own something functional, attractive and durable. If you don't fancy self-assembly the makers can send you your Sandwichbike ready to ride.

217

Fun on Four

The Zox 4 and the Zox4 Hi

Riding solo on four wheels has a quality all of its own. Some just prefer it to other formats. Others like it because they haven't been able to steer confidently on three wheels. They also like the reassurance of stability which four wheels give, and the increased cargo capacity is important to some. The German company Zox produce mainly recumbent trikes, but now offer their Zox 4, and their Zox 4 Hi which has a higher seat position. The electric-assist powers each rear wheel separately so each can be switched on or off as needed. Both versions can be split into two parts for transportation or storage, and a windscreen/roof is available.

Trikes to Fold

Tricycles can be hard to stow or store. Delta trikes (one wheel to front) often have a single frame fold, but you still end up with a difficult package. The Etnnic, from Spain, uses a 'tadpole' format, giving a different (most say better) riding experience. This format cleverly allows the wheels to hinge inwards, giving a full fold. Etnnic also make non-folding versions, and electric versions of each type.

Bikes
from
Bamboo

A concept cycle by Werk Arts in Hawaii, where bamboo is seen as an invasive species.

Why bamboo? It is, of course, an abundant and renewable resource that grows fast and absorbs carbon dioxide. But it's also light and has an ideal strength-to-weight ratio for bicycle frames. Bamboo has a higher specific tensile strength than steel and outclasses concrete in terms of specific compressive strength, which helps control vibration for a more comfortable ride. Bamboo is also versatile: you can cut and join it relatively easily to create many possible configurations.

A lot depends on how the frame is jointed together. High-end cycle makers tend to use carbon-fibre lugs, creating beautiful cycles but denting the sustainability quotient. The alternative is to use layers of resin-saturated flax to form what used to be called lugs. This can result in a bulbous shape which is often left in a natural colour. Others choose to shape these lugs to a more conventional profile and paint them.

Bamboo is not used for cycle forks for reasons of precision, not of strength. Nor is it generally used for handlebars, although Passchier in New Zealand make bamboo laminate bars, their slight natural flex adding to ride comfort. The technology of bamboo bikes has peppered the globe with passionate innovators.

A production cycle from Ghana Bamboo Bikes. They employ around 80 young men and women making various designs of cycle from the bamboo on their doorstep, and they export them worldwide.

Dad made our bike! A first time bamboo bike build using plans from instructables.com.

219

▲ *Calfee are a leading Californian tandem maker. They have a supportive commercial relationship with Booomers Bamboo Bikes in Ghana. Calfee also supply DIY bamboo bike kits in the USA.*

A bike made from a Calfee DIY kit. ▶

▲ *Bambikes are a social enterprise in the Philippines making a crazy variety of bamboo cycles. They use them for the eco-tours they run.*

The Bamboo Bicycle Club (BBC)

These people don't sell you complete bikes. First come detailed conversations, then they send you a home-build kit. They reckon it takes 12 to 16 hours to put a cycle together, thanks to preformed lugs which the bamboo tubes glue straight into. The diameter of tubing is predetermined, having been split and rejoined for uniformity. So no frame jig needed.

Alternatively you can build your bike under supervision in the BBC's workshop in London, working from basics or with preformed parts. The frame designs include road, hybrid, track, MTB, fatbike, tandem and children's balance bike. There's also a custom kit, but it's not for beginners.

The BBC was founded in 2012 by engineer James Marr and has become a community of learners, makers and users. Members connect, exchange ideas, and inspire one another. James works with universities to continually test prototype technology for bikes in bamboo. It lends itself well to prototyping due to its inherent strength and to not needing initial investment in moulds or weldings. James shares his knowledge with BBC members and through educational programmes in schools.

Commuter bike by Becca. She made it herself from a kit at the Bicycle Bamboo Club workshop. She opted for smoothed-off resin-layered joints.

BBC construction plans for a custom build.

The BBC's e-cargo trike is an affordable delivery cycle with a load capacity of 250kg (550lbs). It's available in kit form using bamboo, flax, recycled aluminium and commercially available cycle parts including a differential drive.

Open Source Cycle-Making

XYZ Cargo is a movement as well as a social enterprise. It originated in Copenhagen in 2011 under the splendid name of 'Urban Realm Art Collective N 55' and there are now sub-producers in Denmark, Germany, Spain and the UK. Their aim is to create affordable cycles based on bolted, modular construction using simple designs described as orthogonal ('involving right angles'), aided by advanced 3D design tools. These cycles are conceived to be easy to customise, rebuild and recycle. XYZ Cargo cycles aim to encourage DIY ingenuity and participation instead of 'rigid predefined solutions'. Any frame built can be rebuilt and adapted as needs change or can be recycled as raw materials.

It's open-source, so people can build their own XYZ Cargo under a Creative Commons license. But it must not be for financial gain and any resulting design must also sit under Creative Commons licencing. Clients tend to be in the third sector, and mainly community groups. The UK sub-producer, based in Edinburgh, sells complete cycles but also runs workshops for self-builders. Models built in the UK are CE rated and use components from reputable manufacturers.

XYZ Cargo see themselves as an alternative small business model based on principles of fair, local and environmentally responsible production.

XYZ offer supported self-build sessions: this one in ▶
Edinburgh.

A Fondness for Oneness

Photo: Jason Patient.

In 2006 a video was released which amazed millions. *Into the Thunder Dragon* showed the breathtaking adventures of Kris Holm and Nathan Hoover as they unicycled across the massively mountainous Kingdom of Bhutan. It boosted, almost overnight, the popularity of municycling (mountain unicycling).

At the other end of the wheeled universe are unicycle fans who use theirs mainly for short journeys, especially commuting and shopping. It's faster than walking and needs less effort. It leaves both hands free to carry a load (or an umbrella). You can also take a unicycle on buses and underground trains, and into shops and offices, without ever having to fold it. Unicycles are great for inspiring children to learn balance and in Japanese schools they are often an item of play equipment. Unicycling is about individuality and mastering unique challenges. It also harks back to the days of the high bicycle, where direct drive to a single wheel gave a sense of simplicity and of intimacy with your cycle.

There are many other ways to unicycle. There's racing, on machines with a standard 24″ wheel. The 100m record stands at around 13 seconds. There is also an unrestricted class at some race events. This gives freedom of expression to those who like to ride big wheels (up to about 43″) without restrictions on crank length or other forms of gearing. A typical offroad unicycle has a fat mountain bike tyre, a strong 24″ to 29″ wheel, disc brake, and sometimes a front handle.

Artistic unicycling has become especially popular in Japan, the USA and Puerto Rico. It has something in common with figure skating but toe loops and salchows are replaced with moves such as wheel-walking, spins and riding without saddle. There are also pairs and group categories.

From 'Into the Thunder Dragon'. Photo: Kris Holm and Nathan Hoover.

223

Fantasy and Wonder

If it can be pedalled it can become mobile art, enabling artists and creatives to introduce movement, dynamism and surprise to any event or public space. The cycle becomes an incursive platform for the exotic, abnormal and challenging.

Eric Staller is an American mixed-media artist and inventor living and working in Amsterdam. He uses cycles as art on the move, emphasising wonder, love and community. His Bubbleheads, for example, is a kind of human light show crossing Amsterdam at night to create pleasure and amazement amongst people just going about their business. Staller has also created multi-seater 'circlecycles'. He began with the 'Octos',

shown here giving a performance at the Nagoya Museum of Art in Japan. This he developed into the famous (and commercially available) 'Conference Bike'. It was once used in the UK for a 'peace conference' between rival youth gangs. Another Staller cycle-work is the 'Love Cycle': *"I wanted to offer a bike that two people could use; an artwork to ride, inspired by hotrods and valentines."*

Photo: Julianne Mangin.

A particular phenomenon in the USA is kinetic sculpture races. Teams work all year on imaginative creations, which must perform on the day according to specific event rules. They may look great, or perhaps just crazy, but they also have to stay the challenging course. These participants in the Baltimore Kinetic Sculpture Race have to demonstrate their vehicles through 15 miles (24km) of streets, sand, mud, and river. Some creations go for style and practicality and others, such as this mobile terrace of buildings needed an ingenious transition from pedalling on road to pedalling on water. The 'no parking' signs transformed into rudders.

The 'Bug', a creation of Vincent le Bodo, a cycle-loving artist and sculptor in le Havre, France. As it passes by it reveals its inner nature, consisting of a team of humans pedalling away. *Photos: Jorge Nunes.*

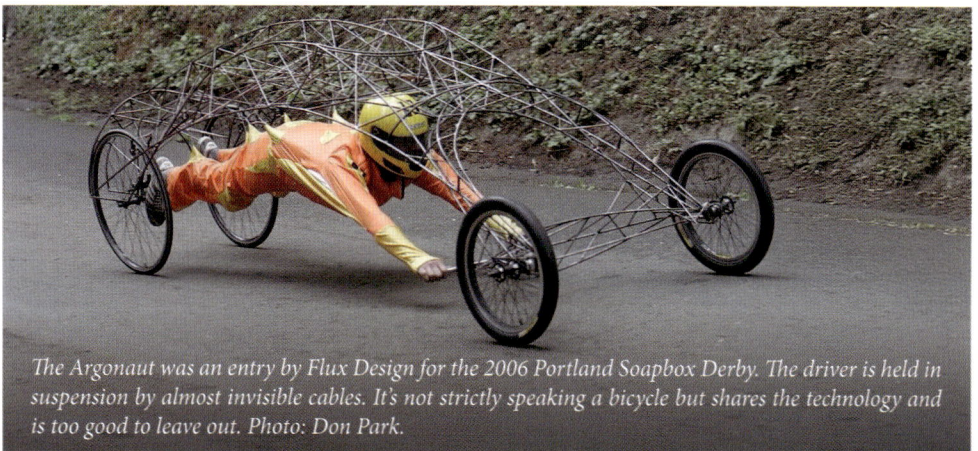

The Argonaut was an entry by Flux Design for the 2006 Portland Soapbox Derby. The driver is held in suspension by almost invisible cables. It's not strictly speaking a bicycle but shares the technology and is too good to leave out. Photo: Don Park.

Fun at the Fair

The Velocipede Carousel, made in France in around 1892, here making a guest appearance on Governor's Island, New York, in 2013.

People have always enjoyed leisure technology which takes them out of themselves. There's a role for the loud, brash and powerful, but there's also a role for human-powered devices which intrigue and excite.

Even better are attractions which depend on people creating their own, human-powered fun: actively creating the experience themselves.

We look forward to the first theme park in the world where everything is pedal-powered and operates at net zero. Surely its time has to come soon.

Pedal power allows performers to move through large crowds and interact. Cargo trikes are used by Island Entertainments of Tasmania for their Sea Shanty Circus amongst other things.

'Looping Bikes' are often seen at Dutch and German fairs and fêtes. Photo courtesy of the operators, augie.nl.

Not quite cycling, but these are still human-powered wheels. In many parts of south east Asia you can see ferris wheels enlivened by agile young men climbing round the spokes using their ever-shifting bodyweight to keep the wheel turning – their acrobatics are part of the show. This example is from Mandalay in Myanmar. Photo: John Bauer.

Something for the children at a closed-road neighbourhood event in York.

Performers from Thomas Trilby Entertainment in the UK. For more about stiltwalking on bikes visit stiltwalkers.co.uk.

Local fairs and fêtes offer opportunities for cycling organisations to present cycling options which people might not have thought of.

Circus Cycling

Beijing circus acrobats demonstrate the traditional 'peacock' display. Photo: Alan Jay Quesada.

Wiki Commons.

The prize-winning China National Acrobatic Troupe.

The early days of the bicycle came as a gift for circuses. It was relatively cheap as a circus item, easily transported, needed no complex setting up, and extended comic potential in a thousand ways. 'Funny scenes on bicycles and rollerskates' proclaims the poster below, for a tour of Germany by Barnum and Bailey's Greatest Show on Earth in 1900. The high bicycle had been introduced just three decades previously, and the safety bicycle just fifteen years previously.

Pedal power still had novelty value and potential for entertainment.

Circuses began exploring the wider potential of cycle technology. Extremely high unicycles wowed the public. Clowns bumped along on bikes with eccentric-wheels, made using spokes with varying lengths. There were also performers who could ride a normal-looking bicycle around the rink while progressively discarding parts of it until they were pedalling nothing but a unicycle.

Photo: Shizhao.

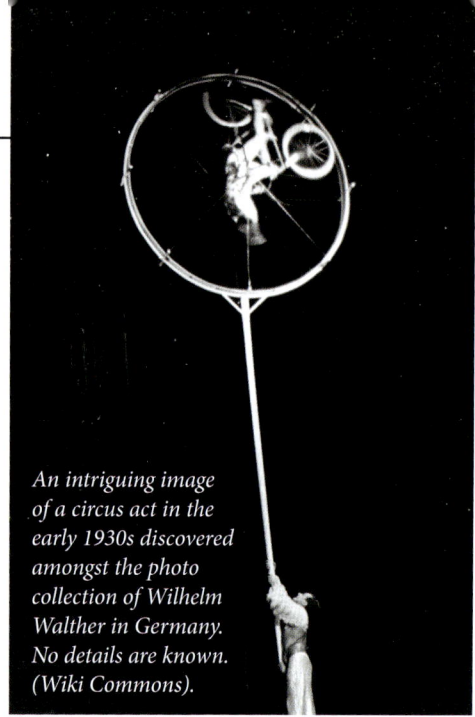

An intriguing image of a circus act in the early 1930s discovered amongst the photo collection of Wilhelm Walther in Germany. No details are known. (Wiki Commons).

Not all cycling acrobatics were confined to the circus rink. 'Professor Arion' (American daredevil Frank Donahue) cycled over the Niagara Falls on a high wire. In 1897 he attempted to ride over a 70 foot high-wire in Long Island. The wire had 500 volts running through it so as to illuminate his costume and bicycle. He fell to his death.

Circuses began featuring comedic acts involving bicycles and some synchronised riding, but the western world was soon introduced to the splendour and ability of Chinese circus acrobats on cycles. They create spectacle to this day with performances moving through a crescendo of difficulty, often ending with the customary tableau vivant where the whole team forms a radiant display on a single bicycle, like a peacock displaying its feathers.

Acrobatic performances on specialised cycles make gorgeous entertainment, amaze the masses and create a sense of wonder and optimism. But acrobatics are also a significant element of traditional Chinese culture and national character. They challenge the limits of artistic movement and mental strength. The Chinese maintain it also helps develop wisdom and self-control. Chinese acrobats bring modern innovations to inherited traditions.

Performers are generally selected around the age of five. Many are brought by their parents from poor rural areas in China to audition in the big cities. Selected children will endure around 8,000 hours of practice by the age of 10. It's a hard apprenticeship, but one which offers a chance of an education, better life opportunities and foreign travel.

Cyclecide

We use bicycles not just as vehicles but as a medium for expressing our interests in art, music, and performance. We see the cycles as malleable machines that can be altered and transformed for the sake of fun.

So say Cyclecide, a collective of around 15 bike-obsessives based in San Francisco. Their workshops are caves of creativity where bits of expired bikes are transformed into crazy cycling concoctions and where scrapyard metal becomes pedal-powered fairground equipment. Out of this creative labour come weird, whimsical and often elaborate creations to become part of Cyclecide's attractions roadshows.

What started as a club in 1996 is now an in-demand troupe of welders, musicians, clowns and generally strange people. Their energetic performances entertain and challenge the public and often involve bike stunts, acrobatics and jousting. There's a 'Heavy-Pedal Bike Rodeo' and the public can enjoy riding off-beat creations such as tall bikes, choppers, sidecar bikes, cycles with no seats, bumper bikes, swing bikes and

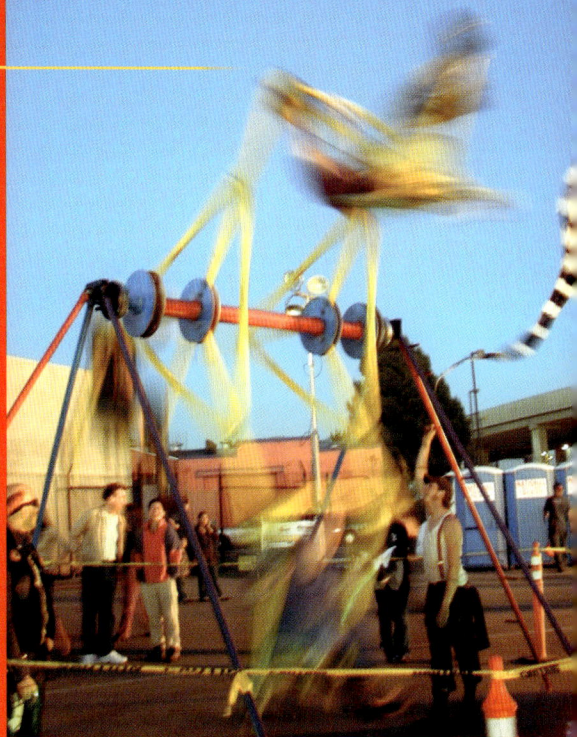

A three-seater ferris wheel developed by Paul the Plumber. Photo: Cyclecide.

customised kids' trikes. Also in their roadshows are pedal-powered fairground rides, designed and built by Cyclecide, and assembled on-site at venues. These include a 'cyclo-fuge', a 'kiddie-carousel', a 'whirl-n-hurl' and a ferris wheel.

It's all mutant merriment taking pedal-power to the edge of the known world.

Cyclecide's pedal-powered whirligig. Photo: Joe Mabel.

Airborne on a pedal powered carousel. Photo: Rhiannon Charisse.

Everybody's Cycling

There are multiple ways to experience the 'cycling message' but few work better than try-out opportunities for people who have lost the culture and habit of cycling. These events need to be fun and supportive, with one-to-one engagement in a traffic-free environment. This is what Everybody's Cycling do. They are a charitable community benefit society who take different forms of bike try-out events and bike loan programmes to city centres, schools, workplaces and community groups.

Everybody's Cycling are based in York, England, and are supported by 52 community shareholders. Their mission is to introduce, encourage and enable. To do this they maintain a large fleet of cycles, selected to balance showmanship with the conventional and the practical. High quality everyday cycles are mixed in with cargo cycles, tandems, tricycles and a few downright exotic machines to draw the crowds. The charity is particularly strong in their disability work and have a fleet of cycles

A pedal-powered wedding near York, England. Around 40 guests accompanied the bride and bridegroom, Laura and David, to the reception. The cycles were supplied by Everybody's Cycling who also provided their pedal-powered 'Bubble Frog' as shown in action above.

dedicated to visiting special schools, care homes and disability support groups.

Everybody's Cycling also operate a range of static pedal-powered 'happening machines'. These include some staples such as a slot-car racing game and a smoothie maker, but there are also unusual music machines and fun devices in the manner of fairground attractions. Popular is the Light-o-Matic: as the rider cranks up the power lights come on in sequence. When the top light is reached the rider is rewarded by a sound and lights show. The operator can alter the resistance level for different users.

Everybody's Cycling also has a pedal-powered velodrome, where two riders compete, with the progress of each shown by the moving LEDs on the track.

The author of this book is a minor community shareholder in Everybody's Cycling Community Benefit Society.

The Light-o-Matic and the Velodrome racing game.

High bikes, each with a different frame design, in Portland, Oregon, USA. Photo: Jonathan Maus.

Kustom Kulture

Builders of exotic cycles like to let their fantasies run free. They create off-beat cycles to amuse, fascinate and inspire. Working alone or with friends, they generally aim for something special, even unique.

Lovers of cycling exotica seem to have a fascination for pedal-powered furniture: sofas, radiators, toilets, bedsteads and more. You might say they are demonstrating the versatility and universal applicability of pedal-power, but you might also say it's beautifully pointless and there to raise a laugh. The sofacycle was made by Mike West.

The Japanese are known for their melding of the old and the new. They design hoodies to look like traditional kimonos. This modern referencing to old crafts inspired this bicycle created by a student named simply Enji, as part of his graduation project. His bicycle honours the traditional lattice work seen on sliding door panels in traditional Japanese rooms and set into the walls of shrines. (@enjiblossomlily)

The Boxer Rocket says 1930s airliners, Flash Gordon, Jules Verne, Wallace and Gromit. It was produced briefly in the UK around 2015 by designer and engineer Jeremy Davies.

This bicycle is rideable. The wheels don't roll at all but an inner section of their tyres is a continuous tread rotating round the hidden rollers at each corner and powered by bicycle chain under the tread. It's a form of caterpillar track. Transmission from the rider is through a chain to one of the rollers. It was made by a team called 'The Q' and you can see it in action on YouTube ('Insane Square Cycling').

Popular amongst amateur fabricators is the swing cycle, a generic terms for cycles with a second steering axis just below the saddle. It means that as you ride you can bring the two halves of the bike close to running parallel. It's not as hard as it looks and it's fun. This is a swing cycle made by the Angels Chopper Bicycle Club in Victoria BC, Canada. Photo: Bruce Dean.

The Cercle Cycle from the UK is made for high-riding, self-sufficient touring. It incorporates a bed, a chair and a table. The cycle also serves as a frame for a full-cover tent. Photo: Cercle the World.

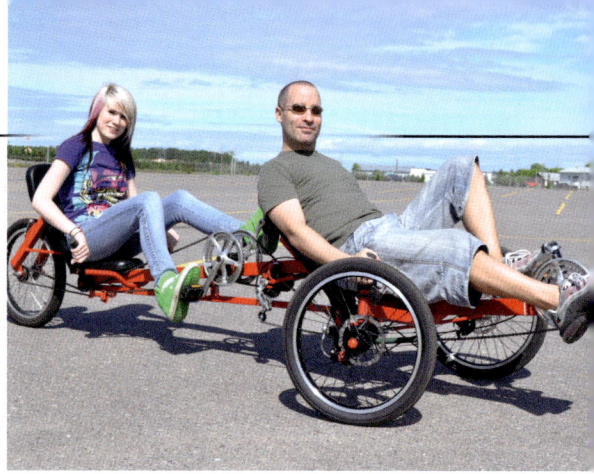

Atomic Zombie

To see how far the definition of 'bicycle' can be pushed visit the website Atomic Zombie *(www. atomiczombie.com)*. It's an international community of amateur cycle fabricators with a love of experimentation. Members share their projects, knowledge, techniques and ideas, and many make DIY construction plans available. There are more than 4,000 creations in the site's builders' gallery and the builders' forum gives insights into creative processes and technology. Some show their work at local community fairs and fêtes: to educate, inspire and raise awareness of the potential and accessibility

of basic cycle technology. Pictured here are some Atomic Zombie creations which verge on the practical, but there is also a medley of more off-the-wall creations on the Atomic Zombie website. The development of Atomic Zombie has been driven by Brad Graham and Kathy McGowan (above), based in Ontario, Canada. Brad is an inveterate inventor and fabricator. His passion was sparked off on a visit to the local rubbish tip. He had no particular interest in bikes but noticed a few bits of cycle here and there and suddenly felt moved to take them home. The rest of the story is not hard to guess.

The Cyclebully electric trailer pushes the bike along.

Orders of Madness

The Ambigram offers surprise and puzzlement. It has the elements of a bicycle but how does it work? Can you ride it? Is it upside down?

A custom build for a client.

> **66** *We create tailor-made works of art. We make the boldest bicycle dreams come true.* **99**

So claim the Polish company Mad Bicycles. One of their boldest creations is *Materialize*, which took three years of design and experimentation in 3D printing and spray-on chrome technology. It consists of 11 parts sliding onto a steel, laser-cut frame, with gold-chromed cubes intersecting to resemble a crystal of pyrite. It can be categorised as a 'show bike' but has an electric motor and can reach 30mph (48kph).

Mad Bicycles aim to give their clients the chance to own and ride a unique and amazing bike. The designer interprets the client's aspirations to create something imaginative and personalised. Their client base ranges from individuals to corporates but they also work on experimental projects of their own – mostly ridable but some not. Started in a basement, developed in a garage, the company has become one of the biggest design and manufacturing studios for custom bikes in Europe. And probably in the world.

Sun Power

Sun Trips

The Sun Trip phenomenon deserves to be better known. It's a series of international human/solar powered long distance races. One version, for example, takes riders 7000km (4.500 miles) from Brussels to the Baltic States, then on a long, mountainous loop down to Romania, Italy and France. Riders clock up around 300km (200 miles) a day and riding is allowed only from 6am to 9pm. The Sun Trip, says one participant, is a great mix of adventure, sport, people and amazing landscapes. It's also a showcase for new forms of mobility. Each adventurer is an ambassador for solar energy and eco-mobility, demonstrating their efficiency and human scale.

En route for the ascent of the Col du Galibier in the French Alps during the 2023 Sun Trip.

Box trike solar conversions

Noël Wilmes is well known as the cycling hairdresser of Maastricht in the Netherlands. He uses his Babboe Carve bakfiets (cargo trike), equipped with solar panels, to ride around 3500km (2000 miles) a year on client visits. In summer he can do this without needing to plug in. In winter the solar cargo bike's efficiency dips to 5% of its summer output, so Noel supplements with mains charging. The outside panels are designed to tuck into the box for storage. Noël cycled his solar-powered cargo cycle to the World Climate Summit in Glasgow to demonstrate solar-powered cycling to delegates. He has set up a company, *solfie.nl*, to market and fit solar-power units to cargo cycles.

Wind power

The Whike is a cycle and a yacht at the same time. You can cycle-sail for impressive distances on roads, or take part in exciting land sailing events. It was created in 2007 by Fredjan Twigt in the Netherlands to combine his love of cycling and sailing and has been in production ever since. The frame is built for maximum stability and control under sail. The wheel hubs are custom-made to withstand powerful lateral pressures. Whiking is road legal for both roads and cycle paths, even under sail, in the Netherlands, the UK and possibly most other countries.

CHAPTER 7
Cycle Sport

Performance, entertainment, controversy

The Urge to Compete

The 'Ultimo Giro' by Jeff Parr.

Cycle sport was born of our natural urge to compete and on a machine which wondrously magnified the athlete's powers – creating excitement and spectacle. This encouraged personal and community achievement at a local level, with local fans. Then came regulation, quantification, record-keeping, globalisation, bureaucracy and commercial interests. An Australian track racer could compete against the recorded time and distance of a Swedish track racer who had died 20 years before.

Meanwhile, a rich hinterland of amateurs has come to populate cycle sport. They compete for the pleasure and the challenge in locally organised events: road and track races, triathlons, MTB competitions, sportives and more. These are also the people who go out alone or with their club each week, wearing lycra similar to the professionals, partly because it's the right clothing for that kind of cycling, but also because many of these weekend amateurs feel an affinity and connection to professional cycle sport. They follow their favourite teams and heroes, though not in any naïve way. Drug scandals have never gone away gone away, and now we hear much more of 'mechanical doping' (tiny concealed electric motors).

Performance statistics and rankings for local amateurs are usually for purely local interest and not taken too seriously. But for professionals those stats and results can be everything, and obsession is personally limiting.

Cycle sport draws in some very varied people. There are dedicated high-performance cyclists who care little for the broader significance of the bicycle to society, and hardly ever ride for everyday reasons; and there are eco-warriors who see cycle sport as an insignificant distraction. And there are the millions of happy cyclists in between.

Cycling professionals are designated as role models and provide the stories and inspiration which draw youngsters (and others) into the local cycling clubs, and some of these young cyclists move into higher level cycle sport, perhaps even with ambitions to represent their country. Stupendous cycling feats by popular professionals mean more kids are keen to emulate their heroes.

Such is the conventional, reassuring wisdom in cycle sport, and there is no doubt some truth in that. But some critics see professional cycle sport and, in fact, virtually all high-level sport, as having low social value. They argue that going a tiny bit faster or further or more cleverly than someone else does not add much to the happiness of the world. There is precious little evidence, they say, that professional sport makes inactive people active. Some go further, saying that high level cycle sport simply puts the unfit and fearful general public off cycling. This cannot be the case. The public have seen enough everyday cyclists in their daily lives to know that cycle sport inhabits a different and separate world. Perhaps it's a world alien to many people's lives. Do the achievements of the professionals indeed draw young people into amateur cycle sport or others into everyday cycling? Or does pro cycle sport offer nothing of great significance to the wellbeing of the many? The debate goes on, and there's precious little attitudinal research to help us understand. And is there any point in trying to?

Cycling has been reborn as a solution to humanity's ills, but cycle sport, and professional cycle sport in particular, are usually left out of that sentiment. A radically minded minority of cyclists feel that international cycle sport in its current form is at odds with the global climate emergency. It would not function without the air miles of thousands of competitors and millions of travelling spectators, but that can be said of many sports. In their development plan, Agenda 2030, the Union Cycliste Internationale (UCI) has fine things to say about the significance of the problem but no practical solutions are offered.

Wiki Commons.

Young Iranians practising Freestyle BMXing in their local park. Where does fun stop and sport begin?

The trickle-down theory

Top level cycle design feeds an appetite for speed and specialisation. It has spawned cycle technology which is reasonably accessible to most of us. We can go out and buy the kinds of bike and equipment which are pretty close to what the top professionals use. There has been an overall rise in product quality over the last forty years but this is not in itself 'trickle-down'. They were already selling aluminium frames in the 1890s. Carbon fibre has rarely entered the mass cycle market, nor should it. Aerodynamic improvements, such as the exotic helmet designs for time trialists verge on the comical and have little relevance to non-competitive cyclists. There are some fantastic components these days, but it's likely that none of them have been critical in the decisions people make as to whether to become cyclists or not.

You can enjoy your bike, and the new technology which cycle sport has bequeathed us. No-one is obliged to engage with cycle sport or even have views on it. Plenty enjoy following cycle sport and not ride a bike. But if it's cycle sport which gets you cycling and keeps you cycling then that's great for you and for the rest of us. But it was never intended to change the world. Perhaps no sport has ever done that.

Ultimo Giro (page opposite) is the work of Jeff Parr, a British artist living in Savoie, France. After a career as an artist and graphic designer for theatres and television Jeff began a new life amongst the French Alps, famed for so many feats and legends of cycling. His passion was always professional cycle racing and he was soon expressing it in his full-time work as an artist. His Ultimo Giro is his homage to the Giro d'Italia, the country's equivalent to the Tour de France. As the peloton flashes by we see 'Il Giro' taking its honoured place in the cultural landscape of Italy. For more on Jeff Parr and his work visit jeffparr-veloart.com.

Road Racing and Time Trialling

The Giro d'Italia 2024.

The great cycling races on the calendar are epics with heroes. Finishing a single stage of the Tour de France demands the kind of physical fitness and psychological resilience beyond most mortals. Life in the peloton of riders is hectic and dangerous as individuals ride as close as possible for aerodynamic benefit. And then, after a gruelling 200km (120 miles) or more, they've got to do it all again the next day.

In other areas of cycle sport professional single-day race distances can take riders up to 300km (200 miles) and even beyond, either from place-to-place or around a circuit. A criterium race involves laps of a closed-road circuit within a single town or city.

Other race formats are place-to-place but ending with laps of a circuit for the benefit of spectators. Some races, known as handicaps, match riders of different abilities and ages.

A World Championships city centre criterium race in Leuven. Belgium, 2021. Photo: Arjan van den Oudenrijn.

The drama final sprint ending Stage 18 of the 2024 Giro d'Italia. Belgian Tim Merlier pips Italian Jonathan Milan by a few centimetres.

When races are in consecutive daily stages the competitor with the lowest cumulative time to complete all stages becomes the overall, or General Classification (GC), winner. Stage races can incorporate other classifications and awards. You can, for example, be an individual stage winner, a points winner, or a mountain climber classification winner ('King of the Mountains'). A stage race can also be a series of road races and individual or team time trials. Important is the aggregate time for completing all stages, so you can win overall without having won all or any of the individual stages. Three-week stage races are called Grand Tours. The professional road racing calendar includes three Grand Tours – the Giro d'Italia, the Tour de France, and the Vuelta a España.

Time-trialists compete against the clock. Riding alone they are not allowed to slipstream other riders, so need to minimise their individual aerodynamic drag. They use low aero bars to give a tucked position, combined with aerodynamic tubing and helmets, and tri-spoke or disc wheels. Time trial races tend to be much shorter than road races, so comfort is less of an issue. Also, control of the bike is less important since there is little chance of bumping another rider. However, there are also team time trials (TTTs), where competitors are, unlike solo time-trialists, allowed to 'draft' in the slipstream of successive teammates.

In both team and individual time trials competitors start the race at staggered times, keeping everything fair and equal.

Ultra-distance races are very long single stage events usually lasting several days, but with the race clock ticking remorselessly from start to finish. Riders take breaks of their choosing and the first over the finish line is the winner. Among the best-known is the Race Across America (RAAM), a coast-to-coast single-stage of around 4,800km (3,000 miles) in about a week.

The radical aerodynamics of a triathlon rider. Photo: Cube Cycles.

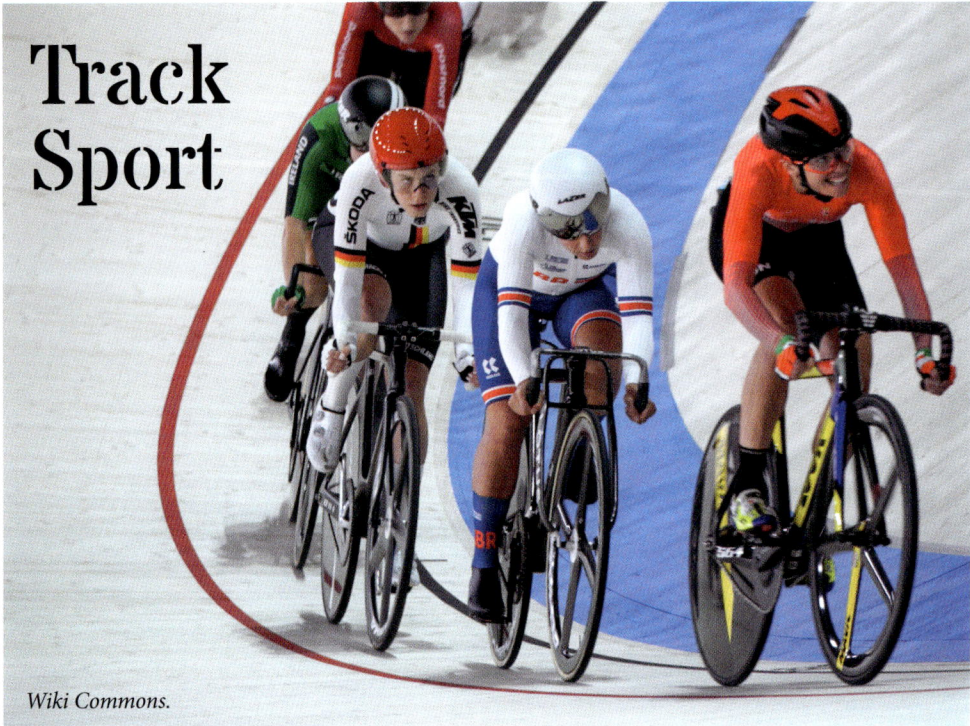

Wiki Commons.

The women's 'points race' at the 2022 European Track Championships: 125 laps including 12 sprints. Photo: Tim Rademacher.

Riders whoosh around the smooth, banked tracks of a velodrome, on bikes with a single gear, no brakes and a high bottom bracket so that pedals clear the banking. On a 250 metre track the banking at each end of the two short straights can reach 50 degrees, and riders can use this height by climbing right up to

Riders from several local clubs competing on the track of the Brownlee Cycling Centre, Leeds. Photo: Otley Cycling Club.

the edge of the track before plunging down to attack. It's a question of race performance versus strength, reliability and safety. There's a thrilling elegance to track racing. On the smooth tracks, with little air resistance, speeds can reach 80kph (50mph), so the stakes are high. Spectators can see every part of the track, raising the excitement levels.

The Track Cycling World Championships, regulated by the UCI, include various disciplines and distances: time trial, keirin, individual pursuit, team pursuit, points race, scratch race, sprint, team sprint, omnium, madison and elimination race. Women's events are generally shorter than men's.

Closed-circuit outdoor tracks, found all over the world, are important community assets. Some are banked, some flat, and circuit distance is typically two kilometres. Outdoor circuits are mostly used by local cycle clubs and may have a clubhouse attached. They can also give a home to other cycling activities, such as sessions for riders with disabilities on adapted cycles.

Not every city has a velodrome, so it's not exactly an accessible sport. However, many velodromes offer a beginner's package involving bike hire and a training session: novices have to be confident and safe going at exhilarating speeds on a banked track, and with back-pressure on the pedals as the only way to slow down. It's an unforgettable experience.

Grass track events are ideal for entry level racing. They can be organised on any flat field, including unused sports fields. The track itself can be marked out accurately, so that times can be compared over a series of events, or it can be laid out as a rough oval of markers with a start/finish line. Races are usually short so that riders can experience different race types at any single event. Photo: John Mullin.

Keirin

Keirin racing is the predominant form of competitive cycling in Japan. It's a high-risk event on an indoor banked track. Riders start in single file and jockey for position behind a pacer: it's the human equivalent of greyhound racing.

For the first 1500 metres of the 2000 metre race the pacer continuously cranks up the speed. Spectators bet on the outcome, then watch as their riders choose their positions. When the pacer gets up to around 45kph, and with two or so laps to go, he slopes off the track leaving the riders to explode into a sprint for the line at speeds of up to 70kph.

Keirin has spread worldwide and became an Olympic sport with the 2000 Sydney Games, making it the second Olympic event after judo to originate from Japan.

Paul Keller. Wiki Commons.

245

MTB Sport

Colourbox.

In the early 1970s, after a century of incremental bicycle development, a radically different type of bike appeared, to be later known as the mountain bike or MTB. With it came new attitudes and rapid advances in technology. Many of the forms of MTB sport have been taken under the regulatory care of the Union Cycliste Internationale.

The breed has fragmented. There was a short window of time when a mountain bike was a mountain bike was a mountain bike. Now a broad spectrum of types fill multiple niches and specialisms.

MTB technology has set a fast pace. Modern mountain bike designers need to understand the complexities, and interplay, of lots of factors including platform-valving, high and low speed compression and rebound damping, axle paths and multi-pivot geometry. This technology is powered by the demands for high performance specialisation in competitive sport or solo off-road performance. It is producing some remarkable cycles and components, and the phenomenon is not stopping.

Competitive mountain bike riding can take many forms. One variety is cross-triathlon: races involving an open water swim, mountain biking and trail running.

Wiki Commons.

Downhilling

Well-armoured riders plunge down steep, rough courses and the fastest to the finish wins. A downhill bike needs massive front and rear suspension, large disc brakes and a particularly strong frame. These bikes are almost impossible to ride back up the hill for another descent. So riders usually return by ski lift or motor vehicle. Photo: Steve Peat by Andy Cole.

Akin to downhilling is enduro – usually a one-day event consisting of a long descending course, over several types of terrain. Scoring is complex, with points won on the downhill parts. It requires both downhilling and general cross-country cycling.

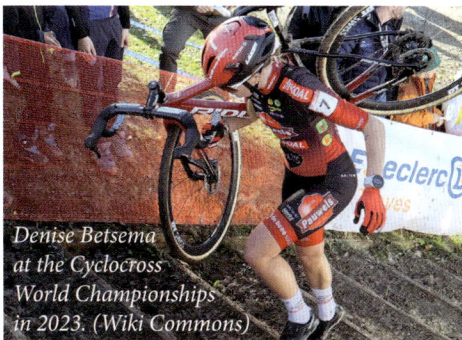

Denise Betsema at the Cyclocross World Championships in 2023. (Wiki Commons)

Cyclo-cross

This predates MTB sport. It shares characteristics with some MTB specialisms, but with cycles more related to road bikes. The terrain is usually varied and often muddy, so bikes are usually carried for short stretches. Success often depends deciding when to switch between riding and carrying. Races take place largely in Europe, in autumn and winter.

Wiki Commons.

XCMTB

Cross-country mountain biking (XCMTB) is an Olympic sport based on long distance or lapped races over rough country routes. It combines stamina with refined cycling skills. Photo: Klaus Nielson.

Wiki Commons.

Trials

This is a discipline in which the rider negotiates an obstacle course without putting a foot down. Performances are observed and scored. Competition trial bikes have a distinctive frame geometry and usually no seat. Gearing is low and single-speed, and tyres are under-pressurised, with the rear tyre particularly thick. Photo: Sandro Halank.

HPV Racing

Semi-faired and unfaired machines on a velodrome near Zürich. From the Journal of the Human Power Institute, www.hupi.org. Photo: Michael Ammann.

Human-Powered Vehicles designed for speed are wildly more aerodynamically efficient, making them much faster than a regular bicycle – even faster than a good time-trial bike. Today top-flight HPVs can hit speeds of over 100kph (60mph).

Since 1934 these vehicles have been banned from all competitions regulated by the UCI. Which means from virtually all cycle sport, and this even applies to unfaired recumbents. So the recumbent virtually disappeared for 50 years, until it was rediscovered primarily by MIT professor David Gordon Wilson and his students. They were instrumental in establishing, in the 1970s, the International Human Powered Vehicle Association (IHVPA), to encourage the development, without artificial design restrictions, of all types of human-powered machines on land, sea and air. This led to experimentation with full and partial fairings, and to the new sport of HPV racing. The aim of the fairing or shell is not primarily for crash or weather protection, but for optimised aerodynamics in pursuit of pure speed. HPVs can be bicycles or tricycles: fully enclosed or with the rider's head exposed, so they can see better, hear more and enjoy some cooling, but with some aerodynamic loss. Races are thrilling but are not mass spectator sports: the audience are mainly the makers, technicians and riders, plus some fans and family members. The ambience is a combination of mutual support and ferocious riding.

The terminology is not easy. HPVs can (to be pedantic) include anything we push or pedal. But the term normally refers to fully or partly faired recumbents, usually in racing. The term 'velomobile' is also used for this category, but is additionally applied to more street-friendly fully-faired recumbents where weather-proofing and comfort are prioritised.

Italian Luca Graziani on an Optima Baron lowracer. Photo: recumbent.news.

The world's biggest Human Powered Vehicle race is the 24 hour Australian International Pedal Prix. It forms the grand finale of the Australian HPV Super Series.

The Fastest Bike in the World

In 2013 Aerovelo set their sights on building the world's fastest human-powered vehicle by surpassing the previous level-ground speed record of 133.8 km/h (83.1 mph). In 2015 their HPV, named Eta, did just that and has since bettered the world record four times, most recently with an astounding 144.17kph (89.59 mph).

Eta gets its name from the Greek letter 'eta' used in engineering to denote efficiency, and Aerovelo's project pursues ultimate efficiency. Based on the measured power input of the pilot Eta boasts a highway fuel efficiency equivalent to 9544mpg (4058km per litre), which is 100 times better than the most efficient electric cars. Every aspect is given careful attention – the laminar front shell has no stickers or seams, not to mention a windscreen. The rider is served by cameras mounted above the rear section. *Photo: Bas de Meijer.*

BMX

Mawaruddin.

The starting gate drops and eight riders power down the first hill, then skid and bounce around the dirt track. Multiple humps throw the riders into the air during a frantic, bobbing charge to the finishing line. BMX is thriving, it's thrilling, it's local, it's accessible – and it's also an Olympic sport. BMX racing has youth in its veins. It's also family-oriented and largely participant-driven. At the other end of the spectrum there are professional ranks for both men and women.

BMX racing has spawned the five types of free-style BMXing. In STREET riders perform tricks exploiting street furniture and other challenges in public spaces. PARK is practised on the riding bowls of skateparks. VERT involves two vertical ramps facing each other. The rider powers up each side to perform tricks in the air while completing a 180 degree turn before landing and swooping across for more acrobatics above the opposite ramp. TRAILS riding (some call it DIRT JUMPING) takes place on tracks of compacted earth built up into mounds for jumping over, often in creative ways. These tracks are typically in woodland. FLATLAND riders concentrate on tricks performed only on flat surfaces. It's a specialism lying somewhat separate from the rest of the BMX world.

▲ Street BMX takes the urban environment as its stage and it's usually sociable and informal. Photo: Klankbeeld

▲ Park BMX and freestyle flatland BMX are mainly urban activities featuring established sequences of tricks mixed with improvisation. Here American Mark McGrade performs a difficult flatland trick called a 'plasticman'.

▲'Vert' in Ukraine. Photo: Colourbox.

▲World-famous street trials rider Danny McCaskill of Scotland performs outside the realm of any governing sports body. He rides a cycle lying between MTB and BMX. Photo: Dave Mackison for Adidas Outdoor: 'Welcome to the Family'.

In the Halls

Artistic cycling

Velodromes are not the only form of indoor cycling. In artistic cycling, known in German as *Kunstradfahren*, performers produce a series of 'exercises', akin to gymnastics or ballet, in front of judges. Routines by solo riders, pairs or teams of four or six last five minutes. Pairs can perform on separate bikes or the same one. All cycles are fixed-wheel with gearing close to 1:1.

Artistic cycling is strongest in the German speaking countries and in Belgium, France and the Czech Republic. Almost all artistic cycling clubs have their own specialised courts, which can also double for the sport of 'cycle-ball'.

The best of artistic cycling can be found on YouTube.

▲ *Synchronised moves by a team from Switzerland. Photo: indoorcyclingworldwide.com*

A handstand plus headstand by world-champion artistic cyclists Katrin Schultheis and Sandra Sprinkmeier of Germany. Their specialised bike is clearly visible. ▶

Austria beating Switzerland in the 2014 cycle-ball world cup. Photographer unidentified.

Cycle-ball

Cycle-ball is played with two teams of two, with either player acting as goalkeeper or field player. They use fixed-gear cycles with no brakes or freewheel. The ball, which can travel at up to 60kph (40mph), is propelled with either the front or back wheel. It's forbidden to use hands or feet to control the ball, except within the goal area, where the goalkeeper is allowed to use their hands to catch the ball and to prevent a goal being scored. A game consists of two halves of seven minutes.

Cycle-ball is popular in Austria, Belgium, the Czech Republic, France, Japan, the Netherlands, Russia and Switzerland, but the centre is Germany, where it is known as Radball. It shares a culture with artistic cycling but most competitors specialise in either cycle-ball or artistic cycling, with very few crossing over. In Germany around 10,000 indoor cyclists hold competitive licences for either artistic cycling or cycle-ball.

Unicycle hockey

This is one of those sports which are more popular than most people imagine. Unicycle hockey has five players on each team. There's no dedicated goalkeeper, although one player usually stays back to cover. Unicycles must have a maximum wheel diameter of 61cm (24″) and a tennis ball is used. The governing body is the International Unicycling Federation which publishes the rules for all unicycle sports, including unicycle basketball.

There are three national unicycle hockey leagues: in Australia (11 teams), Germany (around 90 teams), and Switzerland (around 20 teams). There are also clubs and teams in the UK, France, Denmark, Sweden, Hong Kong, Singapore, Taiwan and Korea. International competition takes place at the biennial Unicon World Championships and there are regional tournaments. *Photo: Rob Varadi (unicycle.com).*

253

Specialised Sports around the World

Rowing bikes ▶

While pushing the pedals on a rowing bike you pull the handlebar towards you. This means that all your main muscles work together, adding combined power to your forward movement. Speed is also enhanced by the aerodynamic profile. Competitive riders can hit impressive speeds. In 2009 Theo Homan 'rowed' 1400km (870 miles) London-Edinburgh-London in three days and six hours, coming seventh out of around 600 on standard racing bikes. The sport has a dedicated following, with owners organising their own regular tours and race events. It's a mainly Dutch phenomenon but there are individual enthusiasts in many countries. *Photos: Dirk Thijs*

◀ Cycle speedway

Four riders head-to-head around oval shale tracks. It's explosive, elbow-to-elbow action. There is cycle speedway racing throughout the UK, and it's thought to have originated on old bomb sites after the war. Countries affiliated to the International Cycle Speedway Federation include Ireland, Poland, Australia, the USA and Ukraine.

Cycle speedway takes place on a banked oval track, usually over four laps of a 70 to 90 metre circuit with a shale surface. There's team and individual racing, requiring fitness, skill and tactical awareness. Each race begins from a standing start with a unique rising gate and typically lasts 40 to 50 seconds.

Sheffield versus Leicester. Photo: Jon Pinder.

Race across America ▶

RAAM is a one of the world's longest annual endurance events, taking riders around 3,000 miles (4,800km) from the west coast to the east coast of the United States. It's several hundred miles longer than the Tour de France but is crucially different in that it is not divided into stages: in other words the clock starts when the rider sets off and it does not stop until they arrive at the east coast. The fastest competitors need slightly over seven days to complete the course. All entrants must succeed in rigorous qualifying events before being allowed to take part.

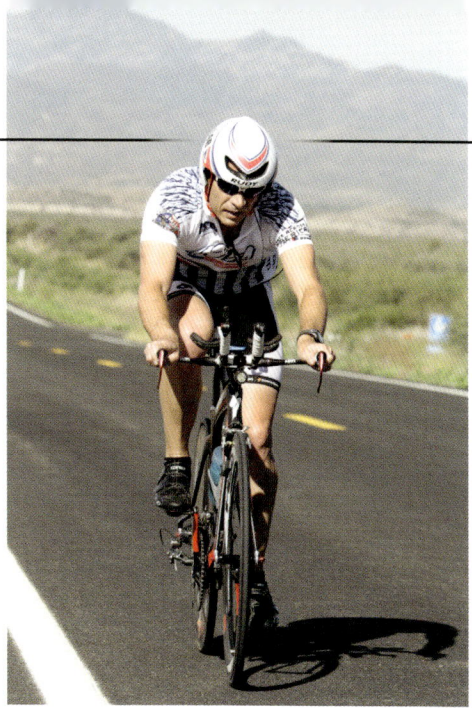

▲ US Air Force Major Justin Martin competing in a Race Across America Photo: US Airforce.

◀ Sidehack racing

A rare and informal sport found here and there worldwide. Pictured is a BMX plus 'sidehack' race in Sitterdorf, Germany. The 'pilot' pedals, steers and brakes. The 'monkey' helps by scooting the outfit up to speed. Then the monkey throws his or her weight around to keep the wheels grounded and to carry speed into the corners.

Trike racing

This is a very British form of cycle racing and requires the skill of cornering at speed to keep more or less on three wheels: by shifting the right amount of bodyweight at just the right time. The cyclists shown are from the tricycle section of Cycle Club Bexley. National racing is organised by the UK's Tricycle Association. *Photo: Martin Purser.*

Unicycle racing ▶

In continental Europe unicycle racing is a big deal but it is also becoming established in the UK. Alongside standard racing comes an exotic variety of unicycle race types, such as wheel-walking and riding one-footed. The IUF (International Unicycling Federation) regulates wheel size and crank length, as both makes a difference to gearing. *Photo: the British National Unicycle Road Race. Unicycle.com.*

◀ Brompton racing

Brompton National and World Championships have an eccentric flavour, with their no-lycra, jacket-and-tie dress code. However, they are highly competitive. There's a le Mans (standing) start to a 15km (9.3 mile) circuit race, with heats. As part of the World Championships are a 500m (547 yards) sprint and a 26km (16 mile) 'marathon'. Those who compete successfully in all three events are eligible for the Brompton Treble, with the winners invited to participate in the annual World Championships. Brompton championships started in Spain and have been in Singapore, but more often in London. *Photo: Prudential RideLondon.*

Bike bog snorkelling ▶

If the definition of a sport requires a mixture of difficulty, competition, entertainment, spectators and record-keeping, then bike bog snorkelling qualifies. The idea for the World Mountain Bike Bog Snorkelling Championship in Llanwrtyd Wells, Wales, originated, as you might expect, in a pub, when, in 1985, a group of friends decided to add a new twist to snorkelling. There'd be an event involving swimming with snorkel in Waen Rhydd Bog, which is filled with dead plants, decaying moss and endless mud. Competitors wore standard diving gear. Twenty years later, it was time to take things to the next level. So they added bikes to the challenge. Each competitor starts with a mask, snorkel and scuba gear and rides a specially adjusted bike with water-filled tyres and a lead-filled bike frame. They compete in wetsuits and wear weight belts.

The race takes place in a 2m deep trench 55 meters in length: out one way, around a pole, and back

to the start. Winners usually complete the course in over a minute. The event has been developed as part of a triathlon, and so is prefaced by a 19km (12 mile) run followed by a 40km (25 mile) mountain cycle.

A rare game of 'penny farthing' polo played in the village of Upper Beeding, West Sussex. Photo: Malcolm Bull.

◀ Bike-polo

Bike-polo in Portland, Oregon. Grass court bike polo such as this is widely played, but is particularly popular in India, with teams of four or five players. Hardcourt bike polo is more recent and saw a surge of interest internationally in the first decade of this century. It has different rules, teams of only three players, and is played in tennis courts or any suitable enclosed space. *Photographer unknown.*

Bikejoring ▶

Bikejoring is a competitive event, mostly in the form of time trials. A team consists of the rider plus one or two dogs. It's well established in Europe and becoming so in the USA. Competitions take place off-road, on soft dirt trails free from problematic obstacles. The time trial format allows competitors (human and canine) not to worry about other competitors in their way. *Photo: Harold Meerveld - Dagscooter / Step. Wiki Commons.*

Paracycling

Albinfo.
Wiki Commons.

Andreas Zirkl at the 2024 UCI Paracycling Road World Championships in Zürich.

The rise of paracycling in sport has produced some remarkable personal achievements, but has also enhanced the visibility and status of people with disabilities. There is, of course, still a long way to go, especially when it comes to securing and adapting the entry-level cycles which beginners need in order to start their journey in sport.

Since there are so many different forms of disability, and degrees of disability within each type, the rules of paracycle sport have become complex. The competitions comprise four groups of handicaps: blind/visually-impaired riders; riders with cerebral palsy; riders with locomotor disabilities, and riders who handcycle. This is meshed with a total of 14 functional categories for men and women in all the age categories defined by the UCI. Riders are placed in the appropriate category in the light of their functional capacity. This causes a lot of discussions and decisions, contrasting with the individual's will to compete and the sense of freedom which comes from the thrill of speed and competition.

Austrian handcyclist Philipp Bonadiman.
Photo: Bauken77.

2024 UCI Road and Paracycling Road World Championships in Zurich. Photo: Albinfo.

CHAPTER 8

Bicycle People

Joseph Coltman

An unusual hobby-horse rider was the Reverend Joseph Coltman (1776 to 1837). He served as Vicar of Beverley Minster, Yorkshire, for almost a quarter of a century, and was said to be the heaviest man then living in England, weighing 238kg (525lbs or 37.5 stone). This silhouette is from around 1830. His hobby-horse became his principal form of mobility.

Reverend Coltman was in clerical charge of Beverley Minster, and apparently rode his machine right into the building. He had trouble with the steps up to the altar so three vergers were tasked with rushing the priest up a specially placed ramp and into the pulpit. There are also accounts of Coleman hobbying around his parish assisted by a boy who used a rope to pull along both man and machine (which on other occasions travelled with him in his carriage).

The Reverend Coltman was much loved by his parishioners, who admired his considerable intellect and persuasive powers as a speaker and writer. He had liberal views and supported the emancipation of Catholics. He was a great benefactor to local schools and a believer in education for all. A plaque in Beverley Minster maintains his memory to this day.

With thanks to Roger Street, author of The Pedestrian Hobby-Horse.

Richard Lesclide

Lesclide was probably the first ever cycle campaigner and his *Vélocipède Illustré*, published in France from 1869, was the world's first viable cycling magazine. He wrote:

❝ *First came the Rights of Man, now let us secure the Rights of the Velocipede.* ❞

Lesclide's periodical featured Mr Jonathan Schopp, an absurdly rich American and a 'noble republican'. He rode the finest bicycle money could buy, and his manager was known as the 'Napoleon of Velocipedes'. Schopp pedals heroically around the world, facing constant danger, and eventually welcomes the companionship of a lady velocipedist. Of course, the relationship remains at all times honourable. Readers' letters were interesting:

❝ *Sir, would you please give me the address of Jonathan Schopp or of the Napoleon of Velocipedes. I can be of great service to them since I am the inventor of a velocipede which will go at an unlimited speed.* ❞

Another reader had followed Schopp's route through Germany but wondered how the American could have covered the distance in such a short time, and on such roads? And how on earth had Schopp so easily befriended the Germans he met en route?

The Plasterer and the Professor

These are the stories of two men who could hardly have been more different yet were both heroes of the high wheel.

George Waller was a jobbing builder from Newcastle-upon-Tyne and also a local folk hero best known for his successes in six-day endurance races on indoor tracks. In 1879 Waller was the only novice riding in the six-day Long Distance 'Championship of the World' in London. He won, with a handsome fee of 100 guineas, and was to later win it a second time. His winnings bought him a huge marquee and portable wooden track. He used this to tour the region with a 'travelling circus' of professional riders, trick cyclists and musicians. It came to an end when a storm destroyed the marquee and he returned to a quiet life as a jobbing builder. He died aged 45 in a carriage accident.

The Honourable Ion Keith-Falconer was a brainbox, becoming professor of Arabic at Cambridge University in his mid-20s. But not before taking up the high bicycle. He was six foot, three inches (1.9 metres) tall, an exceptional height for the period, even for an aristocrat of well-nourished stock. That he could master a very high machine gave him a competitive advantage. So amateurish was his attitude that he sometimes forgot about racing engagements and turned up at short notice to win in heroic style. Despite his show of dilettantism Keith-Falconer was virtually impossible to beat. In October 1878 he raced against John Keen, the then professional champion, and won. Such amateur-professional matches were exceptional and needed special permission.

Keith-Falconer became a missionary in Yemen, where he died of malaria at the age of 32.

George Waller, jobbing builder.

The Honourable Ion Keith-Falconer, Cambridge Professor of Arabic.

'Wild Woman' Tessie Reynolds

When sixteen year old Tessie Reynolds rode from Brighton to London and back in September 1893, wearing a trousered costume, she became the subject of impassioned argument. Not only had Miss Reynolds worn 'immodest and degrading' dress, she had used a crossbarred bicycle, had been paced by male friends, and had dared to ride strenuously: about 110 miles (177km) in 8½ hours. Afterwards she was examined by a medical professional who confirmed the ride had done her no damage. Tessie Reynolds became a celebrity, and her unapologetic embrace of rational dress may have given other women the confidence to follow suit.

Hélène Dutrieu: a cyclist and so much more

Her life was complicated, fascinating and daring. Hélène Dutrieu, from French-speaking Belgium, became a professional track cyclist aged 18. She hit the heights, winning the women's world hour record, followed by a succession of world speed records. Over seven years she became wealthy, independent and famous.

Dutrieu also became a stunt rider. Her 'Human Arrow' act involved riding to the top of a curved ramp to fly 15m (50ft) upside down, landing on another ramp, to complete the loop. She performed in various European cities, but then moved on to motorbike stunt riding, suffering an accident needing eight months of recovery. Following that she transformed into an actress, touring theatres for three years. Then she took up motor racing before becoming a test pilot for the first aeroplane a company had built. She survived two crashes in which the planes were written off but her aeronautical career blossomed. Her flying achievements brought her more celebrity and the French Légion d'Honneur. In the First World War she was an ambulance driver, then managed the ambulance fleet, before becoming the director of the hospital. Finally, after the war she took up a career in journalism. After such a breathless life she died in 1961 aged 83.

Major Taylor, the 'Black Wonder'

The story of Major Taylor is one of remarkable talent in the face of potent racism. Aged 13 he entered and won his first race, a ten-mile (16km) event in his hometown of Indianapolis, Indiana. He won his first significant cycling competition in June 1895, when he was the only rider to finish a gruelling 75 mile (121km) road race near his home town. He went on to win 159 further races, including several world championships, and established a number of world speed records. In 1899 he won the world one mile sprint title in Montreal.

Taylor's achievements were in spite of opposition to Black athletes taking part in organised professional sports. Members from Southern states objected to Blacks having full membership of the League of American Wheelmen. He maintained throughout a nobility of spirit and became one of the first Black athletes to break into American professional cycle racing, traditionally an all-white sport.

From the foreword to his autobiography, *'The Fastest Bicycle Rider in the World'*, he wrote:

> ❝ *There are positively no mental, physical or moral attainments too lofty for the Negro to accomplish if granted a fair and equal opportunity.* ❞

Taylor showed his talents in many European countries, Australia and New Zealand. He is pictured above in France. This was all a far cry from his early days in cycling, when a local cycle dealer paid him to give trick riding exhibitions outside the shop every afternoon for $6 a week and a free bicycle. The youngster performed in military uniform, hence the nickname 'Major' – his real name was Marshall Walter Taylor.

He was once the fastest man in the world, enjoying a fine lifestyle, but he died alone and penniless after some failed business ventures.

Alfred Jarry
Riding on the wild side

Bound by rods to their machines, the crew of a five-man bicycle hurtle across Europe and Asia in a grotesquely dehumanised ten thousand mile race (*course des dix mille milles*) against an express train. They reach speeds of 300 kilometres an hour powered by Perpetual Motion Food, a volatile mixture of alcohol and strychnine. One of the riders dies in the saddle, an event hardly noticed in the farcical pandemonium. The race is a key episode in *Le Sûrmale* (The Supermale), a novel written in Paris in 1902, which speculates on how our minds and bodies may be overwhelmed by technology. The author, Alfred Jarry, was fascinated by bicycles and was notorious for his wild eccentricity and his outrageously unconventional cycling.

In the thirty year period before the First World War, Paris seemed to have lost itself in an extravaganza of public display, frivolity and self-indulgence. They were heady days, at least for the well off. Society life revolved around café talk, banquets, cabarets, duels, circuses and new technological marvels, such as the cinematograph, the electric bulb and the new chain-driven safety bicycle.

Jarry himself revelled in this new technology. He cycled day in day out through the chaos of Paris traffic. More genteel cyclists congregated in the Bois de Boulogne, a fashionable wooded park. One cycled to be seen, wearing the latest cycling fashionwear. Jarry sent this up by appearing in the tight shirt and trousers of a racing cyclist. He caused a stir by also wearing it at the funeral of the revered poet Mallarmé, after having followed the cortege on his bicycle.

Jarry associated with the avant-garde community of writers and artists. For these people a cycle ride could be just as beautiful or radical as a poem or a painting. For them the bicycle was liberation, a machine to extend the potentialities of the human body. Jarry described it as an 'external skeleton' which allows mankind to outstrip the process of biological evolution.

Such attitudes and ideas were in the air when Alfred Jarry first arrived in Paris, from Rennes. It was 1891 and he was 17.

The intensity of Jarry's personality quickly made its mark on Paris. The literary world was both amused and confused by the disconcerting writing style, rich staccato speech and outrageous behaviour of this pale, diminutive, bandy-legged student. He had already dedicated his life to the pursuit of the irrational and the squalid, with a single-mindedness which led to his early death at the age of 34 as a result of poverty, overwork and alcohol abuse. Jarry soon became notorious. He took, for example, to riding

High society awheel in Paris, in a group portrait of real individuals. Jarry mocked all they stood for.

around Paris with two revolvers tucked in his belt and a carbine across his shoulder. Some say that he fired off a revolver to clear his way. All the same, Jarry was an athletic cyclist who enjoyed tearing around the countryside.

Jarry is now best known for his play, *Ubu Roi*, a grotesque farce and a prophetic satire of modern dictators. It caused a riot in the theatre. By challenging normal ethics and standards Jarry constructed an artificial personality for himself based on the Ubu character he had created, and his behaviour, on and off his bicycle, became increasingly absurd. He gestured regally, used the 'royal we' and adopted a grandiose form of speech. Just the same, he was very well received and we have many accounts of his constant intellectual brilliance, panache and underlying good nature. He knew and influenced important writers and artists. No such testimonial would have been given by the tradesman from whom Jarry acquired a top quality racing bike in 1896. It was a Clément Luxe track machine. Jarry never actually paid for it.

Jarry enjoyed giving friends a ride in a trailer, attached to his bike by ropes. Madame Rachilde, who was his close friend and the wife of his publisher, was once being charioted along in this way when they found themselves speeding down a steep hill towards a hairpin and wall. Each time Jarry braked the trailer overtook the bicycle. After scolding his passenger for speeding ahead of him, he took out a knife and tried to cut the ropes. Then, laughing fiendishly, Jarry threw away the knife and leaped off his saddle, letting himself be dragged along the ground until the trailer came to rest. *"Well, Madame,"* he intoned in his usual staccato manner, *"We believe we were a little frightened... and never have we wanted so desperately to take leave of a woman"*. Madame Rachilde considers the incident as typical of Jarry: half criminal and half noble.

Jarry died in abject poverty. His last request was for a toothpick. When he finally had one in his fingers it seemed, his doctor reported, that he was suddenly filled with a great joy before drawing his last breath.

Diamond Jim Brady

'Diamond Jim' Brady was the most flamboyant figure of the American cycling scene during the bicycle craze of the mid 1890s. He made his fortune selling materials to the railway companies, and he wore copious gold and diamonds to impress.

Diamond Jim quickly spotted opportunities for ostentation in the cycle boom. Both he and his close friend Lillian Russell, reigning queen of American entertainers, were getting porky – so cycling would give exercise and publicity. Jim first ordered an exquisitely finished bicycle from the Columbia factory, especially designed for his ample figure, and equipped with a pneumatic saddle. He hired a former circus cyclist, Dick Barton, as his full-time cycling advisor.

Barton ordered a dozen machines with solid gold frames and silver spokes. The stunned folk at Columbia confessed they could not make such a machine in those metals to support Big Jim or anyone else – but steel machines could be gold-plated. So Barton disassembled the machines every two weeks and took them back to have the plating renovated, so that Diamond Jim always rode a bicycle that looked brand new. He also bought a gold-plated tandem (pictured above). To Lillian he gifted a gold-plated cycle with tiny diamonds studding the frame.

Jim eventually moved on to motoring, and drove Lillian in one of the first electric cars in New York. Its blazing interior lights ensured that the people of New York could easily spot them at night.

Elgar & Mr Phoebus

Sir Edward Elgar, the prominent English composer of the early 20th century, found cycling to be an inspirational antidote to the hours he spent at his desk writing music.

He rode up to 50 miles (80km) a day, in fairly formal dress, along the bucolic country lanes of Worcestershire and Herefordshire. Some of his greatest music was born of these rides, and a number of the personalities depicted in his Enigma Variations were frequent riding partners in and around the Malvern Hills.

Elgar discovered cycling at the age of 43, in the summer of 1900. He bought a Royal Sunbeam made by John Marston Ltd. It had a 27″ frame, 28″ wheels, an oil bath chain-case and three brakes. He called it Mr Phoebus (Phoebus being a poetic name for the sun). After a while he bought another Royal Sunbeam, this time with a freewheel. These handsome cycles were the epitome of quality, selling for 16 guineas, around twice the price of standard cycles and equivalent to six months' average wages in 1900.

Toulouse-Lautrec

Henri de Toulouse-Lautrec was a mercurial artist whose fragile bones and short, knock-kneed legs kept him from cycling – his childhood tricycle had been his last taste of physical freedom. However, he loved to watch cycle sport. He was attracted by the beauty of movement, but also by the smells, sounds and excitement of the spectacle. The race results interested him little and as the afternoon and the drinks progressed, he would circle briefly on the grass enclosure, like a dog looking for a place to lie down, to finally curl up on the ground and sleep. He also liked to go into the locker room, leaning over closely to watch the athletes being massaged.

Toulouse-Lautrec accompanied a team of French racing cyclists to London, in 1896. Although a heavy drinker himself, he was apparently depressed by British drinking habits. Toulouse-Lautrec's one major work on a cycling theme is a poster advertising the preposterous hooked-teeth Simpson bicycle chain, and portraying the Velodrome Buffalo during a bicycle race. Lautrec showed little interest in academic notions of pictorial composition. We see a band playing and in the background are a couple of pacing multicycles. The lone racer's bicycle sports a carefully drawn Simpson lever chain, the message being that all the pacing teams in the world won't help you catch a rider using a Simpson chain!

Grandpa of Steel

It was 1951. Fifty of the strongest cyclists in Sweden were in a 1000 mile (600km) race from the Finnish border to the south of Sweden. But the nation was fascinated by one unusual rider: a 66 year old grandfather with a long white beard. He was riding a heavy town bike with loaded panniers. Gustav Håkansson had not passed the medical, so was riding unofficially, in a home-made bib with a zero on it.

After 8km (50 miles) he was 16km (10 miles) behind the leaders. Soon Sweden noticed that he was going no faster – but was now 30km (20 miles) in front. This was because he was 'cheating'. Unlike the other riders, he did not stop each night at checkpoints. With little sleep he kept plodding on alone in the dark. No-one could complain as he was not an official entrant.

The eyes of the whole country were on this *Stålfarfar* (Steel Grandpa). Might he collapse, or damage his heart? After three days he was leading the field by 192km. By the end of the fourth day, with only seven hours' total sleep since the start, he was 240km (150 miles) in front. Håkansson completed the course in five days and five hours – almost a full day ahead of the leading official competitor. He had achieved 291km (182 miles) per day.

He kept on riding for decades, visiting schools and appearing at public events. He was still cycling at 100 and died aged 101.

Graham Obree
Inventing for winning

Chris Boardman and his Lotus Monocoque were backed by powerful movers in the cycle industry. But up in Scotland Graeme Obree was putting together, on his kitchen table, an unorthodox bike made from scrap metal and repurposed parts. This homemade construct was born of years of experimenting with aerodynamics, durability testing and the acceptance of famously bad ergonomics. It was on this bike that Obree was to smash the world hour record in 1993, and again in 1994. He had been a relatively obscure Scottish cyclist but was embarking on a career of innovation and of rebellion against the sport's governing body.

Obree was single-minded and unorthodox. His bike shop business had failed. He was drawing benefits. His experimentation had to be very low budget, but he was full of ideas, technical curiosity and a boundless ambition to break cycling records. He famously used washing machine bearings when standard bike bearings were not right for his designs. He used a monoblade fork (and sometimes a conventional one). He built his bike to enable a new aerodynamic cycling position, 'the Tuck'. He would ride hunched over the handlebars, arms folded away under the chest. Taken together, bike design and riding position reduced aerodynamic drag by around 15%. So it was that, on 17th July 1993, he broke the world hour record at the Hamar velodrome in Norway, riding 32.06 miles (51.596km) on 'Old Faithful'.

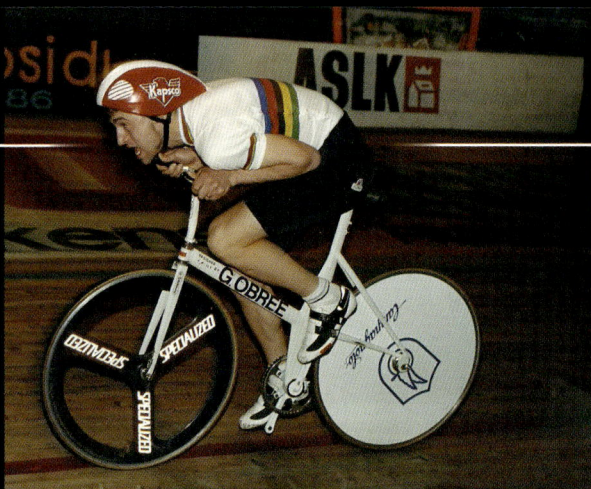

Graeme Obree received his 1993 World Hour Record medal from the Union Cycliste Internationale. In 1993 and 1994 he used the tuck position to take World Championship individual pursuit and national time trial titles, along with the world hour records. The UCI were not pleased, being concerned that technological advances were subverting fair performance comparisons. They banned the tuck, but Obree countered with a new riding stance, the Superman, and this too was banned – for the same reasons they banned Chris Boardman's Lotus.

2013 was also the year when Obree revealed his 'Beastie', a prone recumbent incorporating parts of an old saucepan and a pair of rollerskates bought from a charity shop. He made his own slimline fairing and took it to Battle Mountain, Nevada to compete in the 2013 World Human Powered Speed Championships. He did not fare well against his highly resourced and technically more advanced competitors. But he did set a world record for prone cycling!

Obree is a complex and enigmatic character. He has been very open about his bipolar disorder, depression, three suicide attempts and homosexuality. He uses his experiences to encourage other sportspeople to talk about their own mental health and other challenges.

Obree on his Beastie, minus its fairing. Photo: movie n co.

Beryl Burton
Seven-times world champion

Beryl Burton was a unique and enigmatic athlete. She dominated women's cycle sport in England, set numerous national records and won seven world titles. She also set a women's record for the 12-hour time trial which exceeded the men's record for two years. She is regarded by many as Britain's greatest athlete: little known in the UK outside of cycle sport but now widely celebrated. A no-nonsense Yorkshirewoman, she lived simply, working on a rhubarb farm during the week and turned her back on going professional.

At the age of ten Beryl contracted St Vitus' dance, a form of rheumatic fever which often weakens the heart. She emerged as a timid and awkward teenager but was soon attracted to the Morley Road Cycle Club. She described her entry into competitive cycling:

❝ *When I got there I would curl up with embarrassment if anybody talked to me. I started taking part in the odd ten-mile event and I felt a bit embarrassed that I wasn't going fast enough, so I rode with my hands on the tops of the bars so people would think I was just riding socially.* ❞

Beryl began to show real promise in events. She also married club member Charlie Burton. Money was short and he gave up his own cycling career to support her. Both had to work full time to finance the travelling to events, the bed and breakfasts and the cycling hardware. For the first few years they could afford to keep just the one bike on the go, using it for both time trial and track events. At weekends they adored cycling 100 miles (160km) in a day through the Yorkshire Dales, with daughter Denise on a childseat.

Beryl Burton was a ferociously competitive sportswoman, ignoring the heart arrhythmia which she knew was always there. She died aged 58 of heart failure during a social ride.

▲ She was a seven-times world champion but worked almost all her life in the fields of a local rhubarb farm, where the friendship of co-workers was important to her. She never turned professional. Here, with husband Charlie and daughter Denise, Beryl starts a time trial.

◀ *Towards the end of her career Beryl's achievements were better recognised by the world of cycle sport. Here, in around 1974, she is a celebrity congratulating two Australian champions of the track.*

Chris Boardman

A life of many courses

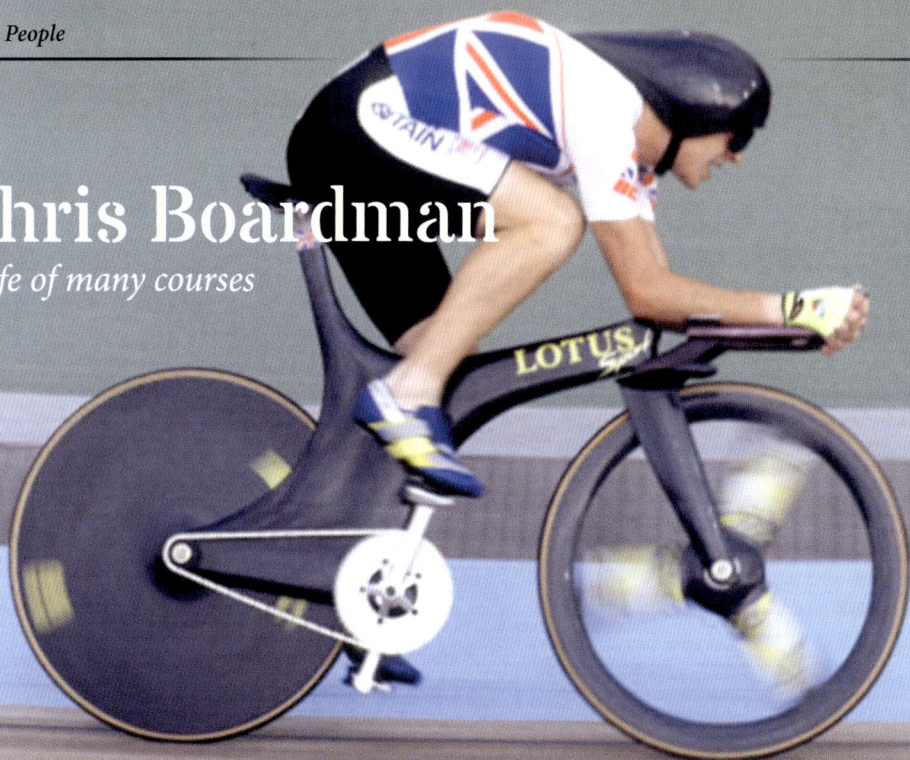

Chris Boardman has ridden many roles: as a celebrated performance cyclist, a cycle design consultant, and then an articulate advocate for everyday cyclists.

His cycling career is peppered with Olympic golds, world hour records and Tour de France prologue wins. He will always be associated with time trialling on the monocoque monoblade Lotus 108 bicycle designed by Mike Burrows. On this machine (above) he won the 4km individual pursuit at the 1992 Summer Olympics. The Lotus design was soon after banned by cycle sport's governing body.

Boardman later became involved in the development and successful commercialisation of Boardman-branded road bikes, but also became a consultant and advocate for walking and everyday cycling across the UK. His resolve was strengthened in 2016, when his mother Carol was killed by a motor vehicle while cycling (for which the driver was jailed). Boardman became Greater Manchester's walking and cycling commissioner in 2017, and in 2022 he was appointed National Active Travel Commissioner by the UK Government. He has become a familiar face and a persuasive voice on national television.

Ed Pratt

The adventure which is youth

What does a 19 year old English lad do if he has just finished school and doesn't want to go to university? Obviously, he needs to unicycle 35,000km (22,000 miles) around the globe, alone, over four continents, in 1,200 days, cranking out twelve million pedal strokes.

Ed Pratt set off in 2015, to become, it is believed, the first to circumnavigate the globe on one wheel. He rode a 36″ wheel Nimbus Oracle with a bespoke rack for tent, sleeping bag, and more.

He experienced the cultures of many countries en route and his choice of transport opened up many a conversation. He rode through Eastern Europe, Turkey and Kyrgyzstan, where he stopped off for six months to top up his finances by teaching English: then Singapore, Australasia and the USA. All land journeys were covered by riding or pushing his cycle. His journey was followed by hundreds of thousands who enjoyed his daily video dispatches. A tracker on his cycle showed followers exactly where he was on the journey.

Ed had hoped his adventure would raise money and awareness for the 'School in a Bag' Initiative, providing school bags filled with useful learning tools, for disadvantaged children in poor countries. He had hoped to raise £7,500 but actually raised over £300,000.

In 2024 Ed took on a more local adventure. He kayaked the length of the River Thames from source to sea to draw attention to river pollution while raising funds for The Rivers Trust. ▼

Anne Mustoe
World cyclist

At the age of 54 Anne Mustoe was unfit and overweight. She had studied classics at Cambridge and was newly retired as headteacher of an expensive, academic girls' school She had solid status in society, but there were signs of changes to come.

She was planning her exit: "*l always knew I was, to an extent, play-acting... I was doing a job, but it was only a job. I don't think women get carried away by position.*"

But she had not cycled for 30 years, had no bike repair skills and hated camping, picnics and discomfort. Nevertheless she set out, in 1987, on her custom-made Condor bicycle, completing 12,000 miles over 15 months.

Multiple rides and books were to follow. Mustoe liked to follow historical routes: Roman roads across Europe, Alexander the Great's route from Greece to the Indus Valley, the Australian Outback, the Gobi Desert, the Silk Route from China.

All her journeys were recounted in a warm, accessible prose coupling a wry humour with enthusiasm and optimism, making light of robberies, injuries, freak floods, storms, desert heat waves, blizzards in the Rockies, and Patagonian winds.

She developed views about possessions. "*I gradually came to realise how little I could manage with. There was a part of my life when I thought it was nice to have a house full of nice things but when I got that I found I wasn't particularly interested in it.*"

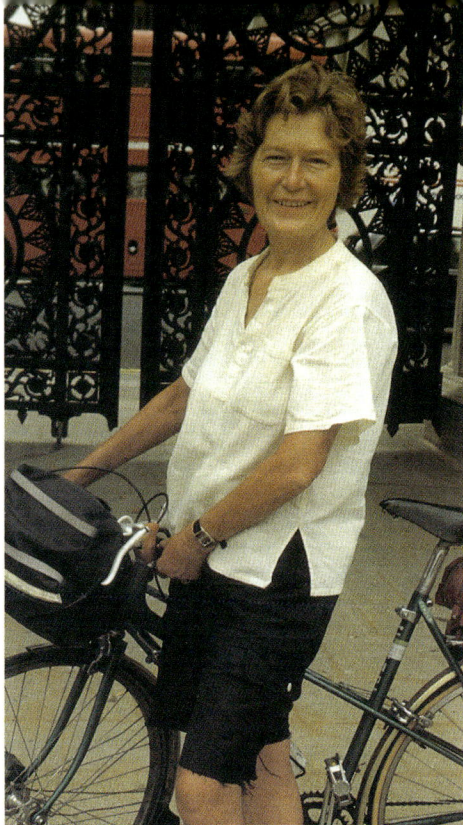

Lone Traveller
One woman, two wheels and the world

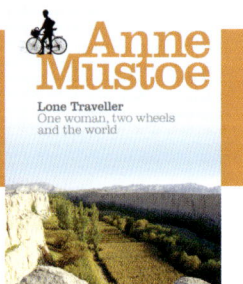

Anne Mustoe's cycles served her well:

❝ *Mechanically, my bicycles are never a problem. If anything goes wrong with them, I just wheel them to the nearest cycle shop. I don't mend my car, so I don't see why I should have to turn mechanic for a bike. In these days of Kevlar tyres and thorn-proof inner tubes, I ride across whole continents without a single puncture, even on stony nightmares of roads... The bicycle is such a straightforward machine that it can be mended anywhere in the world. In countries where everyone cycles, there's a repairer on every street corner, and every wayside tree has a tyre hanging down to advertise bicycle services... A puncture repair in many parts of the world costs as little as 10p. For me, that's a negligible sum, but for the man who does the repair, it's enough to feed his family for the day. It makes sense to help the local people help themselves.* ❞

Readers warmed to her endearingly uncontrived account of riding dirty and waterless through India, of finding the Turks the kindest of people, of sleeping in company with rats and goats, of the generosity and goodwill she received. They were charmed by this unlikely world-traveller from the upper echelons of English respectability.

On her last expedition, in 2009, she became ill in Syria and, aged 76, died in Aleppo, of unclear causes.

Josie Dew
Unorthodox traveller

Where Anne Mustoe was a purposeful, calm-natured traveller, Josie Dew began world-cycling with the impetuosity and irreverence of youth, mixed with fascinating insights into people, lands and cultures. She tells us, for example, that on the Hawaiian island of Haleakala the god Maui lassoed the sun's genitalia.

In her book, *Travels in a Strange State,* she describes sitting alone on top of a mountain on a small Hawaiian island, looking at a chain of islands, and then deciding to career down into a deep gulch for the hell of it:

66 *Then BOOMPH! I was brought rapidly down to earth. My front wheel sank into sand and I shot from my saddle, torpedoing through the air to land flat on my back on a fiery-red dune. Suddenly the wind had gone. The speed had stopped. All was silent and I lay still – very still. I opened my eyes and stared at the sky. With torn shorts and ruddy, mud-splattered face, I thought: What am I doing? Is this normal behaviour for a 26 year old? I thought back to home – to my friends, a lot of them married, with children, with 'sensible jobs.' Should I, I wondered, be behaving with a little more sophistication, a little more panache? In short: should I be acting my age and not my shoe size? But why? Hawaii had caught me, picked me up and spun me around. I loved the place. I was happy. And I thought: What a feeling – what a day!* 99

We learn of the natural wonders of America, but also of how very, very strange some Americans are. The book gives us some unforgettable detail, such as drivers stopping to expose themselves, and being exposed in turn to Josie's put-downs. We learn of an encounter with a prophet called Light, who claimed he came from nowhere and had just materialised from a greater spiritual power. We learn of how Josie encountered the Rodney King riots when 5383 fires ate through Los Angeles and 55 people died. She met one other cyclist in the city and he carried a revolver in the back pocket of his lycra cycling jersey.

▲ *Josie reaches the heights of exhaustion at 2,969 metres elevation on the mountain called Haleakala (Hawaiian for 'House of the Sun.')*

By the age of 58 Josie Dew had covered almost 600,000 miles and written seven books. Her fans have followed her life journey as she brought up a family on bikes and continues as an advocate of everyday cycling and an icon of adventure cycling.

From Travels in a Strange State:
Cycling across the USA. Warner Books.

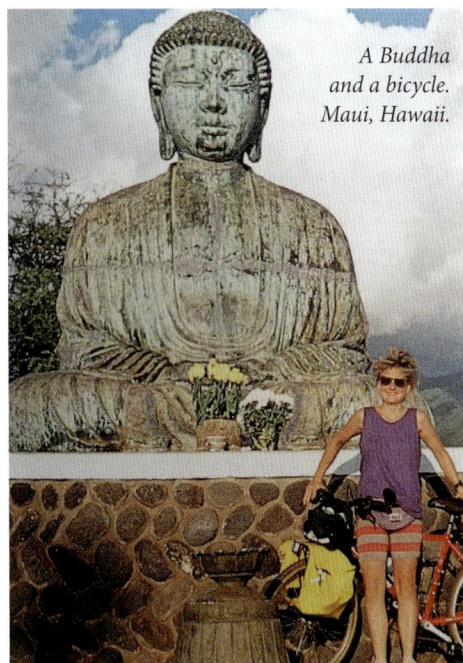

A Buddha and a bicycle. Maui, Hawaii.

Isabelle Clement
Champion of inclusion

Photo: Wheels for Wellbeing.

Isabelle Clement, now in her late 50s, has been disabled for almost all her life. Her parents dearly wanted her to ride on two wheels but she lacked the balance or foot control. That was in France, her country of birth. It was not until her 30s, working in London, that she discovered you can clip a handcycling attachment onto your wheelchair. This changed her life utterly, so much so that she is Director of Wheels for Wellbeing, a London-based charity which works with around 1,300 disabled people each year.

Isabelle aims to bring an understanding of cycling to disability groups and of disability to cycling groups. As an urban commuter handcyclist she has personal experience of what it takes to enable everyone to cycle. She is a leading influencer in the field of inclusive cycling and has the ear of the government.

She initiated more recently Beyond the Bicycle, an alliance with parent cyclists and cargo cyclists who encounter many of the same issues as disabled and older cyclists. Her overall aim remains: to see inclusive cycling become the norm in the UK.

Bilikiss Adebiyi-Abiola
Nothing wasted

She holds higher degrees in business management and computer science from top US universities. But on a visit to her native Lagos Bilikiss Adebiyi could see how so many of the city's 16 million inhabitants had no basic waste management services, with the risk of disease. Nigeria's capital was producing 15,000 metric tonnes of waste every day with only 40% collected by the municipal government.

In 2012 Bilikiss returned to Lagos to co-found Wecyclers, a for-profit social enterprise. It began collecting and recycling rubbish from poorer households – incentivising householders with rewards of points per kilogram of recyclable waste. These could be exchanged for cash or essential goods like food and household items. Wecyclers began with a single cargo bike, and soon there was a fleet of them. There are now over 26 Wecyclers franchises across Nigeria. It all began with a single cargo trike and a woman with determination.

Kacey Wong
Artist, Critic, Exile

Dr Kacey Wong is a visual artist, educator and activist. He was Assistant Professor at the School of Design, Hong Kong Polytechnic University. He was also one of Hong Kong's best-known provocateurs, satirising and criticising those in power. His mobile art creations investigate the relationships between people's living environment and their social relationships. His tricycles give access to public places and opportunities for engagement. His *Wandering Space (Camper Bike)* explores why we live and relate in certain ways. Following the Chinese government's displeasure at his political activism and art projects Wong exiled himself to Taiwan where his life of art continues.

Kacey Wong created his Egg Bar and took it around downtown Hong Kong to serve egg waffles free of charge, to stimulate awareness and discussion about the authorities' suppression of traditional street food vendors.

With Wandering Home 2 Kacey Wong challenged affluent Hong Kong citizens to consider how big a house they really need for a happy life. His miniature house on a tricycle stimulated new thinking about the living environment in the city. It also used nostalgic architectural elements to pay tribute to old Hong Kong.

Ayesha McGowan

Racing and beyond

Ayesha McGowan has interests and achievements which are rare in cycle sport. As a young adult she studied and taught music, and for seven years she commuted by bike. It was, she says, "just a form of transportation, freedom and fun". Then, in her mid-twenties, it occurred to her that black women were practically non-existent in professional cycling. She began racing in criteriums and was soon winning them. She was on the way to becoming the first African-American woman professional cyclist in modern history, riding for Team Liv Racing.

McGowan has ambition and drive, but you can't call her single-minded. She thinks deeply about social justice and is an advocate for diversity and inclusion in cycling, especially for women and ethnic minorities. As her racing career scales down her social justice interests take up more of her life. One of her many initiatives is her online blog, A Quick Brown Fox, where she encourages more women and ethnic minority people to take up cycle sport. She has nearly 40,000 followers on social media, hosting conversations about race, racism and sexism in the world of cycling and beyond. As she recently wrote: *"You can't fight for women and not fight for black women, trans women, disabled women, or any of the other intersections where anyone who identifies as a woman resides."*

Music teacher, professional cyclist, diversity and inclusion advocate: that's quite a life so far. But Ayesha McGowan sometimes wonders if what she is doing really matters. In an interview with *Bicycling Magazine* she said:

❝ I don't think I'm helping people. I don't think that riding bikes professionally is helping anybody. Some people have social missions like, 'Let's get little black kids out the hood'. Yes. Do that. Sure. But that's not what I'm trying to do. It's more (that) I feel like everything is terrible, and the world is a shitty place. I'm driven by the idea that you need to find joy. ❞

Photo: Jeff Clark.

CHAPTER 9
Books and Bikes

Personal Emanations

Paraclèse Bellencontre

In *Hygiène du Vélocipède*, published 1869, Dr Paraclèse Bellencontre put forward some explicit arguments towards women taking to pedals.

❝ *(When dancing) habitually naked shoulders become covered in sweat, affording open and undefended passage to all pulmonary and catarrhal infections. The waist is locked into its tight prison of gauze, satin and flowers, and the respiratory system fails to furnish the body with blood, being troubled by the air fouled by the flames of the chandeliers and by personal emanations... A velocipede, be it ever so flighty, would never encourage our mothers, sisters and daughters to wear those scanty dresses of flimsy, transparent material... designed to entice the male dancing partner looking down.* **❞**

This is how, in lascivious language, Dr Paraclèse Bellencontre predicted that the velocipede would "*distract young people's attention from other passions and prevent them from abandoning themselves prematurely to the pleasures of love.*" It would also, said he, help keep young men away from "*the dirty and unhygienic atmosphere...of the tobacco saloon, bar and tavern.*"

Bellencontre warns that during intimate waltzes a young girl might plan with her partner ways of giving her mother the slip. None of this can happen on a velocipede, he asserts, since velocipeding couples need to keep a distance from each other to avoid collisions. He recommends that velocipeding become an important part of girls' formal education, and that it be used in the treatment of "*pale, anaemic girls with a tendency to scrofula, and those for whom the onset of menstruation is proving difficult.*"

Blanche d'Antigny painted by Betinet in around 1868. (Museum of the Isle de France)

While Bellencontre was urging restraint and decorum in Rouen the launch edition of the world's first cycling magazine, published in Paris, was striking a different note. It portrayed a daring young woman in the style of Marianne, the symbol of revolutionary vigour. She is powering forward, showing leg and shining the light of progress.

Nothing to Hide

Take these Wings! by Maurice Leblanc

Voici des Ailes ('Take these Wings!') is a daring French novel of changing relationships, adultery and bicycle-love, centred on two couples on a cycling tour of Normandy and Brittany. The author, Maurice Leblanc, also wrote the Arsène Lupin detective books. *Voici des Ailes!* was written in 1898, when many adults were enjoying the relative novelty of riding safety cycles on pneumatic tyres.

The men talked bicycles. Pascal Fauvières came back to his theory of aesthetics:

❝ What makes the bicycle beautiful is its sincerity. She hides nothing, her movements are apparent, the effort she puts in is clear to see and easy to understand; she proclaims her purpose, she tells us that she wants to go fast, go silently, go lightly. Why is the automobile so ugly, putting us so ill at ease? Because it hides its inner organs as if ashamed of them. We don't know what she wants. She seems incomplete. We wait for something to happen. She seems made to carry, rather than to go forwards. Look at the locomotive, on the other hand: how beautiful it is! Those muscles of iron which extend and contract, those arms making circles, and those legs powering through. It's all a mighty and noble organism: that broad chest, that ardent breath, that exhalation we can all see. ❞

But Guillaume d'Arjols started up a discussion on the position of the feet on a bicycle. Fauvières attached no importance to the issue. *"That's a mistake, my friend!"* exclaimed d'Arjols, who was more expert in these matters. *"The foot has its role, its duty. It has to bring back the pedal and encourage it to rise again. That is the relevant principle here."*

He curved his hand into the shape of a swan neck to demonstrate the mechanism of the movement. *"Besides"*, he concluded, *"that's what the English, our masters in questions of sport, call ankle play."*

Meanwhile Madelaine was saying how much she disliked the things women had to wear. On a bicycle she found the skirt ungainly. *"So"*, questioned her friend (Régine), *"no skirt because it's ugly, no culottes because they lack grace, no culotted skirt because it's ungainly. What then?... Pascal, what are your views on cycling jerseys?"*

But d'Arjols was engaging Pascal on the subject of cycle brakes: *"The brake? Useless? Yes, people make fun of me on the subject, but there's no escaping the issue. Ask anyone who matters. What about Dupont, the road racer, for example? Now he uses a brake."* The authority inherent in this name knocked Fauvières back, and from that point on he acquiesced to all Guillaume's ideas on saddle position, gear ratio and crank length. This all strengthened their liking for one another, stimulated by the coffee and cigars.

This book has been 'rediscovered' and is in print in French and in English editions. The translation here is my own. The usual translation of the book title is Here are Wings! (author)

The Excitement never flagged

The Wheels of Chance *by H G Wells*

Wells wrote several novels involving cycling but his major cycling work was *The Wheels of Chance* (1896).

The hero, Hoopdriver, is a draper's assistant, just as Wells had been. The bicycle became an aid to Hoopdriver's social mobility. He devotes his annual holiday to a ten-day cycle tour of the South Coast, along a route previously taken by Wells himself, who had just learned to cycle. Hoopdriver sets out one morning, in his new brown Norfolk cycling jacket.

❝ *There is only one phrase to describe his course at this stage, and that is voluptuous curves. He did not ride fast, he did not ride straight, an exacting critic might say he did not ride well – but he rode generously, opulently, using the whole road and even nibbling at the footpath. The excitement never flagged. So far he had never passed or been passed by anything, but as yet the day was young, and the road was clear. He doubted his steering so much that, for the present, he had resolved to dismount at the approach of anything else upon wheels. The shadows of the trees lay very long and blue across the road; the morning sunlight was like amber fire... Whoops for Freedom and Adventure... talk of your joie de vivre!* ❞

Hoopdriver's bicycle transports him to a new world: 'Here was quiet and greenery, and one mucked about as the desire took one, without a soul to see... Once he almost ran over something wonderful, a little, low, red beast with a yellowish tail, that went rushing across the road before him. It was the first weasel he had ever seen in his cockney life. There were miles of this, scores of miles of this before him.'

His mode of transport brings him into contact with a New Woman, an independently minded young lady from the upper middle classes cycling unchaperoned well away from home. Infatuated, Hoopdriver rescues her from her pursuing suitor who claims that she has sullied her reputation by leaving home with him (the suitor) on a bicycle, and therefore has no option but to marry him.

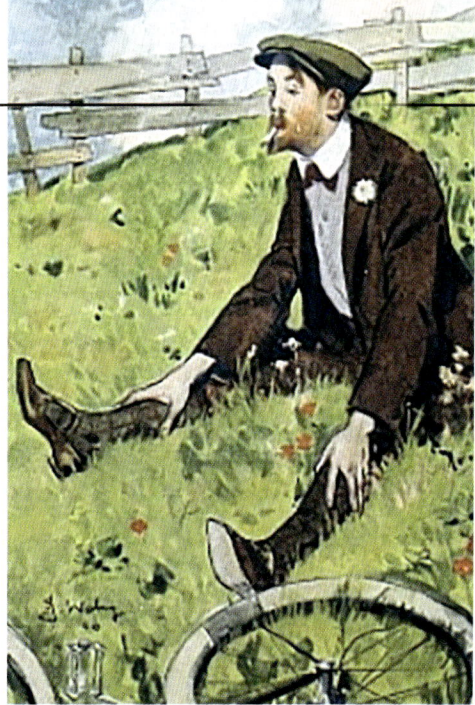

The shift in social perspectives, as exemplified by Hoopdriver, led Galsworthy to later claim that the bicycle had 'been responsible for more movement in manners and morals than anything since Charles the Second'.

H G Wells with his wife. He was an enthusiastic cyclist even before the peak of the bicycle craze in 1896.

Bells and Whistles

Ireland, a Bicycle and a Tin Whistle, by David A Wilson

In *Ireland, a Bicycle and a Tin Whistle* (1995) returned exile David A Wilson, a Canadian professor of Celtic Studies, cycled through Ireland in search of authentic traditional music, and carrying his tin whistle by way of contribution. He discovered everywhere the 'spontaneity, devilment and irreverence' of the Irish.

At Garron Point, I took the tin whistle from the pannier, climbed over a fence, sat down on coarse grass and started to play. A soft tune wafts over the fields, and drifts into the spray of the sea – a piece composed three centuries ago by the blind harper Turlough Carolan for Fanny Powers, the daughter of one of his patrons. Then a jig, *'Out on the Ocean'*, skipping over the water, light as a summer's day. The music is made for meandering, and the meaning depends on the mood – the state of your mind, the direction of the wind, the sounds from the sea. A Jig or a reel will never sound quite the same way twice; the ornamentations, elaborations, and syncopations will twist and turn through the melody, changing its character as it is played. There is the tune, and there is the way you play the tune; there is the map, and there is the way you choose to travel.

You could race through Ireland in a car, sticking to the main routes; but if you take a bicycle, breathe in the air, and wander off into the side roads, you'd be closer to the spirit of the place. You could learn traditional music by the book, sticking to the main notes; but if you take a tin whistle, breathe out the air, and wander off into the variations, you'd be closer to the spirit of the piece. Riding a bicycle or playing a whistle, the journey becomes more than a means to the end of reaching a destination; it becomes an end in itself, its own destination…

At a village shop I met up with an old fellow whose molecules were mixed into an equally old bicycle; he was dressed in a faded brown suit and looked as if he'd stepped out of a sepia photograph. He inspected my bike carefully and closely, with its wide tyres and its multiplicity of gears, and marvelled at the technology. I inspected his bike equally closely, with its heavy black frame and its complete absence of gears, and marvelled at his stamina. *"You'd need to be in pretty good shape to handle these hills on that bike,"* I said.

"Well now," he replied, *"I'm getting on a bit, you know, so I have to walk up a few of them."* And off he went, bolt upright on the saddle, cycling steadily up a hill that would break your back, waving goodbye without turning around and probably smiling to himself as well…

Time to move on; the tin whistle is tucked back into the pack. Apart from anything else, it's the ideal travel instrument; it's easier to carry on a bicycle than is a guitar say, or a piano. The whistle is also the ultimate democratic instrument; for the price of a couple of pints (the universal unit of currency for wastrels and minstrels), you can enter the world of jigs and reels, of songs and laments. And as you make the journey, you learn the music by listening to the people who play it, and you soak up the spirit by going to the places where they play it – the kitchens, the pubs, the festivals, in towns and villages all over the country.

Ireland, a Bicycle and a Tin Whistle is published by the Blackstaff Press in Belfast.

Half Bike, Half Human

The Third Policeman, by Flann O'Brien

Flann O'Brien was an Irish novelist whose work is suffused with the quixotic and comically surreal. The Third Policeman is permeated by an attraction to bicycles. Its content is half bike, half human and richly comic.

When the main character ends up at the police station the policemen presume to ask: *'Is it about a bicycle?'* Bicycles occupy the psyches and conversations of the policemen. They wonder over wheels, saddles and handlebars. They ride bikes everywhere and treat them as equals. They even believe bicycles can committing crimes without a rider.

The police's belief system goes even deeper. They tell the narrator that:

❝ people who spent most of their natural lives riding iron bicycles over the rocky roadsteads of this parish get their personalities mixed up with the personalities of their bicycle as a result of the interchanging of the atoms of each of them and you would be surprised at the number of people in these parts who are nearly half people and half bicycles...when a man lets things go so far that he is more than half a bicycle, you will not see him so much because he spends a lot of his time leaning with one elbow on walls or standing propped by one foot at kerbstones. ❞

At one point, the narrator admits that he's never ridden a bicycle and the police officers stare at him in silent disbelief. The bicycle is a fundamental truth, on a par with as celestially an imperative as gravity or time.

Our narrator is in trouble. He has just killed a man, and experienced a supernatural conversation with his victim. The police stop talking about bicycles long enough for them to incarcerate the narrator, and the surreal continues to flow quixotically to the end of the novel. Then the narrator has a chance to make a getaway – on a bicycle, of course. The escape goes fluidly, as if the bicycle itself is complicit and willingly aids him on his way. True to the policemen's worldview, the bicycle has been kept all this while in its own cell in case it tried to do something sneaky or illicit, and so the two make a lovely pair as they glide away, experiencing a weirdly beautiful bicycle ride:

❝ I knew that I liked this bicycle more than I had ever liked any other bicycle, better even than I had liked some people with two legs. I liked her unassuming competence, her docility, the simple dignity of her quiet way. With a start I realised that I had been communing with this strange companion and – not only that – conspiring with her. Both of us were afraid of the same Sergeant, both were awaiting the punishments he would bring with him on his return, both were thinking that this was the last chance to escape beyond his reach; and both knew that the hope of each lay in the other, that we would not succeed unless we went together, assisting each other with sympathy and quiet love. ❞

Our thanks to Evan P Schneider whose work informs parts of the above.

Flann O'Brien (pen name of Brian O'Nolan) completed The Third Policeman in 1940 but the book was published only in 1967, after his death.

◀ *Irish policemen from around the time O'Brien wrote The Third Policemen.*

Wiki Commons.

He Followed no Rules

The Wild Hills,
by Rupert Croft-Cooke

The attitudes and escapades of Richard Blake Brown were, to say the least, unconventional. He lived and cycled in the rural Cotswolds and London, in the mid-1930s.

He cycled for pleasure and alone and he so loved and trusted his bicycle. He made of cycling more than either a sport or a necessity, a gesture of defiance of all the advancing forces of destruction. He rode with a suggestion of contempt for both car drivers and pedestrians – for him this was the best, the only enjoyable means of transport. It was a cult, not a hobby.

He used his cycle for some impertinent escapades which laid him open to snubs, prohibitions, even penalties. He cycled about London oblivious of frayed tempers in drivers or police, conforming to traffic regulations as much as he could conform to anything but with an air of *droit de seigneur* which must have been very infuriating to hard-pressed motorists. Sitting upright, dressed in elegant town clothes, he would ride down Piccadilly as though it were the drive of his private park. He cycled into the Tower of London and was saluted as a returning officer, he cycled into the grounds of royal palaces and private mansions, calmly to ring at some stone carved entrance and demand to see the building. He cycled up to the doors of the Berkeley or the Dorchester and coolly handed his bicycle to an usually over-tipped and self-important doorman with instructions to look after it while Richard was dining. (The unfortunate man would find himself holding the thing before he realised what had happened.)

He sometimes gained access to houses which were not open to view while the family was in residence. When I protested at this he looked puzzled.

'But they must surely have been delighted that someone gay and amusing appeared unexpectedly. I know I should be!'

At night in my cottage, he would recall the adventures of the road. During the time – less than two years – that he remained in Salterton he must have visited every Cotswold village and seen every large building, ecclesiastical or domestic, of note. He had a good eye for comic or pretentious detail and an amusing love, as wayward as Betjeman's, for Victorian Gothic. But he saw landscapes, too, and fine architecture and beauty unspoiled in the grey stone villages.

The Wild Hills was published in 1966 by W. H. Allen and is out of print.

Bucolic on Bikes

The Little World of Don Camillo, by Giovanni Guareschi

This book, published in 1948, is infused with the author's love for the people of the Po Valley in post war Italy, and their bucolic, bicycle-riding lives little touched by industrialisation.

The Little World revolves around the entertaining power struggle and mutual respect binding together the priest, Don Camillo, and his adversary, Peponne, the Communist mayor. The work is filled with comic incidents, several involving bicycles. The bicycle was an important part of life in the Po Valley, at a time when car ownership was unimaginable. Guareschi explains that: *"the peasants for the most part use women's models, and the paunchy landowners trundle along on old-fashioned contraptions with a high seat which they reach by means of a little step screwed onto the rear axle."* Guareschi describes Po Valley bicycles as heavy and ramshackle, braked by applying foot to tyre rubber. *"City people's bicycles,"* he says, *"are utterly laughable. With gleaming metal gadgets, electric batteries, gears, baskets, chainguards, speedometers and so on, they are mere toys and leg-exercisers."*

Po Valley bicycles, on the other hand, blend in with the landscape, never trying to be showy: *"as opposed to racing models which are like third-rate chorus girls next to a substantial housewife. City people can't be expected to understand these things."*

Cycling is central to the life and duties of the priest Don Camillo. On one occasion his beloved cycle is stolen. He begins the long walk home trying to come to terms with this:

❝ The fact that a country priest, with twenty-five lire in his pocket, had been robbed of a bicycle was a private and moral problem, and not one to be introduced into the public domain. Your rich man, to whom it is all a matter of money, may rush to report a theft. But to the

Photo: Sue Darlow

Italian clergy are increasingly seen cycling. During the Annual Congress of the European Cycling Union In 2019 Pope Francis declared that cycling promotes patience, integrity, altruism, and team spirit.

poor it is a personal injustice, in the same class as striking a cripple or knocking his crutch out from under him. ❞

After a while Don Camillo comes across his bike leaning against the parapet of a bridge with the thief resting by the river below. He is full of remorse that the bicycle belonged to a priest – unemployment and hunger had driven him to the crime. Don Camillo takes the man to his presbytery and cooks him a meal. Before long he had given the man a job as the parish bell-ringer.

On another occasion Pepponi, the hot-headed mayor, sets off on an ill-advised mission with a machine gun strapped to his bike (not all weapons were handed in during the post war amnesty). Don Camillo cycles at speed in pursuit, and the two meet by a bridge. Somehow Peppone ends up in the river below and so Don Camillo kindly returns to the village with both cycles. When the bedraggled Pepponi returns hours later he finds that the machine gun has inexplicably disappeared from his bicycle.

The Little World of Don Camillo is published in English by Pilot Projects.

Photo: Todd Cravens, Unsplash

The Kingdom of the Pedal

China Cyclist, by John Stuart Clark

China was still very much the Kingdom of the Cyclist in 2006. John Stuart Clark describes his learning curve while cycling in Jingdezhen.

I found myself in Jingdezhen, some 300 miles south west of Shanghai, in a province best known as a seedbed for Mao's particularly vicious brand of Communism. My mountain base nestled among strange conical hills, dense with temperate jungle – the model for 'mountain and water' blue-and-white decorations on Ming vases.

While the plague of motorists might have swept through megacities like Beijing and Shanghai, the denizens of Jingdezhen (JDZ) simply weren't rich enough to buy into the boom. Taxis, buses and trucks constituted the bulk of motorised road transport, all driven by government employees or sub-contractors whose lives would be worthless if they so much as clipped a *laowai* ('foreigner') pedestrian or cyclist. I concluded that cycling in JDZ was in fact safer than in my home town of Nottingham, provided I never forgot that anything goes on thoroughfares where bullocks and carts, tricycle freight carriers, 'bang-bang' men and even dog walkers all consider they have the superior right of way.

I'm tall, so the bicycle I settled on was predicated by frame size. I bought new, and was to learn how the trade operates. Forget about test rides and after-sales service. You get what you get, and if something needs sorting you take it to one of the bicycle-repairmen found on virtually every street corner in downtown China. When the chain snapped on my maiden voyage I made the mistake of doing my own repairs. The crowd that instantly gathered meant I spent a good half an hour on an operation I later discovered my local repairman, Mr. Wang, could perform for close to nothing.

Bicycles and tricycles are still exploited for everything from taxi services to fast-food cafés, freight haulage to personal transport, but they are rarely used for distance cycling. In the three months of my sojourn, I saw only one group of Chinese on their equivalent to a club rider's Sunday pootle. The more I came to meet Jingdezheners who pedalled, the clearer it became that to ride a death trap sporting one brake block, two buckled wheels and a set of pedals reduced to spindles was *de rigeur* in China.

I never once feared for my safety either on the road or amongst the people. The landscape I cruised through was like nothing I had ever seen, and by restricting myself to a single province I know I returned with a better understanding of the land of the Han than any of my friends who ticked off the grand tour. Of course the beauty of pottering around on a Chinese bicycle was that it not infrequently needed attention, leading to even more remarkable encounters with a population who still largely believe Westerners are 'barbarians'.

China Cyclist first appeared in Bike Culture Quarterly (no longer published). John Stuart Clark's cartoons, under the name of 'Brick', are featured on page 318 and elsewhere, and his graphic investigation into 'Leonardo's Bicycle' is on page 288. See also brickbats.co.uk.

The Skeleton in the Cupboard

After the Goldrush, by John Stuart Clark

Riding three thousand miles west across the USA, John Stuart Clark (aka the cartoonist Brick) followed the route of the Californian Goldrush. He is almost overwhelmed by the people, terrain and climate. The town of Gerlach, on the edge of the Black Rock Desert, was to offer a particularly unexpected experience.

Ahead, white rectangles in a green blur suggested this time I really was approaching Gerlach… An hour and a half later I was close enough to confirm the blur was the oasis. Between me and the gallon of root beer I had fantasised about for most of the day lay a moat of porridge. Whichever tack I took, I ran into gloop. Finally, I gave up trying to pick my way through and slopped straight across three miles of alkaline mud dragging the bike, never thinking I was wallowing in something vicious. It was another hour and a quarter before I crawled up the beach to the isthmus of sand on which Gerlach rested. From knees down, my skin was on fire.

I staggered into the Texaco station like Swamp Thing emerging from the quagmire. It was more a workshop with a broken drinks machine than a service station with a mini mart. The mechanic pointed me in the direction of Bruno's restaurant and bar. I tried to saunter in nonchalantly but blew it when I fell against the bar and whispered beer.

"Wassat? Where you ridden from?" Bruno asked.

I muttered. *"Ha!"*

Bruno was a man of few words and those he shared were short. The woman sat next to me at the bar explained his attitude problem was probably a product of Italian-Basque parentage. She cleaned the motel for him.

"The blockhouse you passed after the gas station."

"I did?"

"You're in a kinda state." she observed.

The cleaning lady took charge of me. She ordered another round of drinks, handed over the key to a room in Bruno's motel and sent me away to sort myself out. Leaning on my bike, I cheated back down the road to the blockhouse and flopped onto the bed. I could have drifted into oblivion but badly needed to attend to my burning flesh. Stripped and aiming for the shower, I stumbled into the bathroom and immediately jumped back in surprise. There was a skeleton in the cupboard.

I hadn't seen myself naked in a full length mirror since Paul and Arlene's place back in Nebraska. My collarbones protruded like granite mountains from a playa of stretched skin the colour of terracotta. When I moved an arm you could see every sinew operating. My face, arms and legs were dusted in white compact and streaked with rivers of sweat. My eyes were blood red and, around my mouth, it looked like I'd eaten a meringue off a plate without using hands. Except for stinging skin, a ringing in my ears, a mouth washed out with kitchen cleaner and utter exhaustion, I felt better than I looked. In ten days time I was due to meet my wife at Sacramento. I imagined Sandy taking one look at my emaciated body and calling Oxfam.

After the Goldrush, written in 2004, is published by fiveleaves.co.uk

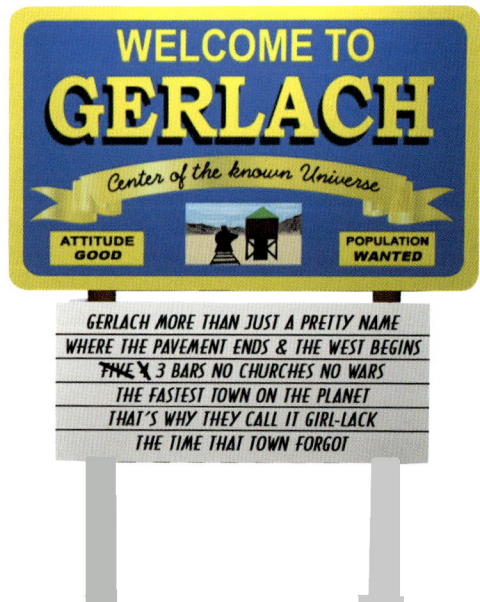

WELCOME TO GERLACH
Center of the known Universe
ATTITUDE GOOD
POPULATION WANTED

GERLACH MORE THAN JUST A PRETTY NAME
WHERE THE PAVEMENT ENDS & THE WEST BEGINS
THE 3 BARS NO CHURCHES NO WARS
THE FASTEST TOWN ON THE PLANET
THAT'S WHY THEY CALL IT GIRL-LACK
THE TIME THAT TOWN FORGOT

Philosophers fall off

La Force de l'Âge (1960), by Simone de Beauvoir

French philosopher and writer Simone de Beauvoir's autobiography, La Force de l'Âge (1960), details some foolhardy cycling adventures with her life-companion and fellow philosopher and writer, Jean-Paul Sartre. Unsurprisingly we also get some bicycle philosophy. As a relief from German-occupied Paris de Beauvoir and Sartre often rode into the countryside.

De Beauvoir studying with bicycle, 1946

66 *Sartre much preferred riding a bicycle to walking. The monotony of walking bored him, while the intensity of effort and the rhythm of a bicycle journey varied constantly. He would amuse himself by sprinting on the hills. I would become winded and fall behind him. On level stretches he pedalled with such indifference that on two or three occasions he landed in the ditch. 'I was thinking of other things,' he would say. Both of us loved the freedom of downhill runs. The scenery flew by more quickly than when we were on foot. Like him, I was quite willing to swap my old passion for walking for this new pleasure.* 99

De Beauvoir was no more skilled at cycling than Sartre: '*I really handled it with ease, except one time I crashed into a dog and another time I collided with two women, and I was very happy.*' She also writes of a cycling accident when out with Sartre in which she lost a tooth in a downhill crash.

Sartre and de Beauvoir had an open relationship. In her wartime diary, de Beauvoir describes how she learned to ride using a bicycle loaned by her former student and then lover, Nathalie Sorokine. It was probably one of many bikes her lover had stolen to repaint and sell.

Sartre, being Sartre, liked to examine intellectually the meaning of a bicycle. Looking at it or touching it are not enough. Just riding it is not enough. The bicycle needs tasks, purposes. But these trips themselves disintegrate into '*a thousand appropriative behaviour patterns, each one of which refers to others*'. Luckily he helps us grasp this better by concluding that '*handing over a bank note is enough to make a bicycle belong to me, but my entire life is needed to realise this possession.*'

Jean-Paul Sartre in occupied Paris, riding an astonishingly modern looking folding cycle, 'le Petit Bi'. This picture was recently discovered in Signal, a propaganda magazine produced by the Nazis trying to show that life was normal for the French people under the German occupation.

Very few examples of this cycle have survived. We know it was invented by Andre Jules Marcelin, a French physicist and Nobel Laureate. He received his first patent in 1939, but little progress was made, presumably because of WW2.

Leonardo would have Laughed

The Curious Case of Leonardo's Bicycle, by John Stuart Clark

In his satirical, comedic whodunnit the author and illustrator tells of intrigue, greed and the human condition. It's an unlikely but valuable book, a panorama of humankind's optimism, idiocy, tragedy and occasional brilliance. Its comic edge keeps us reading as it cycles through social movements and the foibles of individuals humble and grand. Our tour guide pedals round Italy and France popping up here and there to set the scene. But not before he frames the bicycle as "a vehicle of delights that flies the rider high above their worldly cares and woes". The journey begins, contexts are drawn (literally) and we experience history as rarely recounted: in fast-mode and with attention-grabbing transitions in time and place.

In his introduction John Stuart Clark claims his motivation was to clear Leonardo's name and to reinstate Karl von Drais, inventor of the steerable 'running machine', as the man who revolutionised transportation forever. Leonardo's Bicycle achieves much more than that. Skilful, discursive cartoons present us with political intrigue, chauvinism, the collaboration of the Catholic Church with the Nazis and Fascists, Italian cycle race fanaticism, academics' arrogance, artists' venality, crass commercialisation, and of course, the true genius of Leonardo. Humour and broad-ranging insights reveal universal truths.

Whodunnit?

The initial culprit was someone unknown, within the slapdash restoration workshop of the Biblioteca Ambrosiana in Italy. He elaborated on an existing pair of compass circles to sketch out a bicycle. It was then hidden by being pasted to the back of another sheet. The sketch was not intended to be found, but was revealed by other restorers and announced to the world by Professor Augusto Marinoni in 1974 (deceased in 1997). Marinoni promoted the Leonardo's bicycle fallacy with little academic rigour and evidence. His unapologetic ghost haunts the final pages of John Stuart Clark's graphic enquiry. Involved in the final demolition of the myth were Hans-Erhart Lessing, Head Conservator at the Museum of Mannheim, and Emeritus Professor Martin Kemp of Oxford University.

John Stuart Clark is also known as the cartoonist Brick. www.leonardosbicycle.co.uk.

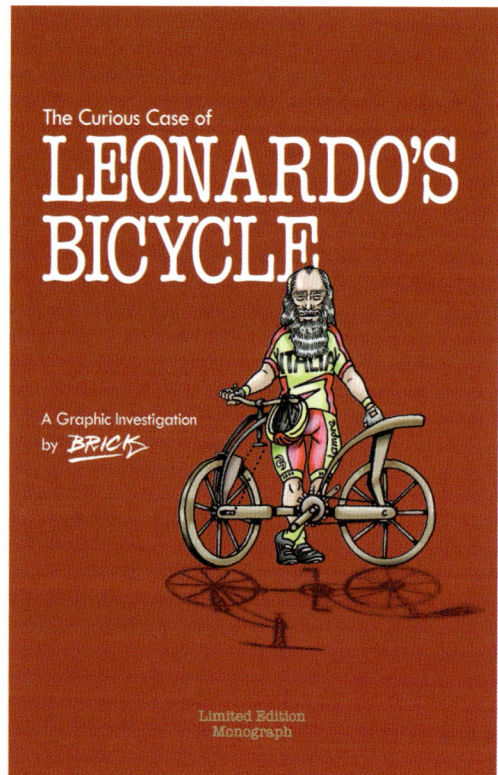

Brick ridicules the argument put forward by Marinoni that the Maestro found the time to perfect what the more technically advanced 19th century took 80 years to crack.

The power behind the myth was the juggernaut of commercial interests squeezing maximum profit out of all matters Leonardo. Even today many commercial exhibitions around the world feature the 'Leo-bike'. Mini wooden kit versions are available online or through the gift shop.

We learn how the ash from the eruption of Mt Tambora in 1815 caused crop failure and famine in Central Europe for several years, and the death by starvation of many horses. Brick and others believe this shortage of horses, central to human activity, gave impetus to the invention of the running machine as a replacement. It was first demonstrated two years after the eruption.

IN FACT THE FIRST MACHINE APPROXIMATING THE FRAUDULENT DESIGN DIDN'T APPEAR UNTIL THE 1880'S, ...

DOOR TO SAME DOOR, HE CLOCKS 15K IN UNDER AN HOUR, FASTER THAN THE MAIL COACH!

The narrator finally found the truth behind the farago of incompetence and deception.

Encounters

Many prominent authors have recounted interesting cycling experiences.

Connections

In his book *The Man who Loved Bicycles* (1973) American Daniel Behrman has a theory that: *'Bikes talk to each other like dogs, they wag their wheels and tinkle their bells, the riders let their mounts mingle.'* He describes the sheer serendipity and pleasure of his encounters with other cyclists in Paris:

66 *A cyclist with a load of 'Le Mondes' on his handlebars asked me how much I paid for my black bike, the one that a bike racer's son made up for me for city riding and occasional country sprinting, not a Ferrari but still an Alfa. I tell him; he thinks I got a good buy. A Portuguese labourer catches me on the squirrel cage at Longchamp; I speed up, we go round together, he asks me where I am riding next Sunday. We have a lot in common, we are both cyclists, we are both foreigners. I sneak up on a young man in the Bois de Vincennes. I get into his slip-stream then I race by him in the hope that he won't be able to get into mine, but he does. He's a salesman, it's not an easy life, he has heard that things are better in America. I give him the embassy's phone number.* 99

Obsession

A love of bikes can also isolate. In his book *My Bike and other Friends* US writer Henry Miller describes his cycling obsession as a youth in New York, around 1912.

66 *After a time, habituated to spending so many hours a day on my bike, I became less and less interested in my friends. My wheel had now become my one and only 'friend'. I could rely on it, which is more than I could say about my buddies.* 99

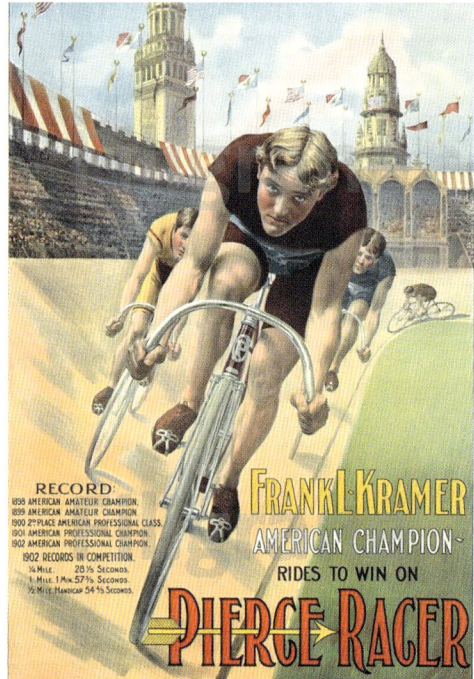

RECORD
1898 AMERICAN AMATEUR CHAMPION.
1899 AMERICAN AMATEUR CHAMPION
1900 2nd PLACE AMERICAN PROFESSIONAL CLASS.
1901 AMERICAN PROFESSIONAL CHAMPION.
1902 AMERICAN PROFESSIONAL CHAMPION.
1902 RECORDS IN COMPETITION.
¼ MILE. 26½ SECONDS.
1 MILE. 1 MIN. 57½ SECONDS.
½ MILE HANDICAP 54⅖ SECONDS.

FRANK L KRAMER
AMERICAN CHAMPION·
RIDES TO WIN ON
PIERCE RACER

However, cycling did bring this socially disengaged young man close to his idol, Frank Kramer, the champion sprinter:

66 *Once I managed to stay right behind him during one of his practice spins from Prospect Park to Coney Island. I remember him slapping me on the back when I caught up with him and, as he slapped my back, said – Good work, young fella. Keep it up!* 99

Betrayal

Sometimes the act of riding a bike, when the social climate is not with you, creates a sense of solidarity. This can be challenged by unwelcome facts. In *All the President's Men* (Carl Bernstein and Bob Woodward, 1974) Bernstein describes what he discovered while investigating the Watergate scandal:

66 *His mind was on Jeb Magruder. He had picked up a profoundly disturbing piece of information that day: Magruder was a bike freak. Bernstein had trouble swallowing the information that*

a bicycle nut could be a Watergate bugger. And Magruder really was a card-carrying bicycle freak who had even ridden his 10-speed to the White House every day. 🙶

Independence

Even fleeting encounters can be meaningful. In *Hovel in the Hills* (1977) Elizabeth West describes how she and her husband Alan had exchanged their city jobs for a subsistence living in a small, remote cottage in Wales. They often cycled out to forage for fruit:

🙶 *With the bikes leaning up against a farm gate, we were sitting at the roadside munching apples. The scent of wild rose and honeysuckle filled the air and the sounds of summer were all around us. I felt absolutely in my right element. I was not just living through a summer's afternoon – I was part of it. Suddenly a car came round the bend and drove on towards Colwyn Bay. A woman looked out of the side window and for an instant. We would have been about the same age. I imagined*

what it must have felt like to her, sitting inside that car – all clean, tidy, nylon-tighted and upright, with the hot interior car smell of fumes and warm plastic. What would they do when they got to Colwyn Bay? She would get stiffly out of the car, straighten her dress and find her handbag. They would walk around for a bit, go into a cafe and have tea, and then drive home. I lay back on the grass; I was dusty, sweaty and absolutely content. I would not, under any circumstances, wish to change places with that woman. And she, looking out at me sitting on my backside at the edge of the road, and probably felt exactly the same 🙶

Incomprehension

Sometimes cyclists face the incredulity of people who don't understand their passion. Dervla Murphy, a much-admired Irish lone-cyclist, describes one incident of mutual incomprehension in her book *Full Tilt, Ireland to India with a Bicycle* (1965). As she neared the border with Afghanistan, happy on her bicycle Roz, an American engineer pulled up in his jeep to investigate. His question: *"What the hell are you doing on this goddam road?"* Dervla took an instant dislike to him, and simply answered: *'Cycling'*, and added that it was *'for fun'*.

The American became insistent:

🙶 *Are you a nutcase or what? Give me that bike and I'll stick it on behind and you get in here and we'll get out of this goddam frying pan as fast as we can. This track isn't fit for a camel!* 🙶

Dervla wasn't having that:

🙶 *When you're on a cycle instead of in a jeep it doesn't feel like a frying pan. Moreover, if you look around you you'll notice that the landscape compensates for the admittedly deplorable state of the road. In fact I enjoy cycling through this sort of country – but thank you for the kind offer. Goodbye.* 🙶

"I regard this sort of life," (she tells the reader) *"with just Roz and me and the sky and earth, as sheer bliss."*

Dishonour

Lance Armstrong is an intelligent and articulate athlete who had become, it seemed, a role model for the ages. He no doubt inspired millions, helped by his 2003 autobiography, *Every Second Counts,* co-written by a sports journalist. The book is full of wholesome homilies:

❝ *When you win, you don't examine it very much, except to congratulate yourself. You easily, and wrongly, assume it has something to do with your rare qualities as a person. But winning only measures how hard you've worked and how physically talented you are; it doesn't particularly define you beyond those characteristics...*

Each time I encountered suffering, I believed that I grew, and further defined my capacities – not just my physical ones, but my interior ones as well, for contentment, friendship, or any other human experience. ❞

In 2012 Armstrong was stripped of his seven Tour de France titles and in 2013 he finally confessed that he had used doping during the height of his career.

Armstrong's belief in the potential of will power also informed his extraordinarily successful battle against Stage 3 testicular cancer, but will power is not in itself a moral value.

Integrity

Far, far away from the murky world of some professional cyclists are the millions of gentler spirits who just love cycling to get about. One such is Alan Bennett: English playwright, social critic, and a 'national treasure'. He says:

❝ *I don't think of it so much as a hobby, more as a way of getting around. But it puts me in a good mood, particularly if you're cycling past lines of cars waiting in a jam.* ❞

In Bennett's first television play, *A Day Out* (1972), a Halifax cycling club set off on a day trip to Fountains Abbey. The eleven male companions meet early in the deserted streets to negotiate the town's challenging hills and cobbles. En route to the Cistercian ruin, the pals exchange banter and deal with punctures and spills. It's 1911, the First World

War is round the corner. There not much action, but gently and persistently the story picks at issues we'd later recognise as classic Bennett themes: class, social hierarchies, overbearing mothers, the kindness and cruelties towards those with learning difficulties. Reassembling after the First World War on Remembrance Day, the club's depleted ranks provide an eloquent reflection on the Edwardian ecstasy and the catastrophe that brought about its end. *(Our thanks to cycling-books.com.)*

Pretensions

In his book, *Bike Snob,* Eben Weiss (aka *BikeSnobNYC)* takes us on a tour of all the eccentricities, pretensions and absurdities of fellow cyclists. Despite the title it's not snobbish. It burst bubbles and encourages us to see humour in the many subsets of bicycle lovers. It's a curious mix of insights, humour and information. Here, for example, the author warns, encourages and amuses all at the same time:

❝ *Subcultures aren't all bad. Sometimes you're attracted to a look or a machine (such as a bike), you try it out, and you discover something you love. Then again, sometimes the subculture can be all about the trappings, in which case it's mostly just a trap. Not only can fussing with the trappings keep you from enjoying the valuable thing that lies beneath your own subculture, but it can also keep you from exploring a different one. The only thing worse than obsessing over your race bike is obsessing over your race bike you'll never race. It's like tuning an instrument you'll never play. And swearing an oath that you will only ride one type of bike ('Fixed Forever!') is almost as bad as never riding at all. As a physical endeavour cycling requires some thought about equipment and clothes, and where there's equipment and clothes there are subcultures. But the most important thing to remember is that nobody has stewardship or dominion over the joys of cycling. Just treat all the posturing like a BMX race – a bunch of nonsense that evaporates the second the gate goes down.* ❞

Bike Snob is published in a US edition by Chronicle Books, San Francisco, and in a UK edition by Hardie Grant Books.

CHAPTER 10
The Art of Cycling

Early Days of Cycle Art

Artists of the 19th century were enthused by cycling as a novel and thrilling activity.

▲ *Illustrators took either a lighthearted view of hobbyhorses, or emphasised dangers. But this work, from 1819, does both – there were such velocipede versus horse races. Entitled 'March against Time' or 'Wood beats Blood and Bone', it shows both riders in jockey attire. (From the collection of Roger Street.)*

This scurrilous print of 1819 ▶ *shows the unpopular Prince Regent and his friend Lady Hertford having a relationship on a hobbyhorse. There is no evidence he ever rode one. The print is by J. Lewis Marks.*

A P---e, Driving his Hobby, in HERDFORD !!!

▲ Boneshakers (velocipedes) in the USA. This image of 1866 exudes elegance, propriety and fashion. Courtesy of the Federal Highway Administration.

'A Meeting on the Road from Layston Villa to Hormead Cottage', a watercolour by James Wilcox, from 1849. It's a fascinating picture since it shows a tricycle and a quadricycle of a type virtually unknown to cycle historians. The are clearly propelled by feet on the ground, since pedal-power had yet to be invented, and they feature the large wheels then common on horse-drawn vehicles to counteract the state of the roads. These are moneyed gentleman, riding sedately, three decades after the short-lived two-wheeled hobbyhorse craze. (From the collection of Cycling UK.) ▼

▲ Looking like a French fashion-plate of around 1890, this picture of a ladies' high bicycle race is probably wishful thinking on the part of the unknown artist. The scene has been overlaid with the aura of fashionable horse-racing with its elegant Longchamps grandstand, notice-boards for the odds and the riders' bonnet-like jockey caps. The winner's immodest posture was calculated to titillate and shock, as she flings a well-developed leg over the bars to slow down her machine. We see the reaction of the genteel lady who appears to be fainting away in horror.

The Velocipede Race

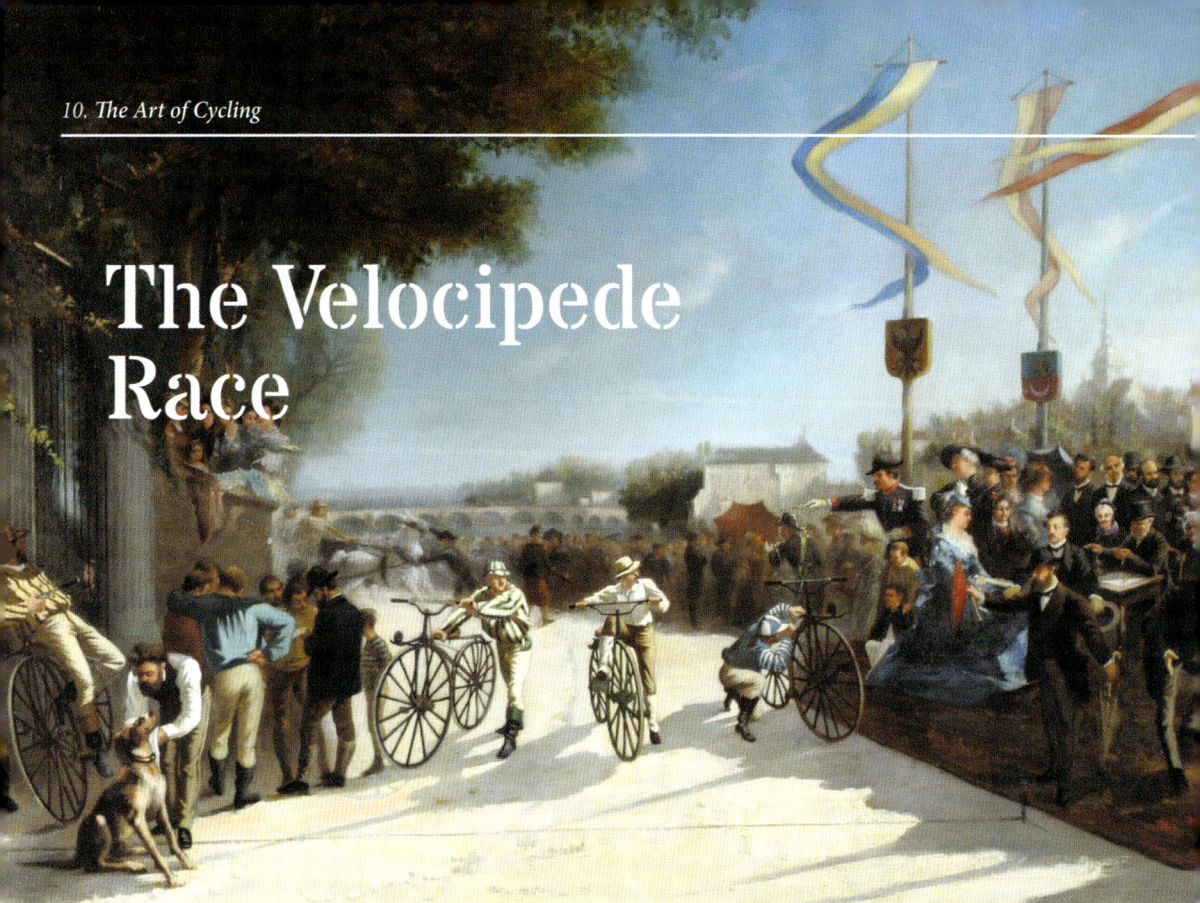

In the late 1860s the French velocipede craze was at its height, so it is little surprise that 22 velocipedists were willing to bring their machines to the small French town of Gray, to compete in its *Course de vélocipèdes*. There were many such events across provincial France, but this one was captured in magnificent animation by local painter Joseph Roux. Only four or five years had passed since velocipedes had first been seen on the streets of Paris and the sense of excitement and novelty is felt in all the busy detail and movement within this painting.

The Course de vélocipèdes: le départ, painted in 1869, is delightful social history. It is also a rarity in that, although the artist had the formal, classical training of the time, this painting is anything but classical: it shows ordinary people taking unsophisticated pleasure in a real event. We also see local dignitaries, many of whom have been identified by name and social position. We see the artist's brother, editor of the local paper, huddled with riders and taking notes. We see the professional riders in jockey-style clothes, and the plainly dressed local amateur riders. We see details which probably relate to incidents on the day, and possibly living on as in-jokes around

the town. For example, what is going on with the seemingly out of control horse carriage about to burst onto the scene? Did the sweaty dog being wiped down chase the riders round the 5km (3 mile) course? What is up with the disgruntled rider far right?

This happy race day becomes poignant when set against the backdrop of history. It was the time of the Second Empire. France was doing well economically, commercially and technically. Napoleon III was delighted by velocipedes and had one made for his own use, in aluminium: a newly discovered metal and very expensive. The Gray cycle race exemplifies a similar innocence at play: all to be shattered just 14 months later by the Franco-Prussian War. France was heavily defeated, the Emperor deposed, and the town of Gray occupied by the Prussians.

'The Velocipede Race' is owned by the National Cycle Museum 'Velorama' in the Netherlands. Their English-language book, 'Joseph Roux and the Course de vélocipèdes', dedicated to just this picture, is elegantly written by cycle art historian Scotford Lawrence and we have drawn here, with permission, from his work.

Painting the Big Wheel

▲ *On the Beach at Ostende by Robert Alott (1859–1910). This strange work, in oil on panel, was painted in 1888, towards the end of the high bicycle era. An elegantly dressed lady gazes at us while a very improbable high bicycle rider approaches from behind. Will she be shocked? It's not clear why the people in the water are such giants.*

The Mount, by Gaines Ruger Donoho, from around 1884. Born in Mississippi, he studied at the Académie Julian in Paris. He remained in France from 1878 to 1887, spending time in the south of the country, where this oil on canvas was probably executed. Courtesy of the Stent Family Wing Archives of the High Museum, Atlanta, USA. ▼

The Explosion of Colour

How two technologies boomed together

▲ *This impressionist painting by Joseph Crawhall III of Newcastle upon Tyne captures in a few brushstrokes the movement of the rider. It became a popular postcard image.*

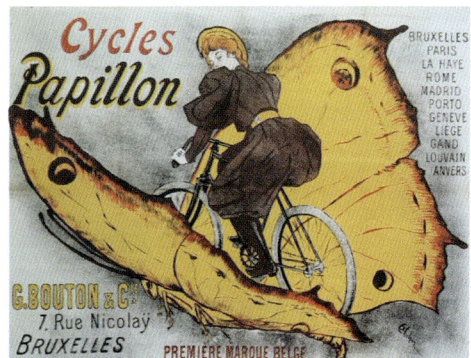

By the 1890s the high wheeler had been superseded by the safety bicycle, enabling the less adventurous to take to the wheel. A bicycle craze amongst the moneyed classes coincided with the proliferation, primarily in France, of luxuriously colourful advertising posters, many of which promoted tyres, bicycles and velodromes.

It is no accident that the golden age of poster design coincided with a golden age of cycling in the mid-1890s. In the closing decades of the 19th Century both industries experienced a technological revolution that commandeered the public's attention. Both expressed a *joie de vivre*, and brought colour and excitement to the

▲ *A bold and whimsical image of flight and freedom, from the Belgian company Cycles Papillon, 1896.*

grimy streets of industrialised cities. And as consumerism gathered pace in western culture, manufacturers, artists and designers enjoyed a creative relationship which revitalised the art of advertising.

The end of the 19th century was a turbulent yet optimistic time. France had patched itself together after the Franco-Prussian war. The French had ripped out the seedy centre of their capital and were rebuilding to shape the majestic Paris we know today. Cycling added to the new sense of vigour and progress.

Idealised, goddess-like women were portrayed in suggestive proximity to bicycles. The use of erotic, mythological and allegorical themes gave products an aura of fantasy, exoticism and even grandeur, as well as revealing a classical bias in the artists' education.

Technical advances also led to a boom in illustrated periodicals, and pictures sold magazines. New, large-page formats made these pictures very popular: readers could cut them out to hang on the wall.

▲ *A French poster within a poster advertising an indoor cycling centre with a thousand metres of track.*

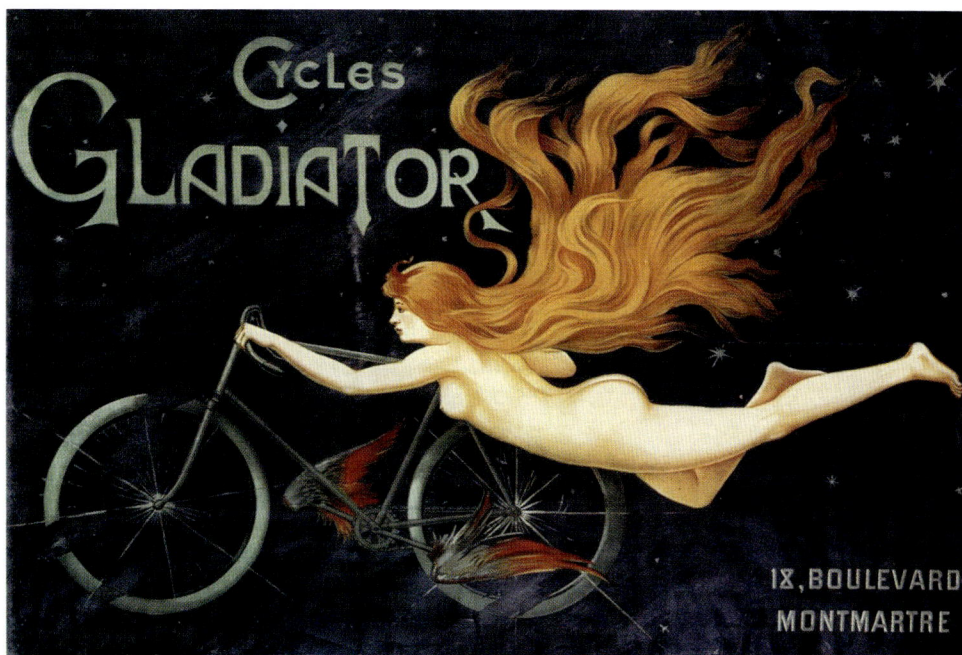

▲ *The unknown artist of the infamous Cycles Gladiator image managed to combine virtually all the touchstones of 1890s cycle art – flight, fantasy, mythology, powerful hair and sexual attraction. Gone is the voluminous clothing worn by most women in European advertising art of the time.*

▲ *Buy a bike which impresses the ladies! A French advertisement for an English cycle.*

◀ *In contrast with naked goddesses and butterflies is this message by Austrian arms manufacturer Swift-Steyr in about 1895.*

Postcards were a major platform for cycle art. Some promoted products, others sold happy feelings. This water colour of 1897 by the Munich artist Ernst Platz evokes bucolic conviviality. 'Versuchung' means 'temptation'.

In reality cycling was intensively regulated by the Bavarian police and prosecutions were common.

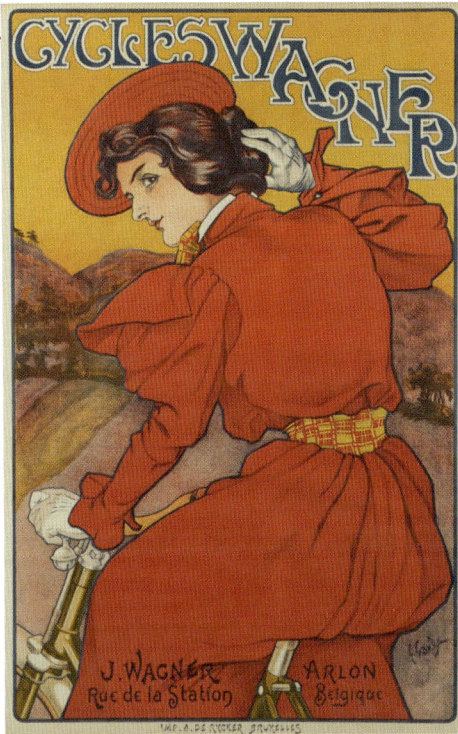

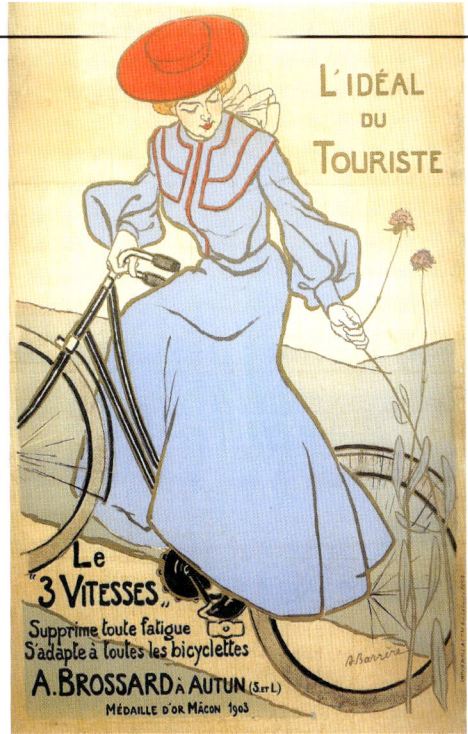

▲ These two posters (1900 and 1903) show that sections of the commercial art world in Europe were moving on: to cleaner lines and flatter renditions. The advertisement above right was for three-speed hub gears, which 'suppress all tiredness and can be fitted to all bicycles'. Thanks to her gears this lady cycles uphill with ease, and she's relaxed enough to pick flowers on the way.

This poster by Dutch artist Daan Hoeksema in 1907 shows how far European cycle advertising had come since the fashionable cycling boom of the late 1890s. The simple shapes and coloration complement the very name of the product: Simplex Cycles. The message is not a lifestyle one but a technical one ('70% less friction'). Also, the rider is of indeterminate age and class, and could be cycling to work. Times were beginning to change.

▲ A French poster from around 1913. The bicycle, combined with sensible clothing, was bringing new forms of freedom for children, too.

Commercial Art USA

Until the late 1880s posters were seen as adjuncts to commerce, with little artistic value. In 1890s Europe poster art intended for the moneyed classes reflected bourgeois values of ornamentation and excess.

The USA was introduced to Art Nouveau in 1890 when copies of *Harper's Weekly* made their way from France and England. American artists and publishers became inspired by the movement, which emphasised sweeping lines and two-dimensional flatness of surface rather than complexity and depth. They were particularly influenced by the work of Aubrey Beardsley in the UK, and his Yellow Book.

This decorative art form coincided with, and supported, the great American bicycle boom of 1895 and 1896. Mass-circulation magazines published special bicycle issues, and Art Nouveau was prominent on their covers. Bicycle makers rushed to associate themselves with this new art fashion, more so than their European equivalents.

The cover of the May 1894 edition of the 'Century Magazine' in the United States. There was keen public interest in cyclists exploring the world. (Metropolitan Museum of Art)

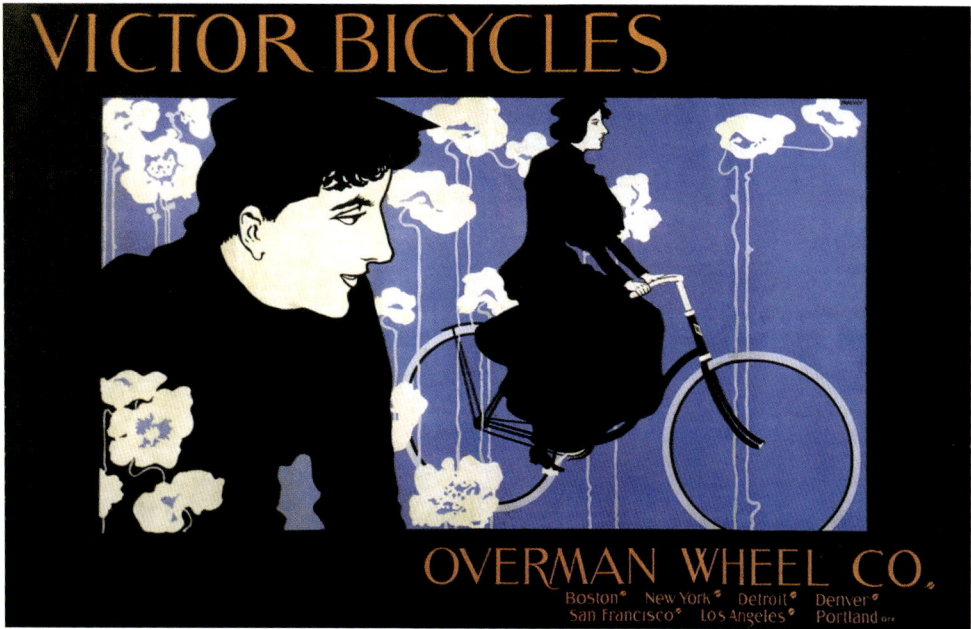

▲ The art of Edward Penfield was steeped in Art Nouveau. His famous illustration for the Overman Wheel Company's Victor Bicycle in 1896 was thought to speak for that company's progressive views, but the company failed soon after, with the sudden collapse of the US bicycle boom.

▼ Penfield's main client was Harper's Weekly but he occasionally created his impassive cycling figures for manufacturers such as Stearns and Northampton.

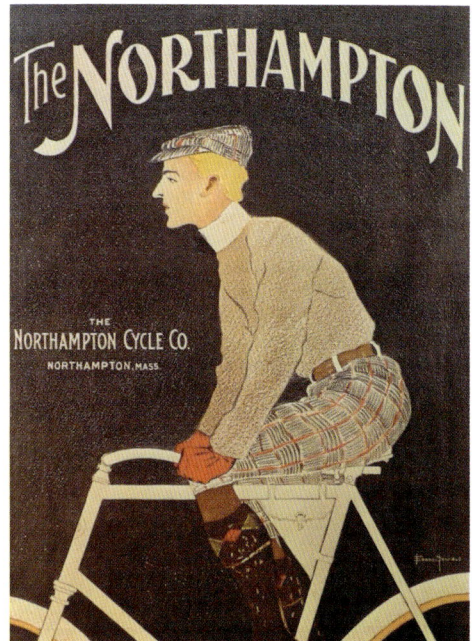

Commercial art USA

▲ Above: two posters from the Pope Manufacturing Company. The cluttered poster from around 1888 is a wordy handbill style of advertising. It was used by Pope before the craze for safety cycles arrived. It contrasts strongly with the Art Nouveau poster for their Olympia Bicycles, about eight years later.

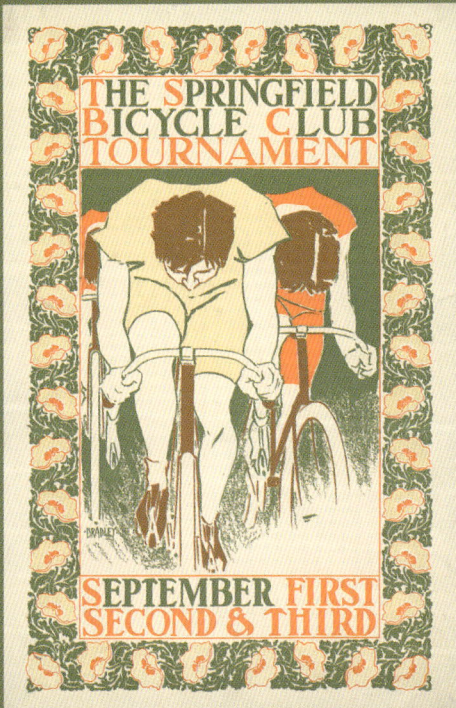

◀ Left: A Will Bradley advertisement for the Springfield Bicycle Club, 1896.

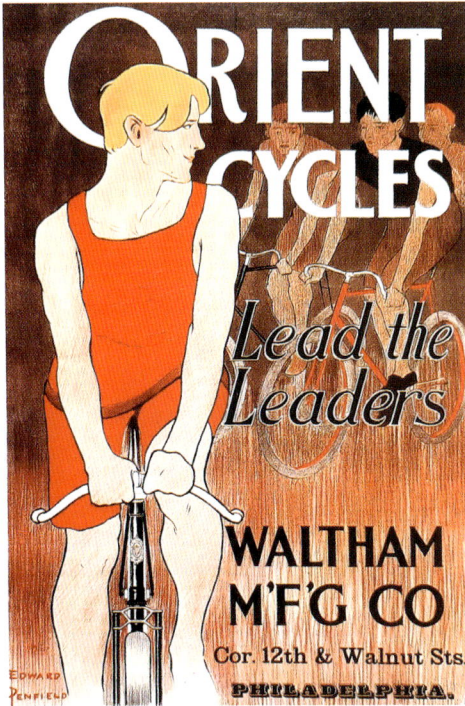

▲ A parallel market for manufacturers was provided by young males with aspirations towards athleticism. These were clean lines for clean-cut customers. This artwork is by Edward Penfield, 1895.

▲ The toff no longer has a need for a carriage and the coachman is not well pleased. Neither form of unmotorised transport was to thrive in the USA.

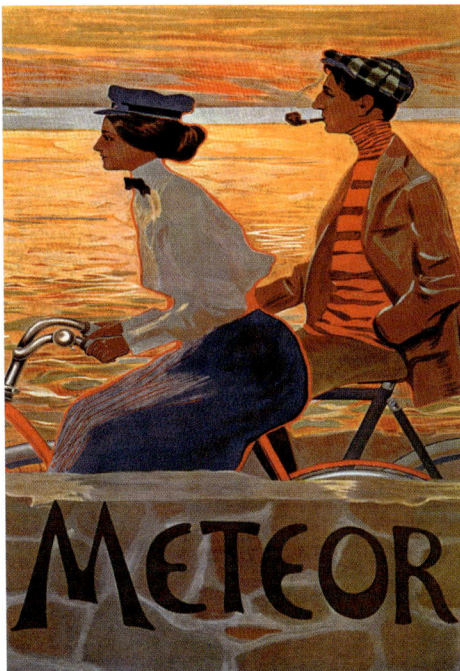

▲ The power of colour, 1910.

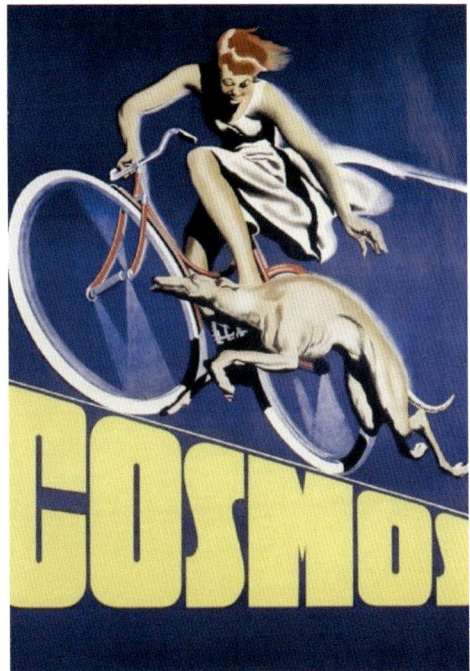

▲ A breathless 1935 advertising image for the Swiss company Cosmos Bicycles.

Cycling in Fine Art

▲ *'The Morning Ride' by Erik Henningsen, 1907. A Danish couple enjoy affection and togetherness in the sun-blessed countryside, contrasting with the townscape of industrial chimneys.*

These scenes of gentle pleasure, entitled 'On a Bicycle', show women friends relaxing. Impressionist painter Federico Zandomeneghi was born in Venice but spent the later part of his life in Paris, where these paintings were probably created in 1896.

▲ *Artist Jean Béraud captured this scene of well-off Parisians at the 'Chalet du Cycle' among the treelined avenues of the Bois de Boulogne, around 1900.*

▲ *'Cycling on the Beach', by Danish artist Einar Hein, in 1894. Courtesy of Skagens Museum (Google Art Project).*

De Fietsster (Woman Cyclist) by Flemish (Belgian) artist Hubert Malfait, probably during the 1920s. His oil paintings show the everyday dynamics of village life during the Flemish Expressionist movement. This image in particular shows the cyclist absolutely dominating the townscape as she powers along, and ignoring the signpost telling her which way to go. Courtesy of the Phoebus Foundation and Wiki Commons.

▲ In 'The Cyclist' of 1913 avant-garde Russian artist Natalia Goncharova conveys her preoccupation with machines and speed. The cyclist's replicated contours suggest a sequence of body positions and movement in time and space. The bicycle also seems to vibrate as it's powered across cobblestones. In the background street placards throw out a jumble of Russian words: hat, silk and thread. Is it pointing to the silk hat seen top right, perhaps representing spurious luxury? The exaggerated cobblestones tell us the worker's journey is a hard one.

In 'The Cyclist III' Cameroonian artist Angu Walters, born 1980, melds elements of cubism and surrealism with humour and an African aesthetic. This is one of a series of cyclist images, created in the city of Bamenda which has found itself at the very centre of a brutal civil war since 2017. The artist is supported by admirers in the US who run artcameroon.com selling prints of his work. Profits benefit only the artist.

Art for the People

LA **DOMENICA** DEL **CORRIERE**

Scene del Giro d'Italia. Un gruppo di corridori, giunto ad un passaggio a livello chiuso,
si scompone, esegue acrobazie, e passa...

▲ *La Domenica del Corriere (The Sunday Courier) was an Italian weekly newspaper renowned for its cover drawings, which often featured events in cycle racing. This is the newspaper's cover from May 1959. The artist gives accurate renditions, in order, of the editor's predictions as to who will win the Giro d'Italia. The favourite, Jacques Anquetil of France, is nearest to us.*

◀ *This cover, from 1946, is an imaginative take on an incident in the Giro d'Italia. The effect is intensified by the animation and excitement of onlookers, all reacting in different ways. The newspaper was distributed free with the Corriere della Sera, and ceased publication in 1989.*

▲ *Commercial art for the Italian cycle manufacturer Colnago, skilfully associating the brand with happy rural values and the delights of the cycling experience.*

A water colour by Lawrence Rooney, with the medium complementing the aqueous message. Entitled 'Summer of 85?', it appeared in Cycletouring magazine in 1986, striking a powerful chord with readers who know that even cycling in elemental adversity can be appreciated. It shows friends of the artist cycling home from Donegal.

Mads Berg, based in Copenhagen, is a respected graphic designer whose elegantly simple illustrations tend towards the art deco style. He creates clear and simple messages by blending classic poster art with a clean, minimalist aesthetic. Several of his works feature bicycles, such as these promoting Copenhagen, the Danish island of Bornholm and the yoghurt of a dairy producer.

The Water-Carriers, painted in oil by Englishman Patrick Cleary, shows a commonplace moment during the Tour de France of 1961 as hot and thirsty riders drink and replenish. They were probably also filling bidons for their team leaders. We can perhaps sense how a sleepy corner of Southern France has been suddenly enlivened by the appearance of these young men doing everything at speed in their individually different ways.

Pat Cleary

The Power of Line Art

In the days before cameras, and long after, illustrators were creating dynamic and exciting work in the printed media. They could use their imagination, rendering the essence of an event with no requirement to replicate reality.

THE ILLUSTRATED POLICE NEWS

THRASHED BY A LADY CYCLIST,
WHO IS NOTED FOR HER ATHLETIC POWERS.

Periodicals relied heavily on line artists giving drama to their stories.

▲ *This pen and ink of the women's cycle race at London Aquarium in 1895 shows power in action. Photography could not have captured such dynamic movement or composition.*

▲ *A David Eccles linocut, from the 1990s shows an exotic Pedersen tandem. The flight of birds and the inclining trees point to a headwind for the tucked-down cyclists. Speed is emphasised by the horizontal streaks which make up the background.*

◀ *'Old school' cyclists appreciate the technical artwork of Daniel Rebour which appeared in the French cycling press from 1945 to the late 1970s. His meticulous and intricate drawings brought grace and clarity which the camera could not easily provide. Rebour was celebrated in the cycling world and was a friend of champion racers Anquetil and Merckx.*

In 'The Metamorphosis' by Frank Kafka the main character wakes up to find he has been changed into a beetle. David Eccles used the concept in this linocut to illustrate an article in Bike Culture Quarterly on the psychological make-up of cyclists.

The linocut technique enables a shadowless flickering effect in Borin van Loon's Country Cyclist. It gives a stark sense of speed, purpose and delight in movement.

An image by Borin van Loon for a magazine cover.

▲ This original and skilfully composed image, probably a linocut, fills the confined space with interest and action. The figure powers out of the black background, with only a tiny part of her cycle showing. We are unable to identify the artist.

The England of Frank Patterson

The work of Frank Patterson (1871–1952) evokes an England which is now mostly lost. He produced ten or so drawings a week, before, during and after both world wars. They were published in *Cycling Magazine* (later *Cycling Weekly*) and the CTC Gazette. The drawing on the right is of and by Patterson himself.

◀ *A common Patterson theme was one of escape. The bicycle so easily transports the day-rider from the dirt and gloom of the city, and from the world of work, into the sunny delights of the countryside.*

Patterson's work resonated with cyclists who knew the delights of meandering down traffic-free country roads. He commonly drew a cyclist stopped to appreciate remarkable old buildings, or chatting with interesting local characters. He was presenting an idyllic England at peace with itself and open to discovery by bicycle. ▼

The 'Time Trial' is a relatively simple sketch showing masterly control of line and tone. It shows a very British form of cycle sport, vividly evoking the excitement of riding against the clock. The rider, clad in traditional black alpaca and with spare tyre round his shoulders, is no doubt doing a 100-miler (160km), or a 12-hour, or even attempting one of the distance records, hence the need for the feeding bottle. The helper's baggy plusses and his patterned stockings put the illustration in the 1930s. The striking perspective of the country lane emphasised by the receding telegraph poles gives added energy to the image.

▲ Cyclists enjoy the simple pleasures and low-cost independence which the bicycle makes possible.

▲ Patterson evokes that sense of contentment which comes after a long day of cycling, with anticipation of an evening in the pub followed by bed and breakfast.

The Craft of the Cartoon

Just as the bicycle says most with least, cartoons carry crisp, concise messages, giving new insights and encouragement towards social change. What they have in common is humour – sometimes black humour. We have chosen cartoons as examples from different times and different cultures. They show how humour has changed over the years.

Young New Zealand: "Oh Grandpapa! What a funny old machine. Why don't you get one like mine?"

Printed and Published by the Artists' Suffrage League, 259, King's Road, Chelsea.

▲ *Bicycles join the cause of emancipation in New Zealand.*

▲ *This illustration appeared in 'de Kampioen', the national Dutch cycling magazine, in 1895. The accompanying text warns women not to try difficult cycle maintenance for fear of injury. With the passage of time it's difficult to work out whether this is meant to be satirical or serious.*

(Eine moderne Köchin.) „Was, die gnädige Frau fährt auch Rad? Da sind wir ja Sportskameraden!"

▲ *Social commentary from a German magazine, around 1898. A lady and her cook come across each other cycling. 'Crikey! Madam rides a bike same as me! Then we're friends in sport.' The lady meets this egalitarian greeting with disdain.*

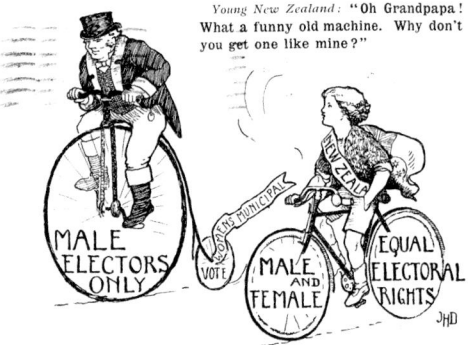

Gertrude. "MY DEAR JESSIE, WHAT ON EARTH IS THAT BICYCLE SUIT FOR!"
Jessie. "WHY, TO WEAR, OF COURSE." Gertrude. "BUT YOU HAVEN'T GOT A BICYCLE!"
Jessie. "NO; BUT I'VE GOT A SEWING MACHINE!"

▲ "My dear Jessie, what on earth is that bicycle suit for?"
"Why, to wear, of course!"
"But you haven't got a bicycle!"
"No, but I've got a sewing machine!"
Punch, 1895

▲ A traditional saucy British postcard by Brian Perry, and probably from the late 1960s. Holiday camps, like bicycles, were still, but only just, significant parts of British working class culture.

▲ English cartoonist BRICK is a prolific and often acerbic commentator.

▲ A cartoon specially drawn for Cycle Magic by Dutch artist Djanko – www.djanko.nl

The work of Zohar Lazar, published in Wired, May 2018.

Neil Scorpen (ko-fi.com/mudcompany).

All the above works are the copyright of the artists.

Satire from Australia

Australian cartoonist Phil Somerville draws for cycling magazines and other planet-friendly publications. He directs his quizzical humour at many aspects of society and is not shy about sending up cyclists.

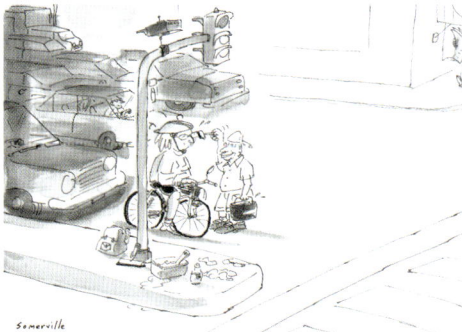

Somerville

Somerville

Somerville

Somerville

Bikes on the Walls

Artist: Caryn Koh.

The murals of Penang

Walk around the sunny streets of Georgetown, capital of Penang State in Malaysia, and you will see why the town is a Unesco heritage site. But you'll also be taken aback by the variety and quality of street art on walls all over the town, some of it devoted to everyday local cycling activities.

It began with Lithuanian artist Ernest Zacharevic painting murals on Georgetown street walls. His colourful, life-affirming work was inspired by real human and animal life in Penang, and the government signed him up for more. The project spread across Penang Island, attracting local and international artists to its patched street walls.

Part-mural, part-montage. Photo: Penang Tourism.

It's a bakery and the children want some of the bread. Photo: Penang Tourism.

An early and very popular work by Ernest Zacharevic. The image makes sense when you put your bike in front of it. Wiki Commons.

Photo: Kirill Kouznetsov.

This mural was created in Moscow by Argentinian artist Mart Aire as part of the city's Bicycle Film Festival of 2014. He began as a 12-year old graffitero on the streets of Buenos Aires in the 1990s. Over time his style evolved beyond graffiti and he became a respected street artist with a unique, imaginative style. His fascination for bicycles became a constant theme and he began painting them at enormous size and with surreal proportions. They conjoin with equally surreal human figures, all creating a kind of happy, colourful, eccentric dream-world enriching the urban environments of many cities.

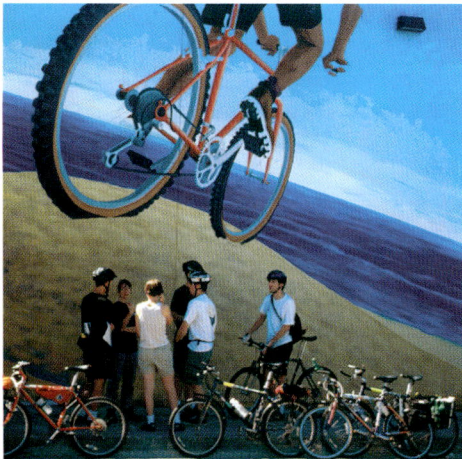

Photo: monacaron.com

San Francisco cyclists use the Duboce bike mural by artist Mona Caron as a meeting point for a ride. This 340ft (103m) artwork was commissioned by the transportation department to celebrate the city's first creation of a bikeway: the very one which runs alongside the mural. Much more of Mona Caron's cycling murals are shown overleaf.

Artist and photographer: Zarateman. (Wiki Commons)

An incongruous orange high-wheeler looks charmingly incongruous in this mural menagerie waiting at the traffic lights. It's one of over 20 murals which have become a significant tourist attraction in the town of Abetxuko (Spanish: Abechuco) in the Basque Country.

Protest and Persuasion: Mona Caron

Mona Caron, is a Swiss artist living and cycling in her adoptive city, San Francisco. Her powerful art supports social and environmental change, especially her images for bike advocacy, contrasting how things are with how they could be. They have proliferated worldwide, which was always one of Caron's intentions.

Caron is clearly passionate about the transformative power of cycling, but her best known artistic activity lies in painting huge murals onto city centre buildings. Each mural features a startling image of a weed or other plant native to the local region, and is beautifully portrayed with a sense of wonder and respect. These plants tower over us, putting us back in our place, superseding the world of concrete. Her artistry, and the basic power of the concept, have made Mona Caron world famous, with commissions from cities on several continents.

◀

A corner-wrapping piece created by Caron in Porto Alegre, shortly after the second World Bicycle Forum in Brazil in 2013. It shows, says Caron, how a simple act, like riding a bike, "can crack the cement of our urban reality."

"I look for clandestine plant life in the city streets. When I find a particularly heroic specimen growing through a fissure in the pavement, I paint it big, at a scale inversely proportional to the attention and regard it gets."

This mural in the city of Curitiba, Brazil, was created in conjunction with the third World Bicycle Forum in the city. Caron's multi-storey murals of gigantic weeds and other plants do not usually contain cycles, but this is an exception.

David Eccles

This image was created by English illustrator David Eccles. It was the cover art for the 1995 yearbook Encyclopedia, published between 1991 and 2000. The Dali clock perhaps reminds us that it really is time for society to change its ways.

David Eccles studied graphic design in the late 60s and then worked in publishing as a book designer. Much of his work has been for the Folio Society who, amongst many prestigious commissions, tasked him with illustrating Flann O'Brien's *The Third Policeman*.

These three Eccles covers for Bike Culture Quarterly were in acrylic paint which dries quickly and is elastic enough to survive being rolled up and sent through the post. He has also long been fascinated by linocuts, creating the images and typography himself and printing on a mid-Victorian hand press. You see his linocut work on pages 314 and 315.

He has never owned or driven a car and has cycled for transport, recreation and on tandem holidays. There was also some time-trialling, on fixed-wheel or hub-gear bikes: he instituted the 'Tin Can Ten' in Nottinghamshire. He continues to ride, though now with a reduced stable of machines. Still at hand is his beloved Dursley-Pedersen made around 1913.

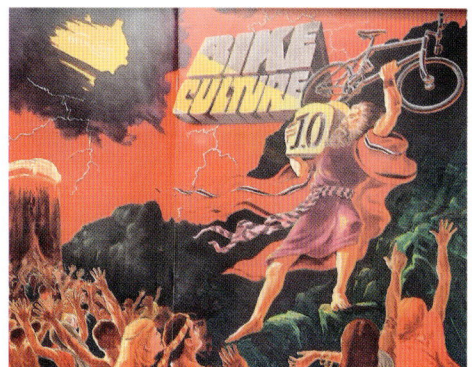

Bikes for a Better World

Posters by media agency OMD for the Singapore Road Safety Council. The dark image below requires close attention.

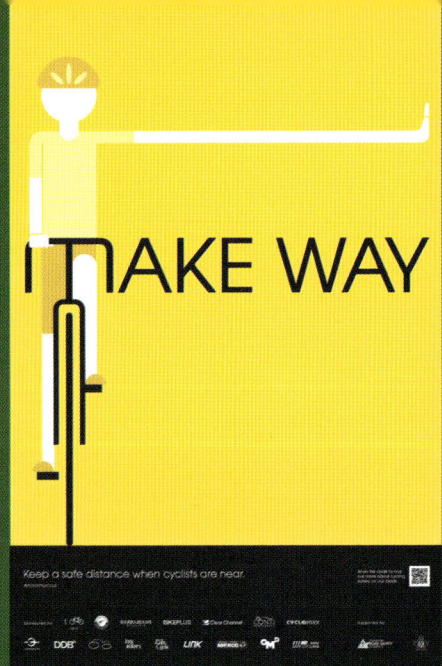

MAKE WAY

Keep a safe distance when cyclists are near.

CYCLISTS CAN BE HARD TO SEE

Look out for bikes when you're on the road.

LOOK OUT

SHARE THE ROAD

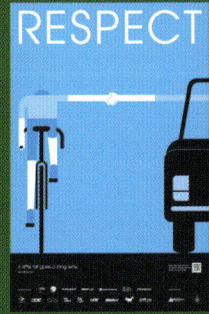

RESPECT

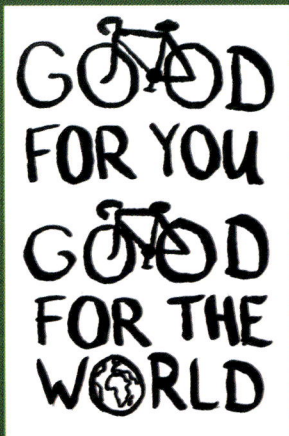

GOOD FOR YOU GOOD FOR THE WORLD

A German contribution to World Bicycle Day in 2018 – so simple and so well executed. We have not been able to identify the creator.

GROTE OPRUIMING!

12 OP DE PLEK VAN 1

Fietsersbond enfb
Postbus 2150, 3440 DD Woerden

'Big clearance! Twelve in place of one!' – a poster by Theo van den Boogaard for the Real Dutch Cyclists' Union in 1993.

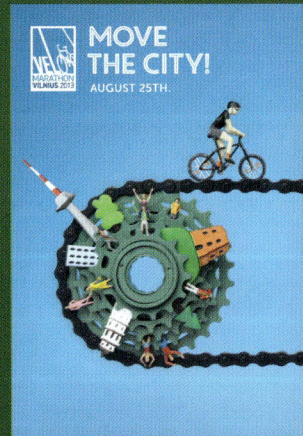

MOVE THE CITY!
AUGUST 25TH.

This clever poster by the McCann Agency publicises an annual mass ride in Vilnius, capital of Lithuania.

RUIMTEGEBRUIK   echte nederlandse fietsersbond   postbus 2150   3440 DD woerden

It had taken months of planning by Daan van Tol and Arne Haytsma and on an April day of 1978 the time had come for a photo shoot of a Dutch street scene.

Arne was standing on scaffolding in the middle of the Hendrik van Viandenstraat in Amersfoort with camera in hand. Down below people with megaphones, backed up by the police, were battling to keep pedestrians and traffic clear of the street. In the side streets 40 cars were waiting

for their photo opportunity. Eventually the eight-scenario task was completed and a composite image created. The *Ruimtegebruik* (Use of Space) poster was to become famous worldwide.

Behind the initiative was the Real Dutch Cyclists' Union (ENWB), formed just three years earlier. 'Real' because it was a splinter movement from the General Dutch Cycling Union, which offered membership services for motorists to the disbenefit of its cycling members.

A Lot
in a Little

The art of the bicycle stamp.

Postage stamps are a demanding art form. A message has to be conveyed in a tiny space and is often destined to deliver a powerful concept to be seen, often daily, by all citizens. There is a community of philatelists who specialise in cycling stamps, and not all are cyclists.

There are several genres of these stamps. Many depict cycle sport. Others carry colourful and pleasing portrayals from cycling history. Curiously, some of the best are from countries with no natural affinity to the mainly European story of cycling which their stamps depict.

Collectors enter arcane arguments as to what qualifies as a bicycle stamp. Basically, a bike or act of cycling must be in the picture. A velodrome image also counts, as does the word 'bicycle' in the native language. The attraction for many collectors goes deeper than that: bicycle stamps (and all stamps) give insights into the cultures and histories of countries around the world, and to possess a stamp is to own a real artifact of that place and time. There are several books on the subject, such as Dan Gindling's *Bicycle Stamps*.

The German Post Office celebrates the Day of the Postage Stamp in 1987.

The USA issued a special delivery bicycle messenger service stamp in 1902.

In celebration of the Giro d'Italia race, 1967.

Millennium 2000, by Cycle Network Artworks. Designed by the UK Post Office.

A attractive but unsettling design for a German road safety stamp of 1991. It only just qualifies as a bicycle stamp, as the cyclists are almost lost within the onrush of traffic.

A Finnish stamp celebrating 100 years of freedom from starvation. The words are in Swedish as well as in Finnish, Swedish being one of the two main official languages in Finland.

The work of famous Swedish artist Lasse Åberg celebrating the activities of the 'springschas' (delivery boy) in the 1940s.

There's a lot in a little with this artwork from Christmas Island.

In 1944, during the difficult times following the end of the Second World War in Italy, the 'Corrieri Alta Italia' was authorised to carry mail between a number of cities. Cyclists riding in relay covered four routes radiating from Venice.

Most Australians know Banjo Patterson's poem 'Mulga Bill's Bicycle', written in 1896. It describes the humorous misfortunes of the hero on a 'penny-farthing' bicycle (which was a rarity by that date).

The Art of The Stencil

Toronto artist Janet Attard never joined cycling advocacy groups. She works best independently and began exploring the potential of stencils after her first ever cycling stencil fetched a high price at local community auction. She finds that stencilling gives opportunities for repeated messaging and attractive patterning, while keeping artistic value. She has her own art studio and gallery where she works for self-fulfilment, creating striking images for cycling event posters, stationery and clothing. She says her cycling stencil activities are not something she's ever really analysed. She makes her art, sends it out to the communities she is involved in, and rarely stops to find out what effect they have. She is in the happy position of making a living from doing what she loves and expressing what she believes in.

The cover of the book you are reading is Janet's work.

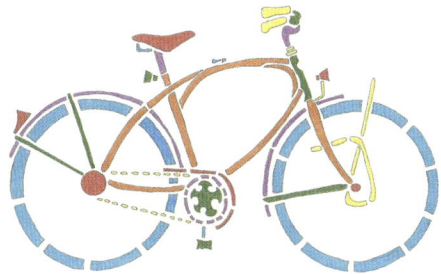

▼ *Hand-cut onto cotton paper: a stencil for Inoperable Gallery, displayed at the Vienna Bike Art Festival.*

CHAPTER 11
Through the Lens

Image: John Bradshaw

Catching the Experience

Photography and cycling were born at much the same time and continue to complement each other. We present images from some of the best cycling photographers, reflecting their differing interests and techniques.

▶

Right top and bottom: Jason Patient captured these two winter scenes in the Scottish Borders in the late 1980s. The staff of a cycle magazine out together for the day, enjoying that kind of crisp winter morning which makes cycling a special delight. The author is centre right, and centre left is Dan Joyce, who later became editor of Cycling UK magazine.

In contrast, a severe image of riders heading for home, with the sombre trees telling of a cold, unfriendly wind.

Ferrying a bike over Lake Malawi in a slim canoe. Photo: 1-2 Travel Africa. ▼

Wiki Commons.

▲ *Alone on a winding road to the sea, in County Galway, Ireland. Photo: Marcello Provenzano.*

▲ *Mick Orloski of Portland, Oregon, expresses a powerful relationship with his bike.*

▲ *Somewhere in China, 1980s. A poor quality picture, but that seems to go with the poor quality air the man has to breathe. This picture would not be the same without his cigarette. Photographer unknown.*

▲ *South African Nic Dlamini heads the pack during the 2019 Tour de Yorkshire. The weather adds to the drama as we sense the danger the riders face. We also begin to wonder whether we need to get out of the way as the arrow of cyclists is heading towards us at speed. Photo: Alex Broadway/SWpix*

▲ *This image of GB cyclist Katie Archibald was taken at Manchester Velodrome in 2016. Photographer Michael Porter admits to some good luck in that the eye focusing on the track ahead perfectly lined up with light reflecting on the visor.*

▲ *An image composed of concentric circles of land mass, cyclists, roadway and spectators. Rwandans have become enthusiastic about cycle racing, which the government have promoted to improve the country's image. Photo: Tour du Rwanda.*

◀

Cyclists in a Smithfield Nocturne ride in London approach a turn. But suddenly the mundane is shot with energy as they become a rocketing mass of colours – without actually going any faster.

Photo: Jeremy Hughes.

The men's sprint semi-final, Rio de Janeiro Olympics, 2016. The photograph's exposure makes an intriguing shape of the four riders in the group, yet the photographer manages to preserve the solidity of the rider in the foreground. It's the work of Fernando Frazão of the Agência Brazil. ▶

Wiki Commons.

Young on a bike

Flying Killerfish. Two forms of art combine here. The wall mural, by the artist Dopie, decorates the Colijntunnel in Delft, Netherlands. It's one of many such images encouraging pedestrians to use the tunnel.

The photographer, Pixel Addict, gives us more. The boy has ducked so as not to spoil the picture, but he has actually made the picture. The shape, movement and colours of the boy and his bike so nicely echo those of the fish.

▲ *Riding in full colour, Angola. Photo: Jason Clendenen.*

▲ *Two siblings return from school in Ghana, 2022. Photo: Kwameghana.*

▲ *Northern England. A boy with additional needs ignores the rain to share the joy of his first ever cycling experience: his new tricycle has just been delivered and the photographer was the delivery driver. Photo: Get Cycling CIC.*

▲ Seven children on a worn out and probably discarded cargo bike. A rear chainstay has rusted through but they have probably not noticed. The quality of this photograph lies in the delight on their faces, and the multiple interactions. Lapu-Lapu City, Philippines, 2023. Photo: Gary Shirey.

▲ Russian children in the 1970s. Photographer unknown.

▲ Bicycle as universal tool. Using a payphone in Porteirinha, Brazil. Photo: Ana Cotta.

Odd Things Happen

◄

An image bursting with energy. A cycle jousting tournament at a Pedalpalooza event in Portland, Oregon. Photo: Jonathan Maus.

◄

An image captured in a Delhi street by photographer Ross Bowling.

◄

Eggheads accost participants during the Great British Bike Ride, Land's End to John O'Groats, in the mid-80s. Photographer unknown.

▲ The Team Educar from Argentina add sunshine to pedal-power during the Atacama Solar Vehicle Challenge in 2011. The stance and gaze of the officer reflect the indeterminate relationship between these two very different road users. Photographer unknown.

▲ Good photographs can transcend low quality reproduction. This moment of menace, intensified by the dog's red eyes, was captured by Richard Johnston during a cycle ride in Oregon in 2015. We presume it came from a rear-facing helmet camera, and that the two riders outpaced the dogs.

Each pole is crowned with a bicycle. This is a vital part of Panjat Panang, Indonesian independence celebrations. Various prizes are hung at the top of heavily greased nut or palm tree trunks. Groups of young men work together to reach the top earliest to secure the goodies. Photo: Ngguhnangguh.

▼

This picture looks great – the interesting layering takes the eye from the active foreground to odd-looking buildings and then to a cityscape of skyscrapers which answer to the towering load. But there's more to this image than first appears. Artist Alain Delorme wanted to highlight the exploitation of migrant workers in Shanghai who transport goods around the city on cargo trikes. He photographed some of them with heavy loads and then digitally altered the images to make those loads look preposterous, in order, he says, to highlight the workers' plight. The altered images have been reproduced all over the world, but with few becoming aware of the artist's message.

▲ *In rural areas of Burkina Faso urine is diverted from household wastewater and collected in jerrycans to be used as a fertiliser on farms. Here the empty jerrycans are being returned to the households. Photo by Happi Raphael, 2009.*

▲ *A school bus in Nepal. 'Education is the Light of Life' says the message on the box, but the children inside are not seeing much of that light. Photo: Paul Jeurissen.*

Delights of the Everyday

These images are by Danish cycling advocate and photographer Mikael Colville-Andersen. His images also appear in other parts of this book, particularly in the section on Denmark.

◀

It takes quick wits to spot and photograph the delightful significance of three generations on one trike in Copenhagen.

▶

A lady in the Dutch city of Maastricht locates her bike in this sea of metal and is rewarded by a shaft of sunlight.

▶

It's summer in Copenhagen and photographer Mikael Colville-Andersen has caught a moment in the daily cycling life of the city. It's almost 'split-screen'. As two cyclists enjoy moving free in the foreground there's a mass of cyclists held back, waiting to surge onto the blue 'magic carpet' which will transport them safely through the city.

People and Their Bikes

▲ A musician on the move in Copenhagen – interesting but that's not all. Cycle history buffs will notice that he's riding a rare Pedersen bicycle. Photo: Mikael Colville-Andersen.

▲ The author's friend, Tom Mason, with his beloved Strutt Worksong folding bicycle. Tom has passed away and the Worksong is no longer produced. Photo: Jim McGurn.

▲ A Chicago cycle messenger looking the part in 2010. The profession was to be undermined by digital transmission but the ethos and fashion style lived on. Photo: Jeremy Hughes.

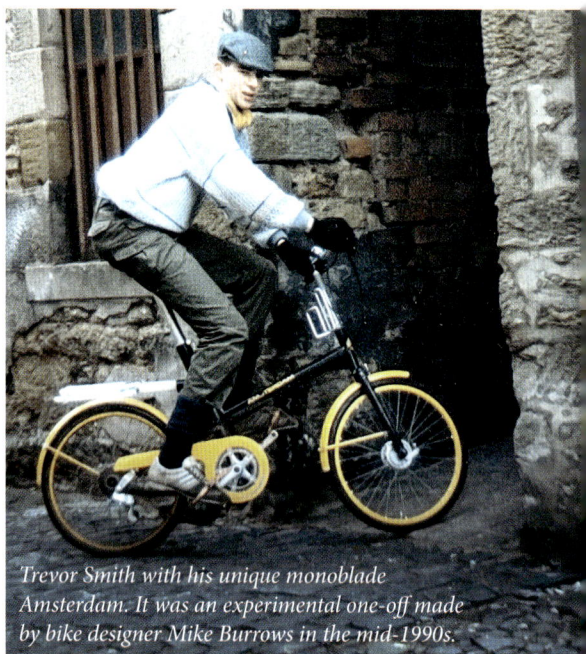

Trevor Smith with his unique monoblade Amsterdam. It was an experimental one-off made by bike designer Mike Burrows in the mid-1990s.

◄ A smile and a wink from a competitor in a folding bike race in 2008. Photo: Jeremy Hughes.

The Power
of Red

Danish photographer Mikael Colville-Andersen spotted the single red bicycle interrupting the monotone wall of the new *Skuespilhus* (theatre) in Copenhagen. Strong reds appeal to him, which is why he also captured the image (below left) of the musician bringing a strong dash of red into a drab background. Photographer Kevin Meredith in Brighton, UK, also welcomes red into his art. Using his classic Lomo camera he caught his friend, the singer Imogen Heaps (below right) cycling in red through the wan whites and greys of the city. He also produced a separate image of Imogen cycling in London. This time it was a planned photoshoot, with Kevin digitally enhancing the image for the cover of Imogen's new album.

The Lomo was produced in the Soviet Union as a simple camera for all, using 35mm film. It has a fixed lens, one shutter speed and manual focusing.

The Familiar with Fresh Eyes

Roff Smith is an English travel photographer. When Covid removed all his employment he took more bike rides around his locality. He wanted to 'see the familiar with fresh eyes', to challenge the notion that 'travel' requires distance.

❝ *I began photographing my morning jaunts as though they were magazine travel assignments. In all of these photos the cyclist in the frame is me – I am both the photographer and the model, a form of photography that took a lot of practice and an entirely new skill set to master. But none of these pictures are meant to be about me. They are about a cyclist in the landscape. It could be anybody: you perhaps. The pictures celebrate the independence and liberation of a bicycle ride, and the simple joys of discovery that are waiting for you on your doorstep if you're willing to look.*

What started out as a lark soon grew into something much more – a celebration of the beauty that exists all around us but we never notice because it's always there and because I was living in a faded old seaside town called St Leonards-on-Sea, in East Sussex, on the south coast of England. It's not on anybody's list of celebrated English beauty spots. Indeed like most of England's faded old seaside towns it's considered a deprived area, of high unemployment and low incomes. Much of my riding was along down-at-heel seafront promenades or across flat coastal marshes. And yet, as I soon discovered, there was so much beauty and interest here. I was astonished I'd never noticed it before.

I found myself leaving the house earlier and earlier – sometimes as early as 3am during the summer months to catch the dawn's first light. And I looked forward to these outings in the way I used to look forward to hopping on a plane to the far side of the globe – before the world became small and shopworn under a surfeit of frequent flyer miles. Later, after the photos from this project were published in the New York Times, and I was being interviewed on the BBC, it was put to me that I must be looking forward to getting on a plane again. I replied that no, I really didn't. There was too much to see and explore right here at home. ❞

King George V Coronation Colonnade at Bexhill-on-Sea.

The Seafront Promenade in St Leonards-on-Sea.

Crossroads, Doleham Lane.

Here I am paying tribute to the English illustrator Ellis Martin who illustrated the covers of Ordnance Survey maps between 1919 and 1939). A great many of his covers depicted a cyclist or motorcyclist, in jacket and cap, paused at a crossroads, consulting his OS map. As a cycling romantic, who loves old maps and illustrations, I couldn't resist turning my hand at producing one, and so this image captured before dawn at a crossroads along Doleham Lane. By way of authenticity I am consulting is an original 1919 Ordnance Survey map with an Ellis' illustration on the cover. For those interested in the technical aspects, I achieved the painterly, 'illustration' feel by shooting in low light using a telephoto lens (70-200 f2.8) and a very shallow depth of field and then flattened the tonal contrast slightly.

A World of Cyclists

Photos by Paul Jeurissen

▲ *Two cycling cultures connect on an Indian road.*

In 2010, Dutch photographer Paul Jeurissen and his partner, Grace Johnson, set off on a multi-year cycling trip to seek out bicycle culture, dramatic landscapes, and remote places.

They have a passion for visually communicating their experiences and created three photo e-books that combine Paul's photography with Grace's writing: *Bicycling around the World, Bicycle Touring Photo Tips,* and *Little Red Cyclist.* These e-books are available for free download on Paul's photography website: *www.pauljeurissen.nl.*

His site also features a collection of bicycle culture photos revealing the diverse ways people use and view bikes around the world. You'll find the colourful bustle of city cycling, bicycle jousting, pedalling musicians, painted rickshaws, overloaded cargo bikes and two-wheelers put to multiple purposes.

For more visual stories from their trips, visit their travel website: www.bicyclingaroundtheworld.nl.

All images © Paul Jeurissen and Grace Johnson.

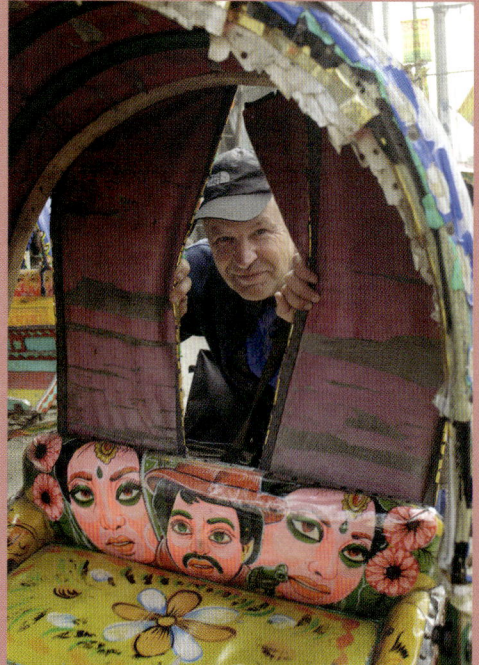

▲ *Paul Jeurissen in Dhaka, Bangladesh.*

▲ *Grace crests the Baralacha La Pass in the Indian Himalaya.*

▲ *A Bollywood film star adorns a mud flap in Northern India.*

▲ *A priest blesses cyclists in Belgium.*

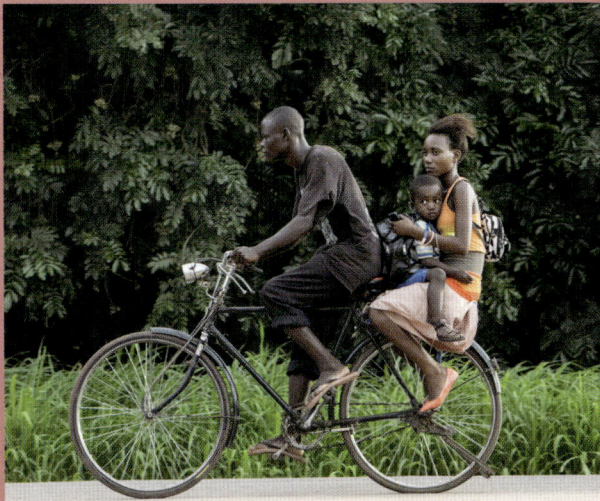

▲ *A bike taxi in Malawi.*

▲ *The aquarium in Antwerp Zoo showing what sits at the bottom of Belgium's canals.*

A candyfloss seller in India. The honest dull browns of his clothes, bags and bicycle contrast strongly with the tower of powerful pink and the light blue wall. Photos above and opposite: Paul Jeurissen.

A river of bicycle rickshaws during the morning commute in Dhaka. The sheer mass of this low-tech transport has denied the street to any other form of traffic. It also seems to have created a great deal of employment and delay.

Africa on the Move

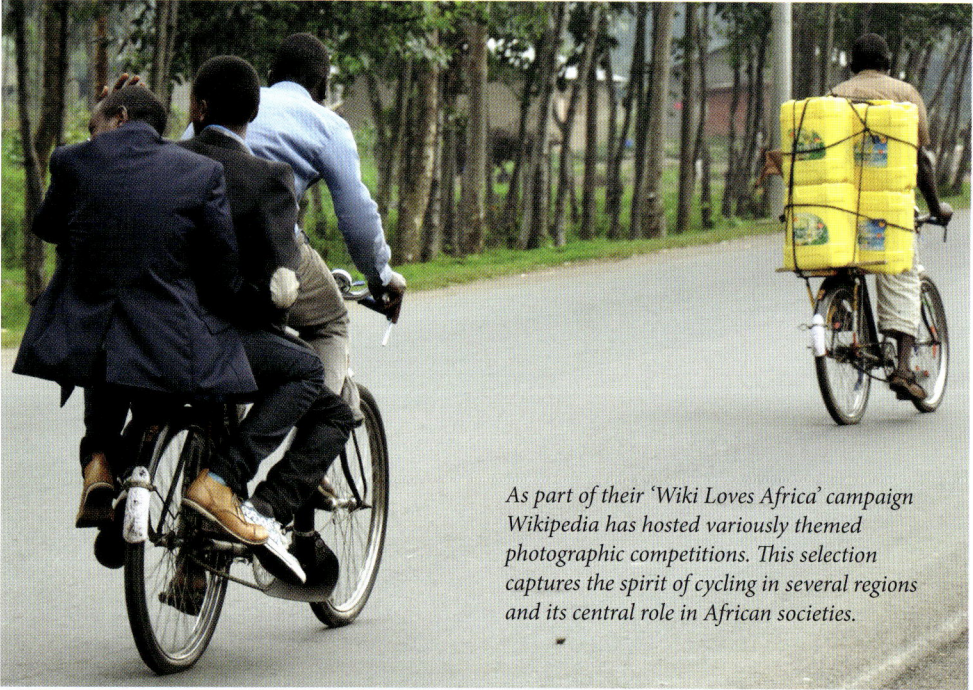

As part of their 'Wiki Loves Africa' campaign Wikipedia has hosted variously themed photographic competitions. This selection captures the spirit of cycling in several regions and its central role in African societies.

▲ *A taxi service in Cameroon. Photo by Happi Raphael, 2016.*

▲ *A Nigerian woman looking stately and stylish. Photo by Periye, 2017.*

▲ *A mixed load impressively transported by bike in Guinea. Photo by Aboubacarkhoraa, 2020.*

▲ On a Buffalo bike in Zambia. Photo by Johanneke Kroesbergen, 2016.

▲ Ordinary bikes are adapted to do almost incredible things. This example in the Democratic Republic Congo shows a bamboo rack supporting bags of charcoal. Photo by Tannoglou, 2013.

▲ This Ugandan boy holds a child-size version of the chukudu, a kind of wooden cargo scooter used by adults. This one was probably used for fun. Photo by Elijah Kennedy, 2019.

◀ Two cyclists in Benin share a load of onions. Photo by Tannoglou, 2012.

Java, Indonesia

Part of an intriguing fancy dress parade down the main street of Surakarta, Java. The tandem in the foreground is a 1950s Dutch Sparta, and the one in the background, which must remain a fascinating mystery, has a Dutch air about it. The riders, perhaps oddly, may be evoking the Dutch influence from colonial days. Photo: Dian Vastho.

Creative Commons.

▲ *Inclusive cycling in Malaysia. The photographer was the young man's mother.*

Caught in Time

▲ *Paris, sometime between 1945 and 1950. This image, by renowned American photographer Benjamen Chinn, asks so many questions. Was the young man injured in the war which just ended? Does he play his harmonica for a living? What is he playing which so pleases the women? What kind of relationship does he want with them? (The exhortation on the kiosk means 'Try your luck'!)*

▲ *Fun and a fag amongst the traffic of Pall Mall, central London, in the late 1920s.*

▲ *Alois Sedlacek (left) built these two recumbents in what was then Czechoslovakia, in 1943. The rider on the right is likely to be his father. Alois gave one of these to his girlfriend and future wife and the couple used to travel on them from Prague to visit her parents in Jihlava, a hilly journey of 126km (78 miles).*

▲ *The torpedo bike (vélo-torpille) encases Berthet-Caseli in 1919, a very early date for aerodynamic fairings. Alongside is the engineer Bunau-Varilla who developed a series of such cycle designs. Photo: Bibliothèque Nationale de France.*

▲ *Sven Turck chronicled, through his photography, the everyday activities of his fellow Danes. This image is from the 1930s. Royal Library of Denmark.*

▲ *The cars, the shops, the clothing, the hair, the first generation Moulton. It has to be 1960s Britain. Photo: Moulton Bicycles.*

▲ *Birthday presents and cakes being delivered by bicycle to the young Princess Beatrix, at the Palace of Het Loo in the Netherlands. Dutch National Archive.*

▲ *The Dutch royal family plus dog showing their common touch by enjoying life in the same way as the general population. Security guards are on bikes in the background. Dutch National Archive.*

▲ A recumbent in Modena, Italy, around 2005. The rider, on a cycle which was rare in the country then, cuts across a traditional perspective. He is framed in the beauty of the trees and silhouetted against the bowl of light. Photo: Sue Darlow.

▲ Netherlands in wartime, around 1944. Tyres and inner tubes had become scarce and people had to improvise. This image was criminal as outdoor photography was banned by the German occupiers. The photographer was Menno Huizinga, member of the Dutch Hidden Camera Movement, which created images of the Occupation for posterity.

▲ Piet van Kempen enjoying a cuppa and a paper on the morning of a six-day event at Wembley, 1936. Photographer unknown.

▲ The peloton encounter an unexpected competitor. Photo-montage by Brian Holt, around 1998.

▲ Stripes upon stripes. A scene from the making of a sci-fi film in the UK, in the 1990s. Photographer unknown.

▲ *Rubbernecking Mennonites in St. Jacob, Ontario, in the early 1960s. Mennonites still ride bicycles extensively. The Amish, on the other hand, generally cycle less, and usage varies from community to community. Photo courtesy of Sani.*

▲ *English engineer, sculptor and inventor Dave Wrath-Sharman designed and made this off-road cycle, the Highpath, incorporating much new technology. Here he rides it shortly after its unveiling in 1985, just as the mountain bike boom in the US was taking hold. The UK cycle industry showed little interest in the Highpath. Photo: Sue Darlow.*

▲ Russian soldiers harassing a woman in Berlin following Russian occupation. Photo: Bildarchiv Preussischer Kulturbesitz.

▲ The Danish resistance celebrate on their bicycles. This photo was taken a day after liberation on May 6, 1945. The bikes may have had symbolic significance since huge numbers had been stolen from the Danes by the Nazis. Photo: National Museum.

◀

An unusual cycle-pram ridden in North London by owner Gladys Armond with daughter Margaret in 1926 or 1927. It was probably custom-made by previous owners. Gladys, husband Frank and Margaret used the cycle-pram on a tour of East Anglia managing 50 miles (80km) a day.

Words and picture from an article by Christine Watts on family cycling in number 183 of the Boneshaker, the Journal of the Veteran-Cycle Club.

To this day companion quadricycles are a staple of the holiday camp experience.

Objects of Art

Good photographers have an eye for creative work in other media. They can help us better appreciate the achievements of artists and designers.

◀ *Startling Eye Bikes photographed at the Burning Man Festival, Nevada Desert, 2010. They were pedalled around the site at night, which must have been an astonishing thing to behold. Photo by Kevin Meredith.*

▲ *Potsdamerplatz (Potsdamer Square) is a busy intersection in central Berlin. Its history includes a Nazi secret prison and party offices, total wartime destruction and the Berlin Wall. With the Wall gone the Square was reunited and 'regenerated', becoming a lively cultural sector. The erection of two large artist-designed neon bicycles loudly announced modern ways of thinking and travelling, while brightening up people's lives. Photo: Fotomatzi.*

▲ *This photograph, taken at the Brooklyn Museum, New York, sets the futuristic design style of the Spacelander bicycle, launched in 1960, against the dull browns and rectangles of the museum's pictures from a different era. The Spacelander was designed by Benjamin J Bowden in the UK. It had a fibreglass frame and was relatively fragile. The bike trade showed little interest and it just did not work as a bicycle: only 522 were ever made and it is now a collectors' item. Photo: Mark of markontour.com.*

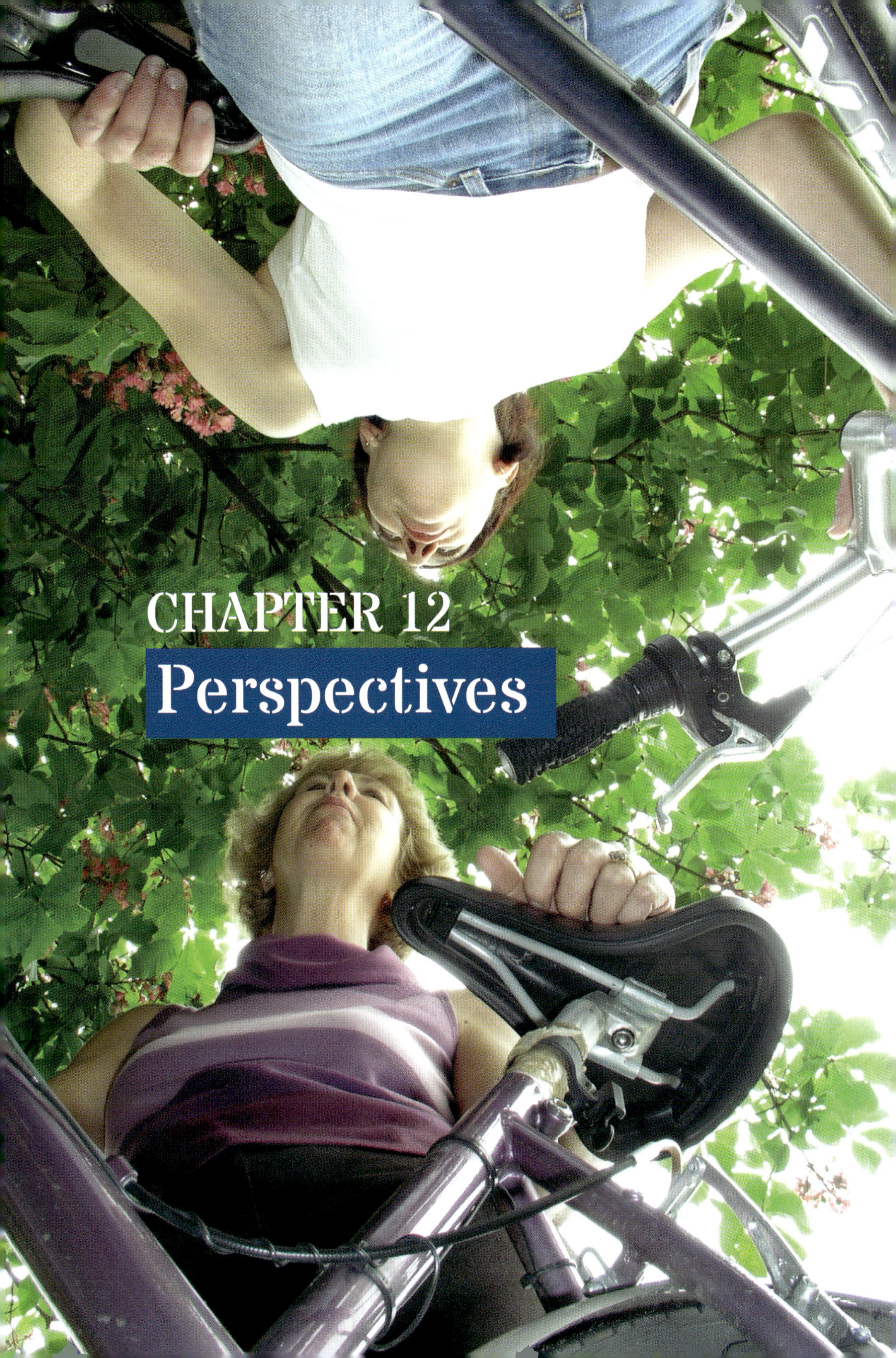

CHAPTER 12

Perspectives

In Search of a Cycling Heaven

All kinds of people cycle in all kinds of ways and for all kinds of reasons. It's not about being a culture warrior: it's about us all having a common interest in cycling in peace and safety. Most non-cyclists are happy to go along with this, but some can be infuriating. Their reasons for not cycling can be illogical, and they show no interest in making it easy for others to cycle either.

People who do cycle have to live within the social structures and value systems around them, but cycling helps them experience the world in a different way and respond flexibly and productively to life's challenges and opportunities.

Cycling can carry us into wearisome engagements with an uncaring world and all we get are slow, incremental changes in the social climate. We need new ideas and a sharper sense of urgency. How can we help now to create more breathing space for cycling? We can begin by getting out there with our bikes – enjoying ourselves, getting our life balances right. Just by making cycling a significant and practical part of our daily activities we show others that cycling has value and benefits. Every time we carry heavy shopping on our bike, in panniers or even in a bike trailer, we are noticed by a silent audience in the car park who may just start thinking... When we go for a ride in the countryside we know why we do it but family and friends notice, as do so many others who see us out there having fun. People who ride to work also get noticed, and by people who might not otherwise get to know an adult cyclist in their lives.

Some cyclists want to be more active in promoting change, or at least in understanding what's going on. Over the next few pages we set out some of the latest thinking and initiatives. They reflect ideas and proposals from cycling advocates and creative thinkers from several countries and specialist areas. Some of these concepts will be familiar and readily accepted; others are radical. Most cannot happen until society has moved on a little, but some may just click into place because they become overpoweringly obvious. We try to show diverse plans and visions for a society which embraces pedal-power, and we hope they serve as signposts towards a more cycle-happy society.

Inspiration for change: car-free Sundays in Bogotá, Colombia.

The Bogotá Institute for Recreation and Sport.

How can we find ways to give cycling its opportunities? Many have contributed their creative ideas, giving us new hopes and visions.

▲ Mixed-mode travel as envisaged in 2002 by Bauke Muntz, a Dutch industrial designer.

A cycle path idyll as imagined in 2004 by English artist David Eccles. He foresaw the need for pathside services, including e-bike charging stations powered by wind turbines. He also seems to suggest a battery swap facility. ▼

▲ Vision goes digital with this concept from Iberdrola, a trans-national sustainable-energy company. Critics claim that elevated cycleways create a lot of concrete and cost, and that there are better ways of spending on cycling.

363

Ivan Illich
The Awkward Critic

Scientist, philosopher, radical Catholic priest, fluent speaker of at least seven languages, and a critic of high technology: Ivan Illich challenged many of the basic principles of western civilisation.

Tools for Conviviality is a remarkable book with a terrible title. By conviviality Illich didn't mean bonhomie but rather happy and equitable living. The bicycle tops his list, in that it can be owned, used and repaired locally. It needs no massive infrastructure. It can carry huge loads using very little energy. Its use does not harm others or restrict their freedom of choice. These arguments, so common now, were pure poetry to cycle campaigners of the 1970s and 80s. The cyclist could now claim to be at the peak of social evolution.

The bicycle is, for Illich, a useful, multi-purpose artefact. Almost anyone (in the West) can afford one and ride one without a licence, and its use does not deprive others of any basic rights or benefits – such as fresh air, freedom from fear, and access to sustainable mobility. We have created divisive technology, he say, out of scale and out of tune with sensible social needs. This has brought inequality, injustice and social dysfunction. We patch up the damage by creating more and more professionalised remedial systems and institutions which in turn undermine the strength and skills of traditional communities.

Illich proposes the development or rediscovery of instruments for the reconquest of practical knowledge by the average citizen. He argues that we need 'convivial' tools, such as bicycles, which can be used for more than one purpose. On the other hand, with complex, capital-dependent machines using external fuel sources, humans become servants, their role being only to operate mega-machines for a unique purpose determined by people who hold power over us. He also believes that modernity is eroding social bonds and undermining cultural goods which are beyond financial value.

Although Austrian by birth, and formidably intellectual, Illich lived most of his life amongst the poor of rural south and central America, with their own varieties of transport inequality. In another of his books, *Energy and Equity: Toward a History*

Teenage schoolgirls, West Bengal, India. Photo: Biswarup Ganguly.

Creative Commons

of Need, Illich has more to say on how he believes modern transport systems leave the poor behind:

> ❝ More energy fed into the transportation system means that more people move faster over a greater range in the course of every day... Extremes of privilege are created at the cost of universal enslavement. An elite packs unlimited distance into a lifetime of pampered travel, while the majority spends a bigger slice of their existence on unwanted trips... Every increase in motorised speed creates new demands on space and time... What distinguishes the traffic in rich countries from the traffic in poor countries is not more mileage per hour of lifetime for the majority, but more hours of compulsory consumption of high doses of energy, packaged and unequally distributed by the transportation industry... Even if planes and buses could run as non-polluting, non-depleting public services, their inhuman velocities would degrade man's innate mobility and force him to spend more time for the sake of travel. ❞

Illich challenges the devotion to technological and scientific development. This where many who study his views begin to question them. Most accept what he says about the role of bicycles and other low-tech tools for living. Most accept what he says about transport inequalities. Not all agree with his criticism, expressed in *Deschooling Society,* of an industrialised education system which, he claims, fails many and teaches all the wrong things. Few accept the full weight of his criticism of the professionalisation of medicine as expressed in *Medical Nemesis*. He also calls for the right to useful unemployment: so that people can be useful to themselves and others outside of the production of commodities for the market.

There remains the question of how Illich defines and values 'tools'. There are many which are high-tech yet very multi-functional and generally accessible. A computer can be used to write this, fly a plane, do a tax return, guide a cruise missile and predict the chance of rain tomorrow, depending on the programme or app that is loaded. What about a helicopter that can be used as an air ambulance in one guise and meeting out death to innocent civilians in another?

Much of Illich's arguments are controversial but his challenges to society have opened up new thinking and perceptions. His iconoclasm and radical teaching in rural Mexico led to a carpeting from the Vatican and resignation from any formal connection with the Church. He spent the rest of his life between guest professorships in Germany and America, with periods living in a Mexican village working on various writing projects. He died in 2002.

The rush hour, Copenhagen. Photo: Mikael Colville-Andersen.

The 15-Minute City

kristofferrolle.com

The idea is simple and radical. In a '15-minute city' people can easily access daily necessities and services – work, shops, healthcare, leisure, education – because everything they need to thrive is within 15 minutes of active travel: a definition which includes public transport. Important facilities are distributed decentrally, so that each district can act like a small town of its own. The movement promises to reduce car-reliance, promote mental and physical wellbeing, support local economies and tackle loneliness and isolation. The 15-minute city is about shortening distances instead of expanding them. It's essentially a set of alternatives to the creation of distance which speed creates. The concept comes at a time when digital technology reduces the need for long distance commuting.

Proximity is important but is not enough in itself: 15-minute cities are also about safe streets, cultural diversity, making urban density pleasanter and boosting 'social intensity.' Progressive planners and politicians argue that this will, in time, bring down the cost of transport investment as infrastructure for pedestrians and cyclists is much cheaper to create. Urban land will then be used in a more efficient and compact way, as car-supporting infrastructure is switched to more productive uses. This will, in turn, strengthen municipal budgets as local tax receipts go up. More bike and pedestrian traffic in cities saves money, as less is spent in the road maintenance and health sectors.

Benjamin Büttner, mobility expert at the Technical University Munich, says that in order to create more sustainable cities things like green spaces, sport facilities, cinemas and shops need to be moved to where people live, not vice versa. And that doesn't mean they have to be demolished and rebuilt, but that already existing public space needs to be rearranged and repurposed.

The originator of the 15-minute city model was Carlos Moreno, a Franco-Colombian urbanist and academic at the Sorbonne in Paris. He has described the key element of the model as being 'chrono-urbanism', or a refocus of interest on time value rather than time cost. Moreno is also working with the C40 global network of nearly 100 city mayors inspired by his views.

The Mayor of Paris is a high-profile supporter. Paris led in a big way with its *ville du quart d'heure* policy. In fact, Mayor Anne Hidalgo won her re-election campaign on the back of her commitment to the philosophy. Paris cycle path networks are being redesigned to make it a 'city of short distances.' The core of the Paris concept sees schools as 'capitals', making them the centre of each neighbourhood. School playgrounds convert to parks after school hours and at weekends, for community activities. Paris also wants to repurpose half of its 140,000 car parking spaces, turning them into green areas, playgrounds, neighbourhood meet-ups or bike parking spots. Streets right across Paris are becoming bike-friendly.

More than 16 cities worldwide have implemented the 15-minute city concept or similar ideas. Bogotá has its *Barrios Vitales* and Melbourne has 20-minute neighbourhoods. Others have focused on individual urban districts or are set on recreating the entire city. In Utrecht, the fourth-largest city in the Netherlands, 100% of people can reach all city necessities in a 15-minute bike ride, and 94% in a 10-minute ride. Barcelona has been experimenting with so-called *Superilles* or *super districts* whereby several housing blocks become a 'super block'. Only residents or delivery services have access with cars, and with a speed limit of 10kph (6mph) an hour. Former car parks are given over to trees, vegetables and flowers, and are now places where children can play and people can relax on benches in the shade. The new districts should reduce motorised traffic by 21%. Traffic reduction is helped by children and parent volunteers riding their bicycles to school in a 'bicibus' formation.

Portland, Oregon, has had a 'complete neighbour-hoods' policy since 2012. Shop owners were concerned that the new localism and car traffic restrictions would cause a collapse in sales. Indeed motor traffic did drop by 20% following the introduction of a 20-minute city concept, but it also led to an additional $1.2 billion staying in the local economy.

The Danes have creating a 5-minute city on the edge of Copenhagen. Nordhavn has been developed from a masterplan drawn up in 2008. One of many innovations is this experimental autonomous bus. Photo: Leif Jørgensen, Wiki Commons. ▼

There are, of course, many limitations to the 15-minute city concept, especially in established urban areas where land use patterns and infrastructure are already in place. Nor will it be easy in areas with low population density, such as those with urban sprawl. The biggest challenge here is to try help create distinct divisions and identify communities. Some will be within areas which have no great sense of social belonging.

People can live in a 15-minute community and yet still identify with their city as a whole. The variegated nature of cities is what makes them dynamic places: as a collection of connected neighbourhoods, each with its own cultural history and identity, and contributing to the identity of the larger city.

According to the World Economic Forum:

66 *The decentralisation of work is not going to kill the city, it's going to save it. There will be a lot of creative destruction along the way, but that is how the city renews itself: from within. The cities that don't decentralise work will struggle mightily in ways both known and unimaginable.* 99

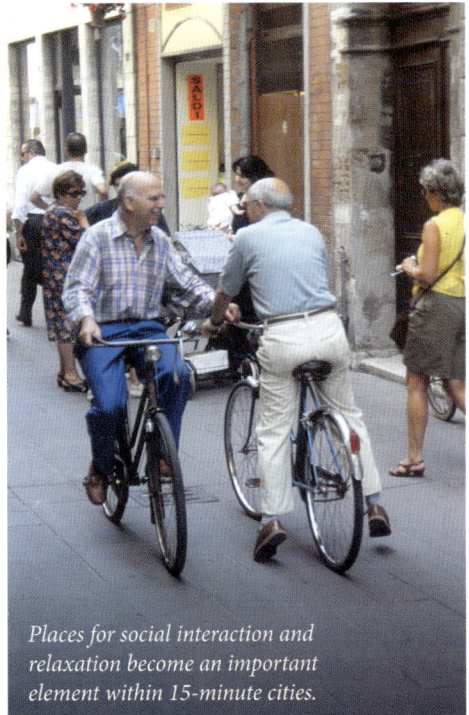

Places for social interaction and relaxation become an important element within 15-minute cities.

Can we make Bikes Sustainable again?

The production of a bicycle is increasingly harmful to the environment while its life expectancy has gone down. There are problems but also solutions.

Photo: René van Leeuwen.

Once, virtually all bicycles had steel frames and parts – easy to repair and recycle. Then along came aluminium, titanium, and carbon fibre, all much harder to repair and recycle. How do they compare when it comes to environmental friendliness?

Bikes create emissions both in manufacture and over their lifetime. There are a variety of emissions but for simplicity we can talk in terms of CO_2 equivalents. Reynolds, makers of steel cycle tubing, calculate that a traditional steel-framed bike emits 35kg of CO_2 over its lifetime, half of it in the manufacturing alone. An aluminium-framed bike emits (also for manufacture and lifetime) six times as much CO_2 as a steel-framed bike, and an aluminium electric bike nine times as much. Carbon fibre frames are even more carbon-hungry and they're not recyclable. Of course, there's also bamboo as a low-emission and renewable frame material.

There are several reasons for the higher emission figures for electric bikes. Their components are more sophisticated, so with more things to go wrong. They offer fewer opportunities for repair, and have a higher rate of technological obsolescence and considerably shorter lives.

The production of bikes of all kinds is, like that of cars, globalised and increasingly focused in China and south-east Asia, with all the problems of carbon-intensive manufacture and shipping costs.

Bike-share schemes

In theory, bike-share and hire-bike schemes should mean fewer bikes need to be produced, and so less CO_2. In practice this is offset to varying extents by the energy used in operating these schemes. Researchers looked at the Vélib bike-share facility in Paris, Europe's largest. It has some 20,000 cycles, half of them e-bikes, and nearly 1,500 hard-wired bike-docking stations with energy-hungry chargers. These heavy bikes experience some rough treatment and were found to have an average lifespan of only 12,250km, compared with 20,000km for a personal bike.

Another problem is that more share-bikes get ridden into city centres in the daytime than get ridden back to the suburbs in the evening. As a result the bikes have to be 'rebalanced' – that is, loaded into vans and driven back overnight to where they're needed again the next morning. The overall result is that a Vélib bike emits three times as much CO_2 per kilometre travelled as a personal aluminium bike, and nearly ten times as much as a steel one. These issues are common to urban bike-share services the world over. In the USA, where they typically use diesel trucks to redistribute the bikes, some schemes have carbon emissions double those in Paris.

Dockless systems, in which bikes can be parked anywhere and located via smartphone, require more bicycles, involve more rebalancing, and have a high loss rate, creating the emission costs of bike replacement. Also. dockless share-bikes require energy intensive electronic components, and the system generates emissions through communication networks. These dockless bikes (which some unfairly call 'litter bikes') are becoming less common.

It's hard to analyse the success of bike-share schemes. Some have higher usage rates than others in relation to fixed costs. Some are better planned and run than others. They all bring direct and indirect benefits to the city as a whole. Vélib in Paris is seen as a massive success, and even a tourist attraction. Bike-share has the potential to make a household's car obsolete and encourage more public transport use by serving as a first and last-mile solution. Plus, the more people that switch to bikes, the less congested our roads become.

So what to do?

It's important to remember that all bikes still generate far less carbon than all cars. They are subject to the same forces of globalisation, non-repairability and obsolescence as other forms of transport, but there are a few things you can do to redress the balance. Go for a good steel-framed bike if you can. Avoid being seduced by the latest wasteful technology by looking up user reports and consumer tests about the lifetime and reliability of different bikes. By all means use share-bikes when away, but if you live in a city with a bike-share scheme don't give up your super-efficient personal bike. And when it starts to wear out use your local bike shop to refurbish it so that you can both enjoy a long and low-carbon life.

Pedalling Forward

By Jim McGurn and Anna Semlyen

Propelling arguments

We can argue till the cow pedals over the moon that infrastructure for safe and happy cycling costs less and achieves more than the money spent on accommodating motor traffic or over-budget high speed trains.

Cycle activists in the UK argue for 10% of transport budgets, to raise cycling levels from the current 2% of traffic. Their case is strengthened by remarkable research by the European Cycling Federation showing cycling generates €150bn in overall benefits per year across the EU, with over €90bn coming from positive externalities like environmental protection, public health and mobility. On the other hand motorised road transport costs the EU €800bn annually in negative externalities. Cycling's benefits also influence areas such as industrial policy, employment, and health. Sadly politicians

worldwide cannot easily act outside of what they sense voters will tolerate, while the excesses of motorism suck in funds which could finance a glorious array of cycle friendly options.

The fairly new concept of 'active travel' includes cycling but sits within a broader context. Active travel professionals recognise that when we walk or cycle we supply the propulsion ourselves with all its societal benefits. Walkers, cyclists and wheelers are encouraged, while car and truck drivers are not. Public transport is usually included as active travel, as it takes cars off the road and because most bus and train journeys involve walking or cycling both ends. Taxis are a flexible resource for people not wanting to own their own car, or with disabilities, so are welcomed in bus and car-share lanes. Hardly anyone argues against active travel.

Demography matters

People make mistakes. Vision zero (VZ) is the 'safe system' policy to minimise all risks so that no-one dies or is seriously injured getting about.

Safe systems are about the speed, mix, volume and weight of all traffic modes, and reducing overall kinetic energy in transport (½ mass x velocity squared). It's the single most effective way to keep everyone safe. It recognises that we all have degrees of vulnerability. For example, the elderly are over-represented in injury data, perhaps due to slower reactions and delayed healing. Dangers faced by children walking or cycling are worse. Research from the USA shows they may not be able to correctly perceive vehicles approaching at speeds over 20mph (32kph). We all need to detect and process the looming of oncoming traffic, but children cannot reliably apply this skill until aged around 14. Risk is increased because vehicles moving faster than 20mph are more likely to cause pedestrian fatalities. *(Research by Julian Agyeman, Professor of Urban and Environmental Policy and Planning, Tufts University, USA, and reported in the Milwaukee Independent.)*

The cheapest and fastest fix

Cycle infrastructure is a cost of allowing motorists to go fast. The United Nation's Stockholm Declaration (2020) says that 30kph/20mph is the safe limit. Lowering speeds makes cycling safer and pleasanter and it costs less. It benefits other road users and is much more effective more quickly than separated infrastructure. There can be insurance benefits. For example, the Esure Insurance Group has reduced its premiums to Welsh drivers living in or near 20mph areas, thanks to lower than expected vehicle damage claims. The company is now committed to reducing policy prices for similar customers within three months of identifying a new 20mph area in the rest of the UK. 20mph enjoys about 70% public popularity. Results from 40 different cities across Europe (including Paris, London, Brussels, and Helsinki) find that, on average, wide area 20mph/30kph speed limits brought a 23%, 37%, and 38% reduction in road crashes, fatalities and injuries, respectively. Emissions came down by an average of 18%, noise pollution levels by 2.5 dB (about half), and overall fuel consumption by 7%. *(Review of City-wide 30kph Speed Limit Benefits in Europe, George Yannis and Eva Michelaraki, National Technical University of Athens.)*

Photo: Mikael Colville-Andersen.

▲ *New cycling infrastructure and 20mph zones are making a difference in London but it will take decades to eradicate cycling environments like this, and it's a problem nationwide. These vehicles are going at less than 20mph but that doesn't make the cyclist any happier.*

20's Plenty

20 mph

Where people are

ZÓNA

(20)

20's Plenty for Us campaigns for 20mph as the default speed limit for urban and village streets where people live, work, shop, play and learn.
www.20splenty.org

20's Plenty for Us is the UK organisation supporting those wanting slower limits where people are. They point out that on average a human is seven times more likely to die if hit by a vehicle at 30mph (48kph) than at 20mph (32kph). Cars have recently bloated, taking up road space and burning more fuel, mostly for no worthwhile reason. Bigger cars are not city-friendly, nor cyclist-friendly. The average weight of a car in the EU is 1400kg, compared to a bicycle which weights around 1.5% of that, and electric cars are pushing average weights up. Higher bonnets of oversized cars mean that if they strike a pedestrian or cyclist they damage vital organs. With smaller cars damage is more likely to be to the legs. This is not an anti-car argument: it's a road safety issue.

Once they've been designated, reduced speed limits tend to gain in popularity and are rarely removed. They need to be wide-area and not just tiny zones. Most drivers do appreciate that a lower maximum speed doesn't affect overall journey times significantly. People's driving gets smoother, with less acceleration and braking – so less fuel use, and less brake and tyre wear. Longer reaction times are created and stress levels lowered. There's no need to rush just to be held up at the next junction or queue.

It is remarkable that 20mph is only 4.5mph faster than the 15.5mph top legal speed for an e-bike in the UK. The corresponding differential in the EU is even lower, at 5kph (3.1mph). So if you and your bike can do your shopping trip at close to the speed of a car, but without the bother and costs, what's to hold you back?

The low-speed fuel myth

You'll soon come across the argument that driving at 20mph uses more fuel than at 30mph. It's false. Like any cyclist a car needs to overcome external forces such as air resistance and the rolling resistance of tyres. These increase rapidly as the speed of the car increases. Air resistance rises with the square of the speed: doubling the speed means you have to push twice as much air out of the way and you're hitting it twice as hard, so overcoming air resistance at 30mph uses 2.25 times as much energy as at 20mph (i.e. 9/4 = 2.25). So driving at a steady 20mph will use less fuel than driving at 30mph. However, fuel use does also depend on driving in the best gear for 20mph. Of course there are other tasks for the engine: it needs to keep itself turning over against internal resistance, and to supply power to lights, internal heating, wipers, etc. For a given engine speed these tasks are nothing like as big as the task of pushing air out of the way and overcoming rolling resistance. All the above applies equally to electric cars.

▲ *Dutch solutions for giving cyclists assured space. Photos: Wikipedia and Jim McGurn.*

Bublr Bikes, Milwaukee.

Minor rural roads, major problems

In the UK, outside of settlements, there are many minor roads with limits of 60mph that are far too high. Some would say 60mph limits on any minor road is far too high. It's a speed which inhibits walkers and cyclists, increasing car dependency. A fully integrated, traffic-free network of long-distance cycle paths is a big ask, and if it happens it will take decades. Lower limits are an affordable and achievable way forward.

The Dutch have clever ways of regulating traffic on minor roads. On both sides of narrow roads they designate a red cycle lane which drivers can enter only if a cyclist is not using it. To overtake the cyclist there must be no oncoming motor vehicle and the overtaking driver can go, often by necessity, onto the cycle lane on the other side to give plenty of room to the cyclist. It's a cheap safety measure, clear to all and well respected. Cyclists are treated as royalty and motorists must overtake with patience, care and good timing.

Show cyclists they're valuable

The barriers to mass cycling are multiple: from disability to status-worry. There is almost always a level at which incentives can kick in and succeed. They might include free access to loan bikes, or shopping vouchers. There are companies which specialise in incentive schemes, mainly for local authority active travel officers.

Such initiatives are often ad hoc and temporary, provided through active travel programmes and employers. The technology used tracks and rewards cyclists who opt to take part, but what if everyone could be offered a permanent scheme which pays them for distances they cycle anywhere? This would need to be a function of central government transport policy.

Society needs to look after its cyclists and appreciate how valuable they are.

Modifying driving behaviours

Normalising 20mph (30kph) limits makes a huge difference. Wales saw a 28% reduction in casualties on its 20 and 30mph pooled roads in the first 9 months of its national default for built-up streets.

Real safety gains also come from ISA (Intelligent Speed Assistance). This is standard in new cars across the Eurozone: though the UK has stepped out of line. Manufacturers will put it into UK cars anyway, but it can currently be overridden. To make compliance with 20mph/30kph effectively mandatory, several tools are needed, including ISA, speed cameras and automatic number plate recognition. Their net cost is low in comparison with road infrastructure improvements. Strict seat belt laws faced 10 years of objections followed by general compliance. These days smoking isn't tolerated in cars with child passengers. Car-free zones in town and city centres were highly contested at first and then became obvious common sense. These are all examples of how social norms can change.

Strict liability law, as used in other countries, is a great way to show that cyclists matter. The bigger vehicle is assumed to be to blame unless the driver can prove otherwise.

Driving needs to become more expensive or bothersome: for example by restricting parking spaces and introducing permits, congestion charges or workplace parking levies.

Mikael Colville-Andersen

▲

Cars have guest status amongst pedestrians and cyclists.

Futureshock

We are on the cusp of big changes. At the micromobility end of the transport spectrum the distinctions between vehicle types are becoming blurred, and electric-assist plays a big part. For example, new designs of cargo e-bike are coming close to matching what a small car can do for short trips: carrying children or goods. Across the world hybrid transport options are emerging which will begin replacing conventional cars in urban settings and it will all demand careful legislation. Also, digital technology is blurring the distinction between public and private transport. Micromobility share-bikes and scooters are already with us, and small on-demand people-carriers, limited to 20mph/30kph of course, may soon be upon us. On top of all this, drones driven by GIS (Geospatial Information Systems) can move cargos efficiently and cheaply, out-performing ground-based deliveries systems in certain circumstances.

Already digital technology could, if allowed to, monitor and control virtually all driving behaviour, making possible enforced 20mph/30kph maximum speeds, with billions saved in car-taming infrastructure and on hospital care after high-speed collisions. Not to mention the human suffering. Of course, these forms of central control would infuriate many and there would be a furore over loss of freedom and privacy. It may also be that too many of us are hooked on speed. The 'Great Acceleration' is reckoned to have begun in the mid-20th century and it shows no sign of slowing. We are getting faster, faster. To slow down will require a detox like no other. We have interesting times ahead of us.

Make that difference!

Just being out there on your bike can change more attitudes than you think. Ride to work for ten years and you'll be radiating the cycling message to hundreds of thousands. Offer to be a cycle buddy for unconfident friends or colleagues. Ask for pro-cycling policies and incentives at your workplace or place of study. Congratulate and publicly praise those making cycling better.

There's power in groups. Join, donate to, or fund-raise for, local or national green transport campaigns or advocacy groups. It's not easy for lone individuals to make a stand, so many prefer to become part of a group with a specific task: perhaps co-organising a ride, or keeping an eye on local planning applications affecting cycling. Make your views known to your social media, public media and elected politicians. Vote for those with proactive travel speed and traffic reduction pledges.

Transforming society's values and the road environment will always be a big job. Local decision-makers need public consent, a clear eye on the intended behaviour change, and the willpower and ability to refashion complex travel infrastructure after many decades of car-centric planning.

◀

The famous rainbow bike path through the university quarter of Utrecht in the Netherlands. It was created on 'Coming Out Day' in 2021 to affirm the commitment of students and staff to values of acceptance, equality and security. There are now other rainbow-themed road markings in the Netherlands, sometimes replacing the white bars on pedestrian crossings.

The Order of Things

DO YOU THINK THEY'RE TRYING TO TELL US SOMETHING, ALF?

There are people who can't cope with the way councils let nature have its way with once manicured areas of grass. They want to see symmetry, tidiness and order in the world. They don't understand how this can harm the complex richness of nature – and the real requirements for human happiness. These are, by and large, decent, caring people, but they tend to resist change. And cycling.

Good order in society has a lot going for it, but it needs to be proportionate and constantly questioned. People have strong views on how we choose to get around. Some who resist change cannot understand cycling. They are usually unaware of the complications in their views, such as the fact that most adult cyclists they see on the road are also car users in other parts of their lives. There are also a few who dislike cyclists because it's an activity which is 'out of order'. They see the very act of cycling as a bit anti-social. It's a challenge to their understanding of progress and the smooth running of society. Cyclists get in the way. They're not licenced. They challenge consumerist values. They have no interest in status. Why can't they go everywhere in cars like the rest of us? They make everything look so untidy. And so on.

Whether modest flowers or proud weeds, people ride bikes for all kinds of undemonstrative, practical, unpoetic reasons. But, intentionally or not, they are also sowing seeds of change on the way. *Jim McGurn*

The New New Rich

Robert Poole

Every age has its new rich – traditionally those who have in one or two generations managed to acquire wealth but not culture. They mistake the sign (money) for the thing (value). They simulate taste by buying ornaments, and popularity by buying friends. They live by conspicuous consumption: waste by any other name.

Times are changing. Waste is out, sustainability is in. In the age of affluence, economy is conspicuous; in the age of cheap dyes, black and white is sophisticated; in an age of noise, silence is precious. Who are the new rich now?

Imagine, say, a young family on a slightly above-average income. They can be highly mobile, but carless, which frees up a budget for flexible travel: cycling, taxis, buses, trains, even hire cars. They are left with enough disposable income for a modest but comfortable and happy lifestyle.

Perhaps they've put down roots, in a town or city with 15-minute journeys. They've made sure to live close to their work, or they can work from home. Their house is modest and was cheaper than most because they need no parking.

Their transport is not their stress but their therapy. They are rich, in both time and resources, precisely because they don't have to spend a fifth of their working life either driving a car or working to pay for it. With what they save they can deploy the labour of others: creating useful rather than wasteful employment. The new new rich don't register very highly on the national income balance sheet, but in terms of resources at their disposal and quality of life, they are economic miracles compared with colleagues who find life hard on twice the income.

The new new rich may be recognisable in you. They have the same sort of problems as anyone else's, but they are probably lean and flexible enough to cope.

Get Bikes into Schools

Bikes at school

In many countries schools teach environmental issues and personal wellbeing, but cycling is rarely prominent. In the UK some children have one-off 'Bikeability' training, but why is cycling not a core part of the curriculum? Why are less academic young people being given lessons in fixing cars when their current form of transport is actually a bicycle, and could remain a bicycle if the school gave it more status? Why do very few schools have a cycle track around their playing fields, with bikes to have fun on? And the big question is, of course: why are there so few safe routes to school? That parents drive their children to school just makes the problem worse. This reflects a general lack of safe cycling and walking routes, but the concept of school streets could at least protect children from car movements.

Roll out the bike bus

A bike bus is not what you might think. It's a term used for cohort of children cycling to school together, supervised by parents and benefitting from the goodwill of other road users. Of course, there are also walking buses getting children to school – it's all active travel.

The bike bus has become a worldwide movement, with best practice shared. Barcelona is pioneering the concept, with over 40 operational. The phenomenon has grown thanks partly to viral videos. Bike buses are sociable and inspiring for parents as well as their children, but the phenomenon relies on volunteers, which generally means a bike bus may be regular but infrequent. To become really significant it needs recognition and specific protection within traffic law. It would also benefit from public sector support.

The concept of 'Kidical Mass' is gaining momentum. These are special events which give children the freedom of entire roads – here, for example, in Barcelona. Photo: Calvox & Periche.

Working Well

A Danish study found that even after adjustment for other risk factors, including leisure time physical activity, those who did not cycle to work experienced a 39% higher mortality rate than those who did. [1]

The arguments are pretty well known. Employees who cycle to work are happier, healthier and more alert. Employees that cycle to work regularly have on average 1.3 fewer sickness days per year. Good facilities and rewards for cyclists create loyal, more productive staff, and good PR.

Employers can encourage active travel but ultimately have no control over how people get to work, But they do generally have on-site car parking, and every parking space helps create a car journey, which affects everyone. Ultimately the general public also pay the opportunity cost of each parking space – related to how productive that piece of land could be if it were not used for storing a car. In the UK that's calculated at £209 per parking space per month and £587 in London.

Employers have options, made urgent if the car park is in high demand. They can work with the local active travel officer to find solutions. The Scottish Government have brought in the Workplace Parking Levy which could lead to some who drive to work having to pay hundreds of pounds a year for a parking space. The legislation allows individual councils to decide whether and how to apply this annual tax.

Few employers want to make their staff pay for parking. An alternative is the removal of parking spaces, with the space saved repurposed to the benefit of the whole workplace, or simply to improve business efficiency and profit centres.

Perhaps car parking spaces are needed less now that more employees work from home.

At the other extreme are nudge-based incentive schemes and consensus-building. Another benefit is Cyclescheme: saving employees up to 42% on a bike and accessories. They pay nothing upfront and the payments are taken tax-efficiently from their salary.

Cycling to work is only part of the story. Progressive companies look at ways to make cycling an integral part of their operations: to improve efficiency and cut costs but also for reasons of public image and staff goodwill. Consultants in active travel analyse the opportunities specific to individual workplaces. Can outworkers travelling locally be given cycling options? What would they need to carry and how? Can mixed-mode train journeys replace some business car travel? If workers need to travel by car can they take along a folding bike for efficient mixed mode transport? Can on-site items be moved by pedal-power? Can they be delivered to customers by electric cargo bike? Would there be cost and efficiency savings by contracting to local pedal-powered delivery specialists? The cultures of workplaces change as society changes. Cycling can be part of that progression.

[1] Andersen, Lars Bo et al (2000). *All-Cause Mortality Associated with Physical Activity During Leisure Time, Work, Sports, and Cycling to Work.*

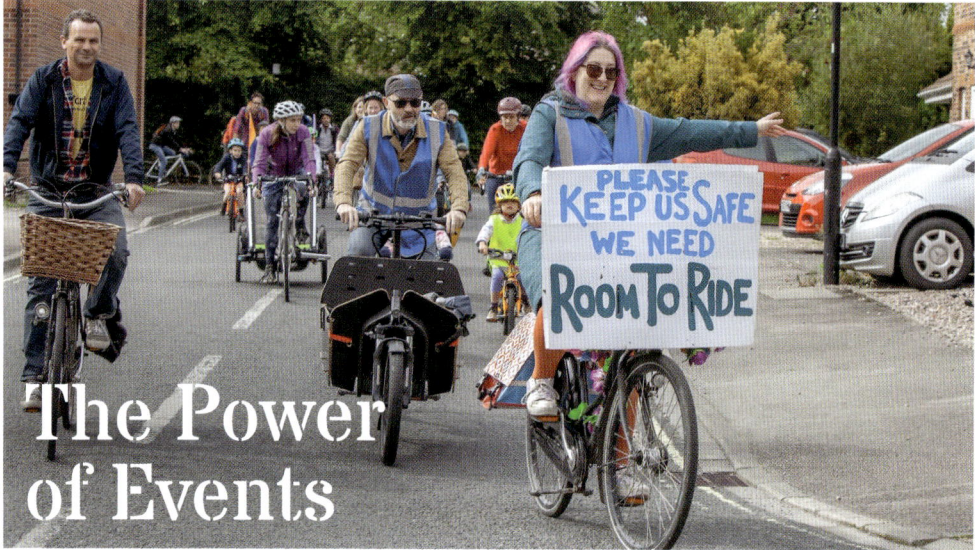

A critical mass ride by York Cycle Campaign

Closed-road Sundays, critical mass, naked bike rides, park events, cycling festivals, sponsored rides. Wherever cyclists get together they can have fun, meet other cyclists and send out a message of wellbeing and solidarity.

Colombia's capital, Bogotá, has its Ciclovía. Every Sunday 120km (75 miles) of urban roads are taken over by thousands of cyclists, walkers, rollerskaters and pedestrians. The originators could see that using already built spaces was the best way to promote bicycles as a part of the new urbanism. Ciclovía has strengthened Colombia's culture of cycling and the goodwill of policy-makers. It has boosted Bogotá's economy and created jobs, mostly informal ones. Ciclovía has kindled a greater sense of community in the city: people of all ages, political views and positions in life are all equal on their bikes in Bogotá each Sunday. There are now Ciclovías in several cities worldwide.

There are many other event forms. On Car-Free Day (a.k.a. In Town without my Car) streets are closed to all but cyclists, walkers and wheelers. There are also critical mass rides where cyclists become the dominant form of traffic. They send a strong message, especially if the local media take an interest, but these events need to be carefully judged to avoid antagonism. Then there are naked bike rides, celebrating the beauty and vulnerability of human power, but often leaving onlookers perplexed. There are also bike try-out roadshows visiting parks and city centres. These introduce the general public to the diversity of cycling options.

A particular British penchant is for sponsored bike rides. These usually serve to raise funds for a charity and draw in non-habitual cyclists – sometimes people who have not cycles for decades. Charity rides introduce or re-introduce many to cycling.

Photo: Jonathan Maus, BikePortland.

The Bike Kitchen in Graz, Austria. ▲

Hubs for almost Everything

There is now a wide palette of techniques for getting people cycling: training, bike loans, bike doctors, try-out events, cycling buddy schemes, to name a few. These are very worthwhile but most are poorly funded and not always built to last.

But what if there were to be viable and prominent cycle hubs offering all this and much more, firmly centred on a cycle path network but within our towns and cities? These would be community-based centres of cycling activity providing tried and tested forms of cycling support, such as offered by 'bike kitchens' and 'bikeability' programmes. A further step might be to offer on-site riding experiences matched to different user needs, with cycle tracks set amongst a pleasant, biodiverse landscape.

This would all need income from multiple sources, which might include cycle retailing, bike repair, on-site cycling fun, children's parties, schools visits, bike recycling, courses, classes, and guided rides. This kind of cycling centre would offer something for all ages, interests and abilities, and give what many would-be cyclists yearn for: a safe, controlled, supportive, enjoyable environment for exploring all the possibilities within cycling.

All of the active travel aspirations of a typical local authority could be included in these hubs, but they could be a base for mobile outreach to local workplaces, schools and neighbourhoods. There are certainly local authorities doing some of this, but rarely at a scale, breadth and diversity to make a large and sustained impact.

The concept might work as a social enterprise in partnership with the public sector, and perhaps also with the cycle industry, but a surer route might be to work with a commercial leisure developer or activity centre operator: people well used to operating attractions within a pay boundary without prejudicing other income streams. They will have the experience and know-how to make it fun and attractive enough to generate repeat visits. The emphasis could then shift towards being a pedal-powered activity park – a visitor centre with a strong local profile, and potential for being replicated in other regions. We could have a lot of fun one day!

Afterwords...

The bicycle is the most civilised conveyance known to man. Other forms of transport grow daily more nightmarish. Only the bicycle remains pure in heart.

IRIS MURDOCH, NOVELIST

If you have ever, just once, sat on a bicycle with a singing heart and felt like an ordinary human touching the gods, then we share something fundamental. We know it's all about the bike.

ROBERT PENN,
JOURNALIST AND AUTHOR

Beyond environmental and pollution reasons, a unique social integration takes place when people of all socio-economic classes sit next to each other in a bus, or stand together at a traffic light on a bicycle.

ENRIQUE PEÑALOSA,
FORMER MAYOR OF BOGOTÁ

It is the unknown around the corner that turns my wheels.

HEINZ STÜCKE, WORLD CYCLIST

A cyclist is a disaster for the country's economy: he doesn't buy cars... (Doesn't) buy fuel, (doesn't) pay to have the car serviced... Doesn't cause any major accidents. No need for multi-lane highways. He's not getting obese. Healthy people are not necessary or useful to the economy... On the contrary, each new McDonald's store creates at least 30 jobs – actually 10 cardiologists, 10 dentists, 10 dietitians and nutritionists – obviously as well as the people who work in the store itself.

POSTED ONLINE BY EMERIC SILLO
(possibly a pseudonym)

A triangle framed bicycle can carry ten times its own weight – a capacity that no automobile, aeroplane of bridge can match.

BILL STRICKLAND, WRITER

My bottom bracket nearly rusted through on a 30 year old Dawes. Mechanic says keep riding but listen for creaks. I think I'll ask him to be my doctor, too.

ROBERT POOLE

During my younger years, six of my friends died or were seriously, permanently crippled in automotive accidents. Motorists kill over 40,000 Americans a year directly, another 30,000 through exhaust gases. If you add up the math, for every 30 people who drive, someone dies for it… So mostly, I got into bicycles because of…childhood friends that I can't talk to anymore. So I'm a very loyal friend. It didn't hurt to discover that bicycles were fun!

CHARLES BROWN, CYCLE DESIGNER

Bicycles may change but cycling is timeless.

ZAPATA ESPINOZA, JOURNALIST

Think of bicycles as rideable art that can just about save the world.

GRANT PETERSEN, BICYCLE DESIGNER

The bicycle can be used for countless self-selected routes, at every hour and in every direction of the compass. It meets the needs of individuals and matches the eternal multiplicity of the human will.

ALBERT HERRESTALL, WRITER

Most cars are parked 96% of the time and driven 4%, yet transport costs are about 14% of household spending – more is spent on transport than food.

RAC AND THE OFFICE FOR NATIONAL STATISTICS

My two favourite things in life are libraries and bicycles. They move people forward without wasting anything.

PETER GOLKIN,
ENGLISH TEACHER AND CYCLIST

Bicycle riding is a beautiful thing. Peaceful and serene, flowing and artistic. Freeing and blissful, pedalling a bike over hill and dale is ethereal. Tack a number on your back, though, and bike racing is a bizarrely unnatural sport.

TED KING,
FORMER PROFESSIONAL ROAD CYCLIST

Photo by Kevin Meredith, a professional photographer in Brighton, UK:
"I got up at 5:30 this morning while it was still dark to take part in the yearly morning low tide bike ride."

THANK YOU!

David Eccles

My Thanks and Acknowledgements

This book has been made possible by the contributions and guidance of a peloton of talented writers, photographers, illustrators, bike-makers, colleagues and fellow cyclists. Any errors of fact or judgment remain entirely mine.

There are many who helped indirectly to create Cycle Magic, by encouraging and supporting me in good times and otherwise. My thanks in particular go to Sara Robin, Dan Joyce, Peter Eland, Tony Hadland, Roger Street, Rebecca Lack, Alan Davidson, Brian Holt, Nancy Woodhead, Mike West, Stephen E Bach and Neil Stanford. I also owe a lot to Joanne Mahon and Chris Pengilley who gave me the freedom to write this book by taking over many of my tasks at Get Cycling.

Main Contributors

I thank Paul Jeurissen, Mikael Colville-Andersen, Jason Patient and Jonathan Maus for their generosity in giving me access to their photo libraries. I thank Grace Johnson for helping to make the book so much better than it might have been. She taught me so much I did not know. I will always be grateful beyond normal bounds to Rob Ainsley for checking and correcting all copy so incisively and diplomatically. Jenni Gwiazdowski pitched in with some fine writing and editing. Robert Poole gave much wise guidance and welcome criticism. I thank Mick Allan for his previous collaborations and his copy-checking support for Cycle Magic. His writings appear here and there in the book, not always adequately acknowledged. David Hembrow put me right on many points, especially about the Netherlands. Anna Semlyen gave editorial support and co-wrote the final 'manifesto' with me. James Pitt tactfully pointed out some weaknesses in my writing. I thank John Stuart Clark and Phil Somerville, each for their generosity regarding cartoons and illustrations. Another prominent and generous contributor has been David Eccles, who has let me make ample use of the artwork from Bike Culture Quarterly covers and elsewhere. Borin van Loon contributed inimitable line drawings. Mona Caron did not hesitate to let me reproduce her artwork. Steve and Jane Caron gave me good publishing advice. Evie Stanford, Alice Thatcher and Richard McGurn skilfully pursued picture research and securing rights. Throughout the complex production of Get Cycling I have benefitted from the talent and calm professionalism of Cycle Magic's designers, Bob and Claire Main of Frozen Marrow. There are many, many others who supported and enabled Cycle Magic in their own ways, and I apologise for those I have unintentionally left out.

Working on Cycle Magic has brought to mind those wonderful people who have left the ride: Chris Hamm, Richard Ballantine, Mike Burrows, Kalle Kalkhoff, Claire Morissette, Tom Riley, Tom Mason, Edgar Newton, Geoff Apps, Graham Bell, Alan Gayfer, Sue Darlow, Hugh McPhearson and others. Their spirit lives on in these pages in one way or another.

Illustrations

That an image is not specifically credited does not mean that it is not under copyright. I have made every effort to secure permissions and acknowledge correctly. This has not been easy as there are over 1000 images. In a very few cases I have not been able to establish the identities and/or whereabouts of some photographers and illustrators appearing in the book. I apologise for any crediting errors or omissions, which will be corrected in future editions.

Jim McGurn

The Transport of Dreams.
Photographed by Mikael Colville-Andersen in Dublin.